Adolescents at School

Adolescents at School

Perspectives on Youth, Identity, and Education

SECOND EDITION

EDITED BY MICHAEL SADOWSKI

Foreword by Deborah Meier

HARVARD EDUCATION PRESS
CAMBRIDGE, MASSACHUSETTS

Second Printing, 2010

Library of Congress Control Number   2008928877

Paperback ISBN   978-1-891792-94-6
Library Edition ISBN   978-1-891792-95-3

Published by Harvard Education Press,
an imprint of the Harvard Education Publishing Group

Harvard Education Press
8 Story Street
Cambridge, MA 02138

Cover Design: Perry Lubin

The typefaces used in this book are Sabon for text and Gill Sans for display.

Contents

Foreword

I was once thinking of writing a book called *In the Company We Keep*, a title intended to remind readers about the enormous changes that have taken place over recent decades in the way adults keep (or do not keep) company with the young. The idea came to me very suddenly in 1984, when I was starting Central Park East Secondary School (CPESS) in East Harlem.

The irony I had noticed was that the closer many kids got to becoming adults, the fewer adults they got to know well—or kept company with—on a regular basis. More than two decades later, there is evidence that a lot of students still feel disconnected from their teachers, and vice versa. When asked if they knew any adults who had gone to college, a group of dropouts I recently saw being interviewed on TV all said no. But even these dropouts had spent ten years in schools, and presumably all their teachers had gone to college. But they didn't count. The teachers didn't *know* their students and the students didn't *know* their teachers. By no stretch of the imagination could one claim they were learning together—keeping company, so to speak.

The most efficient, natural, and powerful way to learn is through the company one keeps. The identification can be vicarious—my brother "kept company" with Joe DiMaggio and learned a lot about playing baseball by watching him play and internalizing each and every moment. We learn from the authors we read, although many youngsters are encouraged to read only books about people much like themselves, generally their own age or one or two years older. Or they read fantasy—stories about worlds with which they can identify on some level but in which the signposts toward adulthood are purposefully blurred.

I wonder about this phenomenon. It's not universal, even within our own local culture. My own grandchildren have taken to adolescence differently and have made friends with adults, or not, depending on their nature. But the kids who did least well at CPESS were those we discovered to be the least willing or able to engage with adults, to join them in conversation, a good joke, a passing comment—much less extended dialogue. The resistance was telling, and I went back to teaching younger children before I had a chance to explore it in more depth. We did all the obvious things. Our staff was racially, generationally, and gender mixed. We had small classes, kept kids together with some of the same staff members for several years, and provided them with a wide range of adults from the larger world with whom they might connect. These were all wise moves, but they were insufficient for many children.

We also worked hard at bridging the gulf between home and school, one often created by schools themselves. We even argued that adolescents needed their families' close support now more than they ever had, which meant that we needed to design the school so this collaboration could be accomplished. A lot of our success, we discovered, was related to our persistent efforts, as well as the families', to use each other wisely.

Yet if there was a book like this for us—one that provided us a glimpse into what our adolescent students might be experiencing and how the world around them could be shaping this experience—we forgot to read it. We read snippets from here and there, but we were mostly re-creating what schools had done for too many of the students we now taught. Sometimes we missed important details. For example, we never learned how to deal with the victimized kid; we were pretty good at preventing the victimization but not at reversing it once it started. We made tentative gestures toward addressing homosexuality but mostly let sleeping dogs lie. We knew that the minority of white kids in our midst were not as carefully and sympathetically at the center of our attention, and that the rare Asian American kid who came our way more often than not was left to sink or swim. As I write these words I feel a bit ashamed, but maybe I'm overstating it, because each student belonged for two years to a small cohort of 12–14 peers and one adult. Maybe more valuable relationship-building went on than I remember.

But as I read this remarkable collection of essays, research summaries, student profiles, interviews, and commentaries about the inner and outer worlds of adolescents, I want to start all over again and try to fit the insights gathered back into our work. I'd like another chance to read these pieces together with young people and get their feedback, their counter-stories. I wish we had talked more with our students about the nature of adolescence. It still stuns me to realize how much we talk *about* them, but not *with* them—even how much of our terminology we hide from them, or they hide from themselves.

I began my first book, *The Power of Their Ideas*, with an account of a trip to upstate New York with a group of 14-year-olds from the city, asking them if they knew what the term "inner-city kids" meant (not to mention "at-risk"). It was a new term for them, but it is a common term used *about* them.

Throughout the course of history, most young people have become members of the adult world by the age of 14. But the young today grow up in peer packs, walled away from us by so many institutional habits. This book offers us a chance to take a clearer look behind those walls, not just for the sake of our own understanding, but so that we may become better teachers and create schools where the deepest, most lasting kind of learning is possible.

The kind of schools that Sadowski and the other authors of this book envision must be very different than the ones most of us have known. They must be sites of resistance—by teachers who refuse to view their students solely as test-takers and by students who refuse to be pigeon-holed or limited by whatever cultural forces or expectations might conspire to hold them down. Forty years after beginning my teaching career, I feel sad that we have made so little progress toward reconceptualizing what such schools must be like. The schools my colleagues and I "invented" in the 70s, 80s, and 90s—progressive-minded, small, self-governing public schools—were pilots that we hoped would take hold and grow like weeds. We were stopped in our tracks by top-down, test-driven reforms. Our collective "resistance" went largely underground.

But there are exceptions that have bucked the tide and continue to give me hope: schools like those started across the country by Big Picture and like Urban Academy in New York City, where a powerful staff surrounds kids with their own passion for learning, becoming their allies and mentors. Educators in these schools have gone back, in a way, to the oldest educational approach that exists—the apprenticeship model, "learning alongside of," "joining with," and "keeping company with" adolescent learners.

I wrote an essay in 1988, during the early days of CPESS, called "The Beautician Question"—trying to tease out why "even" the beautician deserves the best of education, and why cosmeticians were the equals of cosmologists. It rests on the almost unthinkable belief these days that what America, and the best in civilization, is about is our mutual respect for each other, about equality as a prerequisite for a decent and prosperous society. Education where adolescents and adults can learn in the company of one another is the vehicle for forging such respect and decency, and this is a collection of essays and accounts that provides the details of how we must act and what we must undertake to achieve it.

DEBORAH MEIER
New York City

Real Adolescents

MICHAEL SADOWSKI

In the introduction to the first edition of *Adolescents at School*, published in early 2003, I wrote that "standards, accountability, and testing are probably the three words that best sum up the approach to education reform that currently prevails across the United States." More than half a decade later, despite marked shifts in the political climate, there is little evidence of change in our approach to improving schooling on a national level. The headlines are filled with news of schools deemed failing (or, more euphemistically, "in need of improvement") and threatened with closure based on test scores or fixed "school report card" criteria; more and more states now require students to pass exams in order to graduate from high school and, in some cases, advance from one grade to the next; and stories abound of teachers all over the country who are drastically modifying their curricula, often under intense pressure from administrators, to raise their schools' average scores on state standardized tests—at times, it seems, as if the *schools'* scores were themselves the goal.

Certainly, current federal testing requirements have focused some much-needed attention on the overall performance of certain segments of the student population, such as African American and Latino students, who have historically been underserved by U.S. schools. (Under federal law, schools are held accountable not only for their students' overall performance but for raising test scores among various subgroups.) State mandated graduation exams also have helped to ensure that students will, at the very least, be encouraged to achieve at a basic level, even if this achievement is limited to obtaining a passing score on a standardized test. Yet the ongoing standards, accountability, and testing movement is based primarily on a view of students as a group—and the notion that if we can just find the right inputs and apply them in the right amounts, then eventually we'll get the right output from the group, as well as all the subgroups within it for which we're held accountable (i.e., their overall test scores will rise).

To some extent one would expect federal and state efforts to improve education to focus on group-centered approaches, given the number of students whose progress these larger agencies are responsible for tracking. A serious problem arises, however, when these same approaches to improving student learning trickle down to the classroom. The most extreme examples of this are the "drill, test, and drill again" forms of teaching seen in the most fear-driven classroom and school environments, yet even teachers with good intentions and rich curricular ideas can find themselves falling back on mass-produced lessons and group-centered ways of thinking about their students, especially if they are being held "accountable" for raising the test scores of their segment of the school's student body.

In day-to-day teaching, viewing and treating students solely as a group can result in something that feels like success. If the group is relatively compliant and disruptions are few, then students move along with the course content, and each unit may culminate in an assessment that reflects a set of shared understandings, even if demonstrated at different levels. Yet one of the most common laments heard from teachers is of students who "slip through the cracks," a metaphor that implies that all other students "went with the flow" of the program and eventually "made it," albeit in their own time, to a common destination. From the individual students' perspectives, however, their destinations are all but common, and the student who slips through the cracks lands in a very specific place from which she or he alone must navigate.

Group-centered approaches to improving student learning can only achieve limited success because the students who inhabit middle and high school classrooms in the United States are much more than members of a group—they are *real* adolescents living in a *real* culture and attending *real* schools. Beyond stating the obvious, my point in emphasizing the "realness" of each student's life is to underscore the complex and highly charged nature of adolescence, of culture, and of schooling, all of which are central themes of this book (and have inspired the book's new subtitle, "Perspectives on Identity, Culture, and the Classroom"). All three of these elements have strong influences on how young people view themselves, their place in the world, their capabilities, their limitations, and their futures. Said another way, each has a profound effect on a young person's emerging sense of *identity* and, therefore, on her or his learning and life trajectory.

Collectively, the authors in this volume make a powerful case that much of a student's success or failure in school—academically, socially, and personally—centers on questions related to identity: "Who am I?" "How do others perceive me?" "How do I perceive myself?" "What kind of student do I want to be?" "What will my life be like in the future?" "What things are and are not possible for me?" Adolescence is a time when a "perfect storm" of forces—cognitive changes, puberty, greater awareness of social roles, sexual activity, stronger peer networks, and the need to develop future academic and career plans—converge toward what child and adolescent psychology pioneer Erik Erikson (whose theories are echoed throughout this book) called the central "crisis," or turning point, of identity development.[1] Thankfully, as Erikson noted, much of this development happens subconsciously, yet young people are also acutely aware of many aspects of their cultural world—both school, peer, and family cultures and the larger society in which they live—that frame their conceptions of themselves.

Erikson also wrote, in the prologue to his 1968 book *Identity:Youth and Crisis*, that identity is shaped by forces both "in the core of the individual and in the core of his communal culture."[2] As Erikson knew, and as others have articulated in countless ways since he wrote and published his work, adolescents' identities develop in a complex cultural context. For today's adolescents, identity development undeniably occurs in a climate of cultural racism, sexism, classism, homophobia, anti-immigrant sentiment, and a host of other negative social forces that Erikson could barely have imagined. Yet the various chapters of this book are aimed at much more than mere consciousness-raising about these various "isms." Rather, the authors herein explore how these forces work their way into the cultures of schools and into the thinking of adolescents themselves, often limiting their self-concepts and academic performance—and they help to illustrate the various ways educators can work to redirect students' learning experiences and ways of thinking away from the false limitations these cultural forces might impose toward a more expansive understanding of their true potential.

Several summers ago, I cotaught an Advanced Placement (AP) transition class for promising students who had not been in upper-level literature courses previously but were planning to take AP English as juniors. The course was part of the school's effort to increase the number of students of color in its AP program. (Although the school had a racially and ethnically heterogeneous school population, enrollment in AP courses was overwhelmingly white.) A number of the students in the class, many of them African American males, seemed to struggle with reconciling this new "high-achiever" identity with the low expectations they had grown accustomed to from teachers, administrators, peers, and in some cases themselves. In addition, many were wary of being one of only a few students of color in their AP classes in the fall. Having conversations with my students about these issues helped me to understand why some resisted success despite their skill and promise, and others found the personal resources to forge new identities for themselves as learners and took on the challenge of breaking racial barriers in their school's AP courses.

As an advisor to another school's gay-straight alliance, I knew a number of lesbian, gay, bisexual, and transgender (LGBT) students who sometimes chose to stay home from school in order to avoid the harassment they experienced there. (At least one student eventually dropped out altogether.) Yet at the same school I also knew sexual minority students who transformed discrimination into a catalyst for activism and a strong sense of purpose in their lives. Issues of identity obviously were important factors in these students' success—or lack thereof—in school and beyond. Similarly, as an English and drama teacher, I had students with disabilities in several of my classes who seemed to believe that they needed to segregate themselves from their classmates and others who viewed themselves, and were viewed by others, as full participants in the school community. Clearly, how these young people incorporated disability into their identities was central to the ways they connected to, enjoyed, and performed in school.

ABOUT *ADOLESCENTS AT SCHOOL*

Adolescents at School is a relatively simple title for a book about an exceedingly complex topic. Of course, any volume about the ways identity and culture affect middle and high school students will inevitably be incomplete, since there are infinite aspects of adolescent identity, infinite ways these can be influenced by culture, and infinite ways these can play out in academic environments. Rather than a comprehensive text on adolescent identity in the school context (which would be impossible to assemble), the book is an invitation to consider a range of related topics in a variety of ways.

Michael Nakkula's opening chapter, "Identity and Possibility," explores Erikson's adolescent identity development model through a profile of Mac, a 14-year-old who already feels in many ways that his identity is fixed and unchangeable. ("It's who I am, man. I can't change that.") Drawing on the opposing notions of "moratorium" (exploring a range of possibilities for oneself) and "foreclosure" (establishing a fixed sense of oneself without such exploration),[3] Nakkula illustrates how the work of teachers and others who work with adolescents is in many ways about "creating possibility"—helping young people develop ideas about themselves, their abilities, and their futures that they otherwise might not be able to imagine.

The chapters that follow are devoted to specific aspects of identity that can have profound effects on adolescents' learning and school lives: race, ethnicity, immigrant status, gender, sexual orientation, gender identity and expression, social class, ability and disability, and spirituality. Though certainly not an exhaustive list of the factors that affect middle and high school students, these issues can play central roles in the development of their self-concepts, their social interactions with peers, their relationships with teachers and other adults, their goals and plans for the future, and their academic achievement. They also can be associated with the kind of identity foreclosure against which Nakkula warns. For example, if adolescents view themselves through societal prejudices about what it means to be African American or poor or gay or an immigrant, they may have difficulty realizing their full potential as learners.

In the book's final chapter, "Beyond Categories," John Raible and Sonia Nieto expand the framework for understanding adolescent identity, profiling three young people whose lives represent the intersection of multiple identities and experiences. As with the adolescents featured throughout the book, these young people demonstrate how factors such as race, gender, sexual orientation, class, and ethnicity—though extremely useful for understanding aspects of an adolescent's experience—tell only a part of the story, the remainder of which is unique to each individual.

Like the youth and issues about which they write, the contributors to *Adolescents at School* are a diverse group. The researchers, educators, counselors, and education journalists represented here shed light on adolescents' lives from a multiplicity of vantage points and use a variety of approaches. Commentaries, interviews, profiles (of individual adolescents or groups of students), and research features (pieces new to this edition that describe a study or studies about a particular issue) complement the longer chapters and provide additional perspectives on the issues raised in them. In many cases, authors draw on the voices of youth themselves, citing the "real authorities" on the adolescent experience in interview excerpts, anecdotes, case studies, and samples of student writing.

WHAT'S NEW IN THIS EDITION

Two new full-length chapters

This second edition of *Adolescents at School* contains two full-length chapters that were not included in the first edition but that address aspects of identity central to many adolescents' lives at school and beyond. Chapter Three, "Adolescents from Immigrant Families: Relationships and Adaptation in School" by researchers Carola Suárez-Orozco, Desirée Baolian Qin, and Ramona Fruja Amthor, explores the host of issues facing students who are either immigrants themselves or the children of immigrants—now one in five students in U.S. schools—and how the building of quality relationships with teachers, peers, and the act of learning itself can be especially important contributors to school success for this population. In Chapter Ten, "A Question of 'Faith': Adolescent Spirituality in Public Schools," professor and former middle and high school teacher Eric Toshalis tackles the difficult question, "If spirituality is important to the identity of some adolescents, are there ways teachers can support its development without crossing the line between church and state?" For Toshalis, the answers to this question lie in teachers' adopting a more expansive view of concepts such as faith, meaning, and purpose, the kind of "ultimate concerns" he argues are central to virtually all adolescents' identity development and to every academic discipline.

Three new mini-chapters

Along with these two new full-length chapters, this second edition contains three new mini-chapters that bring additional perspectives to issues addressed in longer chapters of the book:

- A commentary by Howard Gardner, who developed the theory of multiple intelligences, about the implications of his theory for adolescent identity development and the way teachers think about curriculum and instruction
- A review of recent research on the "acting white" theory (the notion that some students of color reject academic achievement because they perceive it as "acting white"), and a discussion of why it is important for teachers to understand the nuances in these studies
- "The Story of Matt, 'Transgender Superhero,'" a profile of a female-to-male transgender youth who discusses the challenges he has experienced both at school and at home reconciling his identity with the relationships in his life

Four extensively revised chapters

In addition, four chapters or mini-chapters have been extensively revised (and, in some cases, retitled) to reflect recent social and cultural developments and new data that have emerged since the last edition. These include:

- "Getting the Message Across" (an update of "Writing Their Way Through" from the previous edition), in which high school teacher Theresa Squires Collins discusses the effect that recent technologies such as e-mail, text messaging, and blogs have had on the age-old practice of in-class note writing among girls.
- "What's In a Label? Adolescents and *Queer* Identities," by Arthur Lipkin. Lipkin updates his earlier piece on the word *queer*, adopted by some sexual minority youth to describe themselves, to include all the variants of the word and other identity markers such as *genderqueer, pansexual, and boi* that have become popular in the last few years.
- "Still in the Shadows? Lesbian, Gay, Bisexual, and Transgender Students in U.S. Schools," in which I examine whether recent cultural shifts around LGBT issues have resulted in schools being any safer or identity-supportive for sexual minority students.
- An update of Michael S. Kimmel's piece "'I Am Not Insane; I Am Angry': Adolescent Masculinity, Homophobia, and Violence." Kimmel incorporates the recent wave of college shootings, in particular the 2007 shooting at Virginia Polytechnic Institute in which 32 students and faculty members were killed, into his analysis of how aspects of school culture and society at large may contribute to violent behavior among boys and young men.

Finally, all remaining chapters of the book have been updated to reflect the most current statistics and other information available as this second edition goes to press. Issues for which updated information is provided in various chapters include gender gaps in educational attainment and test scores, graduation rates among students of different races and ethnicities, and the inclusion of students with special needs in mainstream learning environments.

MORE THAN SELF-ESTEEM

Working with young people in ways that reflect an understanding of some of the identity-related issues they might experience and the culture in which they are growing up is distinct from the worthwhile but different goal of helping them build self-esteem. While issues of identity and self-esteem intersect at school, they are not one and the same. Like other educators, I have known students who seemed to have high self-esteem despite poor academic performance, as well as high-achievers who I believe had low self-perceptions. I am not sure whether the students in my AP transition class, for example, felt good about themselves as people. Despite my hopes for all of them, I suspect that some did and some did not. (Adolescents can be notoriously self-critical.) As is true of all students with whom we might work, we will never know everything about what they are thinking, how they feel, or how they see the world. But it was clear to me that, for those students, how they viewed themselves as learners at that point in their lives, what others expected of them, and what it would mean to achieve at a high level in their very specific and *real* school culture affected their academic performance and, quite possibly, their future life chances. I believe that exploring these kinds of questions, as imperfect as my understanding may be, continues to make me a better teacher.

Standardized tests, state curriculum frameworks, and other accountability-based measures have dominated the educational reform landscape for some time now, and these reforms may well have a place in setting the baseline levels of knowledge we want all students to demonstrate before they graduate from our schools. But they also carry with them the risk of seeing each student not as a real person but as a number, a percentile ranking along a distribution of test scores, or a member of a group labeled "proficient," "needs improvement," or "failing." To paraphrase school superintendent Thomas Fowler-Finn, a contributor to this volume, improving achievement involves much more than taking measures to raise test scores. It also involves understanding our students' perceptions of themselves and their world, how they view their relationships with educators and education, and a host of other factors that are central to the *real* lives of *real* adolescents. Fostering *real* achievement may also depend on expanding our definition of what achievement means, and for whom. If we want all students to achieve—not just on tests but in the pursuits that are and will be important in their own lives—then trying to understand as best we can who they are and where they are coming from may be the best place to start.

NOTES

1. Erik H. Erikson, *Identity: Youth and Crisis* (New York: W.W. Norton, 1968). Erikson's work has been widely criticized by later psychological theorists, particularly feminist and

relational psychologists, for presenting normative adolescent development largely in male, white, middle-class, heterosexual terms. See endnote 5 to Chapter 1, "Identity and Possibility," for a more complete discussion of this issue.
2. Erikson, *Identity*, 22.
3. Erikson, *Identity*; James E. Marcia, "Development and Validation of Ego Identity Status," *Journal of Personality and Social Psychology* 3, no. 5 (1966): 551–558.

CHAPTER ONE

Identity and Possibility

Adolescent Development and the Potential of Schools

MICHAEL NAKKULA

It's who I am, man. I can't change that. My family made me this way . . . my neighborhood made me this way. People around here [this school] always want me to change, but I can't change. I mean, I could, but I ain't gonna. I been this way all my life and I'm probly gonna keep bein' this way. This is how I am. They [teachers, counselors, and school administrators] should know that. My mother came in and said to you she don't know how I got this way. That's crazy. She knows I'm just like my father, my brothers, my uncles, and all these crazy people [kids in the neighborhood]. I gotta fight every day after school. How you gonna be any different when you gotta deal with that every day?

—*Mac, 14-year-old eighth grader*

Dealing with it every day—as Mac succinctly puts it—is precisely how and when identity develops. Contrary to popular misinterpretations of identity development theory, identity is not the culmination of a key event or series of events, although key events can play an important role in the larger process.[1] In fact, it is not the culmination of anything. It is, rather, the lived experience of an ongoing process—the process of integrating successes, failures, routines, habits, rituals, novelties, thrills, threats, violations, gratifications, and frustrations into a coherent and evolving interpretation of who we are. Identity is the embodiment of self-understanding. We are who we understand ourselves to be, as that understanding is shaped and lived out in everyday experience.

MAC: A MINI CASE STUDY

What is the "it" that/who Mac claims to be? "It's who I am, man. I can't change that." Mac shared this self-perception in a conversation I had with him following a suspension hearing. (I was his school counselor at the time.) The principal of the middle school Mac attended called his mother and me into his office to discuss potential consequences stemming from Mac's latest fight. As usual, Mac had beaten somebody up . . . well, had sort of beaten somebody up. He had not hurt the boy badly, had not used a weapon, and had not engaged in a prolonged battle that involved multiple participants on both sides of the conflict. (These latter actions come with consequences far more serious than those considered in a suspension hearing.) Rather, Mac had simply "taught the kid a lesson . . . not to mess with me . . . you don't call me a faggot and get away with it. . . . I pulled him in an empty class-room, threw him on the floor, and punched him in the face a few times." There was no "he started it" in Mac's conversation with the principal. He accepted full responsibility for his actions, refused to apologize, and was open to whatever punishment the principal deemed fair. As Mac explained, "It's his school. He has to do whatever he thinks is right. He should pun-ish me . . . he has to. But that ain't gonna change what I have to do to take care of myself."

On the surface at least, the "it" Mac claims to be is a quick-triggered, self-protective fighter. If attacked, he strikes back instinctively, with just enough force to resolve the situation and preserve his integrity. From the outside, he might be defined as violent and homophobic. Those attributes might be seen as central to his identity. But Mac does not define himself by these terms. He views his fighting as a survival tactic within the contexts of a tough family, neighborhood, and school. Thus, Mac's "identity" as a fighter has been shaped by, and in his mind is consistent with, the environments in which he spends his time. Violence to him implies premeditation, maiming, and the use of weapons, things with which he does not associate himself. Fighting in response to an external threat, on the other hand, is seen as a noble act of self-defense. According to Mac, it is important to develop a tough reputa-tion not for the sake of being cool, as many adults assume, but rather to be safe and respected in the environments he must navigate.

A bit more scratching beneath the surface uncovers a deeper understand-ing of the "who I am" Mac claims to be. Fighting under the circumstances in which he lives is one event within a coherent pattern of activity in his everyday interactions. Mac feels a compelling need and desire to be a stable, recognizable part of his environment. "Being known" in a particular way at school and in his neighborhood is important to him. He trusts his own instincts for self-protection, and he wants others to know how he will respond. "I trust myself" and "you can count on me" are two statements that apply equally well to Mac, and each seems equally important to him. He knows himself as a self-protective fighter, and others know him in this way. But he also knows himself as helpful and kind, as honest and stubborn, and others know him by these characteristics as well. He can be counted on. Teachers know this. The principal knows this. His family knows this. His friends know this. He can be counted on to fight and get into trouble, and he can be counted on to help family and friends in need. His word is solid.

This mini-portrait of Mac touches upon many of the themes critical to adolescent identity. It depicts the integration of a stable way of being; it raises questions about the implications of adolescent identity for later development; it points to the complexity of meaning that underlies seemingly straightforward interpretations of identity-related behaviors; and it exemplifies the multiple roles of context, including but not limited to school, in shaping identity. But the core theme of this chapter is that identity development occurs through the interactions among all of the activities and human relationships that take place within specific contexts.

Given the amount of time young people spend in school, the educational context plays a critical role in identity formation. Clearly, however, time spent within a setting has less impact on identity than does the nature of involvement. The activities and relationships most influential to identity development are those in which youth are most invested and through which they experience the deepest gratification and most meaningful reinforcement. Because the answer to the identity question "Who am I?" is inordinately shaped by the contexts, relationships, and activities in which youth are most deeply invested, it is essential that our schools be environments in which young people choose to invest and through which their investment is adequately reciprocated.

ERIKSON'S CLASSIC IDENTITY MODEL: IMPLICATIONS AND LIMITATIONS

When influential child and adolescent psychologist Erik Erikson was constructing his original notions of identity development in the 1940s and 1950s, the world was a very different place. Taking a personal stand to "be" a certain way was arguably easier in the immediate postwar United States, for example, than it is today. In 1950, when Erikson's groundbreaking work *Childhood and Society* was published, there was intense pride in "being an American." Individual identity could clearly be organized around national identity. Perhaps for the first time, and certainly with the most clarity, "American" was embraced as its own nationality, rather than being viewed solely as the melting pot of other nationalities. For adolescents of that era, figuring out what to be and how to be were clearly linked to "what kind of American to be" and "how to be a productive American."[2]

By 1968, when Erikson's second major work, *Identity: Youth and Crisis*, was published, it meant something very different to be an American.[3] Participation in and opposition to the Vietnam War had split the country's loyalties, and the civil rights, women's, and labor movements had raised the national consciousness about what it meant to be an American of a particular race, class, and gender. The largely unified, pro-American identity parameter of 1950 had split into crisis by 1968. It is little wonder, then, that "identity crisis" became a fundamental organizing principle of Erikson's later work and a focal point, in one form or another, of the many identity development models that followed.[4]

In Erikson's widely cited lifespan model of identity development, which begins in infancy, each stage ushers in a unique "crisis" or critical task to be negotiated.[5] Successful negotiation of the task creates a critical opportunity for positive ongoing development; unsuccessful negotiation results in progressively heightened challenges. For example, the crisis of infancy—which Erikson called "trust versus mistrust"—sets the foundation for all subsequent developmental challenges and opportunities.[6] The infant fortunate enough to approach toddlerhood with a basic sense of trust in her caretakers and surrounding environment is provided with a secure foundation from which to negotiate the next "crisis" of "autonomy versus shame and doubt."[7] The infant who has been mistreated or neglected, and as a result approaches toddlerhood with increased levels of fear and anxiety, is more likely to struggle in her early steps toward autonomy and in subsequent attempts at relational connectedness. In short, each life stage is marked by a developmental crisis that brings both risk and opportunity for future growth.[8]

By adolescence, enough experiences of success, failure, and sheer survival have accumulated that the magnitude of the developmental crisis is exponentially compounded. In addition, growth in cognitive development is such that the understanding of one's own situation makes the possibilities for the crisis still more complex. According to this model, adolescence provides the best last chance to rework some of the prior crises, and thus reset the course for positive subsequent development. Erikson's stance on adolescence can be criticized as either idealistically hopeful or fatalistically hopeless. Is it really possible to substantially rework the damages of childhood via a successful identity struggle in adolescence? And is it really the case that the unsuccessful negotiation of adolescent identity leaves one fated to a lifetime of confusion, failure, and despair? The great likelihood is that the truth lies somewhere in the middle. Still, few if any psychologists would argue that the process of identity development is not crucially important and deeply felt during adolescence, even if the repercussions may be less dramatic than Erikson depicted.

CRISIS AS OPPORTUNITY IN ADOLESCENCE

The risk of identity crisis in adolescence is accompanied by a unique opportunity for young people to interrupt the cycle of unhealthy development that may have evolved throughout childhood, according to Erikson's model. If adolescents can experience a "developmental moratorium," in which they have an opportunity to reflect on and experiment with who they are, particularly with respect to their skills, interests, and relationships with others, they are likely to move toward adulthood with enhanced possibilities for long-term health and success. In essence, such a moratorium provides a "break in the developmental action." It allows adolescents to use their advanced cognitive abilities to explore a range of possibilities for future development—to ask, "Given my present interests, aptitudes, and motivations, what life course(s) should I pursue?" Remaining open to possibility is the key to a successful moratorium experience.

The opposite of moratorium in Erikson's framework is "foreclosure."[9] The foreclosed identity results from an adolescent making a commitment to a particular life course without adequately exploring alternatives. We hear the hints of such a foreclosure in Mac's opening statements:

> People around here [this school] always want me to change, but I can't change. I mean, I could, but I ain't gonna. I been this way all my life and I'm probly gonna keep bein' this way.

In many respects, Mac's statements reflect a deeper foreclosure than Erikson had in mind, at least in his early writing. The classical notion of developmental moratorium focused on role clarification: figuring out what role to play in society in relationship to work and career. But Mac is referring to more than a role in the workplace; he is referencing a way of being: "I been this way all my life and I'm probly gonna keep bein' this way." There are tones of both resignation and personal ownership in Mac's comment. He sees himself as destined to fulfill a certain kind of role in society, based in part on his gender, social class, and family history, and this expectation seems to be a deeply embedded component of his identity.

CREATING POSSIBILITY

If Mac's teachers, counselors, or parents wanted to support him in exploring a different life course, what form would a moratorium take? For Mac, and for many other urban teens living in poor and working-class communities, concern over prematurely committing to a working role in society is largely irrelevant. A job, any job, is often viewed as an opportunity too good to pass up. Delaying work commitments to explore more gratifying long-term work-related options is simply unrealistic.

Still, adults who work with adolescents can increase their options for healthy development by presenting them with multiple opportunities to redirect their investment of mental or psychic energy. The psychologists Mihaly Csikszentmihalyi and Reed Larson have shown how development is very much a process of this kind of energy investment. They note that we grow most strongly in the areas in which we most thoroughly invest.[10] Mac has invested heavily in his prowess as a strong, successful fighter and defender of his word. It could be argued that his overinvestment in this area has left him with deficits to contend with in other areas. He has foreclosed on other options in order to support that which he knows best. His identity, from this perspective, will be overly determined by a narrow band of experience.

There is a strong movement afoot in psychology and related youth development disciplines to provide a broader range of developmental opportunities for young people. Rather than viewing Mac and others like him as deficient and in need of treatment, this emerging perspective views them as capable, but in need of a greater number of engaging opportunities. Consistent with this notion, youth development programs and broader community initiatives of all types are sprouting up across the country.[11] Although most of these "sprouts" never make it beyond the seedling stage, others grow and interact with schools to create viable opportunities for developmental experimentation. Rather than creating a space for adolescents to stop and reflect, these initiatives provide them with an opportunity to pivot and reinvest vital psychic energy. As noted previously, identity development happens every day and everywhere, but it develops most actively where energy is invested most thoroughly. In this regard, a program, an activity, or a hobby that calls for a deep investment of time and energy does more than build skills and interests in a particular area; deep investment builds into and upon the very sense of who we are.

Mentoring programs. This kind of youth development work has taken a wide variety of forms over the past two decades. Large organizations like Big Brothers Big Sisters have made an extraordinary contribution, not only by providing thousands of adolescents with opportunities for one-to-one mentoring but also by helping to raise our awareness of the value of adult-youth relationships both within and outside the family. For youth, meaningful exposure to future possibilities and possible ways of being tends to be facilitated by caring adults who can provide guidance and modeling.[12] School-based mentoring is becoming progressively more common as schools grapple with the reality that many young people have little access to caring adult role models.[13] A particular characteristic of many school-based mentoring approaches is the effort to incorporate academic learning into the mentoring relationship. This approach gives youth who are disconnected from school or who may view educational success as antithetical to their self-understanding the opportunity to connect with learning in a different way. Through relationships with their mentors, many such youth come to experience education as relevant to who they are and who they hope to become, often for the first time.

One-to-one mentoring and other relationally based youth development programs might be viewed as contemporary "holding environments," designed to provide youth with some semblance of a developmental moratorium.[14] They are not explicitly intended to help young people explore different career paths or adult roles in society, but they are designed as spaces for self-exploration and development. Such programs cannot and should not jolt young people out of the pressing demands of their everyday lives, but they often constitute an important space for adolescents to pause, connect with the world in a different way, and perhaps experience a change in life course, whether subtle or dramatic.

Sports and other activities. In recent years, my colleagues and I have studied a girls' development program organized around rowing. G-Row (Girls Row) recruits between twenty and thirty middle and high school girls from Boston's public schools to participate in an intensive rowing program. Founded by Holly Metcalf, an Olympic rowing gold medalist, G-Row is explicitly designed to use the activity of rowing to help girls build strength, character, and a sense of self. In a variety of ways, this program epitomizes the role youth programming can have on development generally and identity development more specifically.

For starters, rowing is largely an elite sport, available primarily to young people privileged enough to encounter rowing opportunities in their private boarding schools or colleges. Its availability to urban girls has an immediate impact on the ways in which they encounter a culture quite different from their own. The girls place themselves in relation to rowers in the other boats, who are private school and college students. By placing themselves in meaningful relationship to these rowers, they have entered another world and expanded their own horizons in an important way. It is not that their home environment or community is deficient relative to this new context, but rather that their exposure to and exploration of the larger world has been expanded.

But the identity implications of participating in an elite sport against competitors from dramatically different environments is only a small part of G-Row's impact on participants' experience of themselves. The girls talk proudly about pushing through barriers in ways they could never have imagined, about calloused hands that mark the commitment to their sport, about opportunities they see for rowing in college, and, most important, about the profound implications of connecting deeply with their teammates and coaches. G-Row is about skill development in multiple arenas: rowing, building physical strength, mental focus and discipline, and teamwork. But the guiding center of these self-development tasks is relational connectedness. As one rower explained about her coach, "She's in my face . . . she's on my butt every day . . . she has my back and I never question that. I don't want to let her down in the race by not giving it everything I have."

Such comments were common in our interviews and focus groups as the girls talked about their teammates and coaches. G-Row is much less about the skills and excitement of rowing, or even about individual growth, than it is about relationship development. And relationship development is very much the anchor of identity. Identity from a relational perspective is not just a matter of how I see myself in relationship with and to others; more accurately, it is a matter of how I have come to see myself through the profound influences of meaningful relationships. While I am not arguing that youth development programs such as G-Row can compete with the influences of lifelong family relationships on identity development, I am claiming that such programs can serve to profoundly redirect the investment of vital psychic energy. This redirection, in turn, can set youth on a longer-term course of relational and skill-development experiences that become progressively more central to a core sense of self.

CONNECTEDNESS TO SCHOOL

While activities like mentoring and athletics provide special contexts for identity exploration, adolescents' everyday experiences of family, friends, and school arguably carry the most weight for ongoing identity development. For the vast majority of youth, school is the single context within which the combination of skill and relationship development occurs on a regular basis, day in and day out. Furthermore, the core educational mission of schooling has obvious implications for identity development. For example, students strong in specific academic subjects often integrate these talents into their identities as aspiring college students. But what do schools contribute to identity development beyond the basics of education, and how can they maximize this contribution on behalf of their students?

To reiterate a theme that runs throughout this chapter, schools that promote positive identity development are rich in engaging activities in which students can invest their psychic energy, and they value the role of relationships at all levels of learning. Good teachers teach their subject matter well; great teachers engage students in the learning tasks of the moment and instill in them the desire to keep learning long after graduation. Teachers who have this kind of impact do more than impart knowledge; they engage their students, they relate to them, and in turn they foster their students' relationship to learning. The act of engagement is the key to identity development in schools, as elsewhere. This act can occur in classrooms between teacher and pupil, in gymnasiums between coach and player, in hallways among friends, and in the guidance office between counselor and future college applicant. Engagement that has the greatest impact tends to be reciprocal.

It is not enough for teachers to move students, as this movement is unilateral or unidirectional. Transformational learning occurs when students sense that they too have moved their teachers—through their efforts and accomplishments and through their deep engagement in the learning process. Teaching and learning constitute a two-way street: When they work optimally, all parties are transformed. In the school counseling arena, Sharon Ravitch and I have called this process "reciprocal transformation," based on our repeated observation of the extent to which counselors are affected by the students they counsel.[15] In the athletic arena, examples of reciprocal transformation are readily apparent in the joyous victory celebrations and tearful expressions of defeat shared by coaches and players. Whatever the school-related context, adolescent identity will be profoundly influenced by those relationships in which it is clear to the student that she matters to the adult as much as the adult matters to her.

But what about Mac and students like him who are far more engaged in the street than in school? He is not particularly interested in sports, art, or music, much less math and reading. How can schools engage such students in order to make a meaningful contribution to their identity development?

Through a school-based project called Inventing the Future (Project IF), my colleagues and I reach out to educationally disengaged students in an effort to forge links between their present situations and future possibilities. We learned through the project that Mac wanted to be a fireman. Of all the students in his class he had perhaps the clearest vision of his potential career. We learned that he wanted to be a fireman because he wanted to save lives. Someone close to him had died in a fire when he was a child, and he was committed to saving others from a similar fate. Our project uncovered something about Mac that others in the school had not known. The public expression of his commitment to saving lives moved the adults and students who heard his story during our classroom activity, just as his telling it seemed to move him. Mac could no longer be narrowly defined by those present as a quick-tempered street fighter who had little interest in school. He held a different position in the class after that, and he played a different role.

In order to find what boils beneath the surface of students like Mac, schools must make explicit efforts to reach out and engage them beyond the basic curriculum. The curriculum represents the school's agenda. While it is critical that this agenda be met, it is similarly critical to meet the students where they are and to learn their agendas. Only by meeting the students where they stand now can we actively participate in the development of where they are going and who they are becoming.

NOTES

1. The most widely cited, and often misinterpreted, theory is Erik Erikson's lifespan model, which frames identity development as the hallmark of adolescence (see subsequent notes).
2. Erik H. Erikson, *Childhood and Society* (New York: W. W. Norton, 1950).
3. Erik H. Erikson, *Identity: Youth and Crisis* (New York: W. W. Norton, 1968).

4. William Cross, *Black Identity: Rediscovering the Distinction between Personal Identity and Reference Group Orientation* (New York: Africana Studies and Research Center, Cornell University, 1980); Jean Phinney, "Multiple Group Identities: Differentiation, Conflict, and Integration," in Jane Kroger (ed.), *Discussions on Ego Identity* (Hillsdale, NJ: Lawrence Erlbaum Associates, 1993), 47–74.

5. While identity theorists generally concur that adolescence marks a critical era in the life cycle when experiences from childhood are integrated into a revised understanding of who one is and where one fits within her social context, there is a great deal of debate over the actual nature of adolescent identity development. Erikson's model has been widely critiqued by feminist and relational psychologists such as Miller, Pastor, McCormick, and Fine, for example, as being largely representative of white, middle-class male development. Specifically, their claim is that the model overemphasizes autonomy, individualism, and personal freedom at the cost of relational and cultural connectedness. Although this type of critique questions the potential outcomes of identity development in the human life cycle, it does not contradict Erikson's argument that the "process" of identity development is often defined by engagement in a crisis of self-understanding or self-understanding in relationship to others. See Jean Baker Miller, *Toward a New Psychology of Women* (Boston: Beacon Press, 1976); Jennifer Pastor, Jennifer McCormick, and Michelle Fine, "Makin' Homes: An Urban Girl Thing," in Bonnie J. Ross Leadbeater and Niobe Way (eds.), *Urban Girls: Resisting Stereotypes, Creating Identities* (New York: New York University Press, 1996), 15–34.

6. Erikson, *Identity*, 96–107.

7. Erikson, *Identity*, 107–114.

8. Erikson, *Identity*.

9. The concept of identity foreclosure has been developed further in the work of psychologist James Marcia. See James E. Marcia, "Development and Validation of Ego Identity Status," *Journal of Personality and Social Psychology* 3, no. 5 (1966): 551–558.

10. Mihaly Csikszentmihalyi and Reed Larson, *Being Adolescent: Growth and Conflict in the Teenage Years* (New York: Basic Books, 1984).

11. Peter L. Benson and Karen J. Pittman (eds.), *Trends in Youth Development: Visions, Realities and Challenges* (Boston: Kluwer Academic Press, 2001); Martha R. Burt, Gary Resnick, and Emily Novick, *Building Supportive Communities for At-Risk Adolescents: It Takes More Than Services* (Washington, DC: American Psychological Association, 1998).

12. Jean Rhodes, *Stand by Me: The Risks and Rewards of Mentoring Today's Youth* (Cambridge, MA: Harvard University Press, 2002).

13. Carla Herrera, "School-Based Mentoring: A First Look into Its Potential," unpublished study, 1999.

14. The pediatrician and child psychiatrist D. W. Winnicott originally defined "holding environments" as safe and nurturing spaces for healthy child development. See D. W. Winnicott, "Adolescent Immaturity," in D. W. Winnicott, *Home Is Where We Start From: Essays by a Psychoanalyst* (New York: W. W. Norton, 1990), 150–166.

15. Michael Nakkula and Sharon Ravitch, *Matters of Interpretation: Reciprocal Transformation in Therapeutic and Developmental Relationships with Youth* (San Francisco: Jossey-Bass, 1998).

CHAPTER TWO

"Joaquín's Dilemma"

Understanding the Link between Racial Identity and School-Related Behaviors

PEDRO A. NOGUERA

When I am asked to speak or write about the relationship between racial identity and academic performance, I often tell the story of my eldest son, Joaquín. Joaquín did extremely well throughout most of his early schooling. He was an excellent athlete (participating in soccer, basketball, and wrestling), played piano and percussion, and did very well in his classes. My wife and I never heard any complaints about him. In fact, we heard nothing but praise about his behavior from teachers, who referred to him as "courteous," "respectful," and "a leader among his peers." Then suddenly, in the tenth grade, Joaquín's grades took a nosedive. He failed math and science, and for the first time he started getting into trouble at school. At home he was often angry and irritable for no apparent reason.

My wife and I were left asking ourselves, "What's going on with our son? What's behind this sudden change in behavior?" Despite my disappointment and growing frustration, I tried not to allow Joaquín's behavior to drive us apart. I started spending more time with him and started listening more intently to what he had to tell me about school and his friends. As I did, several things became clear to me. One was that all of the friends he had grown up with in our neighborhood in South Berkeley, California (one of the poorest areas of the city), were dropping out of school. These were mostly black, working-class kids who didn't have a lot of support at home or at school and were experiencing academic failure. Even though

Joaquín came from a middle-class home with two supportive parents, most of his reference group—that is, the students he was closest to and identified with—did not.

The other thing that was changing for Joaquín was his sense of how he had to present himself when he was out on the streets and in school. As he grew older, Joaquín felt the need to project the image of a tough and angry young black man. He believed that in order to be respected he had to carry himself in a manner that was intimidating and even menacing. To behave differently—too nice, gentle, kind, or sincere—meant that he would be vulnerable and preyed upon. I learned that for Joaquín, part of his new persona also involved placing less value on academics and greater emphasis on being cool and hanging out with the right people.

By eleventh grade Joaquín gradually started working out of these behaviors, and by twelfth grade he seemed to snap out of his angry state. He became closer to his family, his grades improved, he rejoined the soccer team, he resumed playing the piano, and he even started producing music. As I reflected on the two years of anger and self-destructiveness that he went through, I came to the conclusion that Joaquín was trying desperately to figure out what it meant to be a young black man. I realized that, like many black male adolescents, Joaquín was trapped by stereotypes, and they were pulling him down. During this difficult period it was very hard for me to help him through this process of identity formation. While he was in the midst of it the only thing I could do was talk to him, listen to him, and try to let him know what it was like for me when I went through adolescence.

As a high school student, I had coped with the isolation that came from being one of the few students of color in my advanced classes by working extra hard to prove that I could do as well as or better than my white peers. However, outside of the classroom I also worked hard to prove to my less studious friends that I was cool, or "down," as we would say. For me this meant playing basketball, hanging out, fighting when necessary, and acting like "one of the guys." I felt forced to adopt a split personality: I behaved one way in class, another way with my friends, and yet another way at home.

THE EMERGING AWARENESS OF RACE

Adolescence is typically a period when young people become more detached from their parents and attempt to establish an independent identity. For racial minorities, adolescence is also a period when young people begin to solidify their understanding of their racial identities. For many, understanding the significance of race means recognizing that membership in a racial category requires certain social and political commitments. Adolescence is a difficult and painful period for most young people. For those struggling to figure out the meaning and significance of their racial identities, the experience can be even more difficult.

Awareness of race and the significance of racial difference often begins in early childhood. We know from psychological research that the development of racial identity is very context dependent, especially in the early years. Children who attend racially diverse schools or reside in racially diverse communities are much more likely to become aware of race at an earlier age than children in more homogeneous settings.[1] In the latter context, race is often not a defining issue, nor is it a primary basis for identity formation. When children see their race as the norm they are less likely to perceive characteristics associated with it (e.g., physical appearance) as markers of inferiority.

In contrast, children who grow up in more integrated settings become aware of physical differences fairly early. Interacting with children from other racial and ethnic backgrounds in a society that has historically treated race as a means of distinguishing groups and individuals often forces young people to develop racial identities early. However, prior to adolescence they still do not usually understand the political and social significance associated with differences in appearance. For young children, being a person with different skin color may be no more significant than being thin or heavy, tall or short. Differences in skin color, hair texture, and facial features are simply seen as being among the many differences that all children have. In environments where racist and ethnocentric behavior is common, children may learn fairly early that racist speech is hurtful.[2] They may know that calling someone a nigger is worse than calling them stupid, but they may not necessarily understand the meaning of such words or know why their use inflicts hurt on others.

Several years ago I was conducting research with colleagues at an elementary school in East Oakland. We were interested in understanding how the practice of separating children on the basis of language differences affected their social relationships and perceptions of students from other groups. As is true in many parts of California, East Oakland was experiencing a major demographic change, as large numbers of Mexican and Central American immigrants were moving into communities that had previously been predominantly African American. As is often the case, schools in East Oakland served as the place where children from these groups encountered one another, and at several of the high schools there had been a significant increase in interracial conflict.[3]

In the elementary school where we did our research, we found that most of the black and Latino students had little interaction with each other. Although they attended the same school, the students had been placed in separate classes, ostensibly for the purpose of serving their language needs. From our interviews with students we learned that even very young children viewed peers from the other racial group with suspicion and animosity, even though they could not explain why. Interestingly, when we asked the students why they thought they had been placed in separate classrooms, most thought it was to prevent them from fighting. We also found that the younger Mexican students (between ages five and eight) saw themselves as white, and the black students also referred to the Mexican students as white. However, as the children entered early adolescence (age nine or ten), the Mexican youth began to realize that they were not considered white outside of this setting, and they began to understand for the first time that being Mexican meant something very different from being white.

Depending on the context, it is not uncommon for minority children to express a desire to reject group membership based on skin color, especially during early adolescence. As they start to realize that in this society to be black or brown means to be seen as "less than"—whether it be less smart, less capable, or less attractive—they will often express a desire to be associated with the dominant and more powerful group. This tendency was evident among some of the younger Mexican students in our study. However, as they grew older, the political reality of life in East Oakland served to reinforce their understanding that they were definitely not white. As one student told us, "White kids go to nice schools with swimming pools and grass, not a ghetto school like we go to."

In adolescence, awareness of race and its implications for individual identity become even more salient. For many young men and women of color, racial identity development is affected by some of the same factors that influence individual identity development in general. According to Erik Erikson and other theorists of child development, as children enter adolescence they become extremely conscious of their peers and seek out acceptance from their reference group.[4] As they become increasingly aware of themselves as social beings, their perception of self tends to be highly dependent on acceptance and affirmation by others. For some adolescents, identification with and attachment to peer groups takes on so much importance that it can override other attachments to family, parents, and teachers.

For adolescents in racially integrated schools, racial and ethnic identities also frequently take on new significance with respect to friendship groups and dating. It is not uncommon in integrated settings for pre-adolescent children to interact and form friendships easily across racial boundaries—if their parents or other adults allow them to do so.[5] However, as young people enter adolescence, such transgressions of racial boundaries can become more problematic. As they become increasingly aware of the significance associated with group differences, they generally become more concerned with how their peers will react to their participation in interracial relationships and they may begin to self-segregate. As they get older, young people also become more aware of the politics associated with race. They become more cognizant of racial hierarchies and prejudice, even if they cannot articulate the political significance of race. They can feel its significance, but they often cannot explain what it all means.

For a number of years I worked with a group of racially integrated school districts in the Minority Student Achievement Network (MSAN). At the racially integrated high schools in MSAN, students often become much more aware that racial-group membership comes with certain political commitments and social expectations. In these schools, high-achieving students of color, like my son Joaquín, are sometimes unwilling to enroll in Advanced Placement courses or engage in activities that have traditionally been associated with white students because they fear becoming estranged from their friends. If they appear to engage in behavior that violates racial norms, they may be seen as rejecting membership in their racial group and run the risk of being regarded as race traitors. For this reason, I have urged the districts in MSAN not to rely upon student initiative to break down racial barriers but to put the onus on school leaders to take steps that will make this border crossing easier and more likely.[6]

THEORIES OF THE IDENTITY-ACHIEVEMENT CONNECTION

For educators, understanding the process through which young people come to see themselves as belonging to particular racial categories is important because it has tremendous bearing on the so-called achievement gap. Throughout the United States, schools are characterized by increasing racial segregation[7] and widespread racial disparities in academic achievement.[8]

Blatant inequities in funding, quality, and organization are also characteristic of the U.S. educational system. Despite overwhelming evidence of a strong correlation between race and academic performance, there is considerable confusion among researchers about how and why such a correlation exists.

The scholars whose work has had the greatest influence on these issues are John Ogbu and Signithia Fordham, both of whom have argued that black students from all socioeconomic backgrounds develop "oppositional identities" that lead them to view schooling as a form of forced assimilation to white cultural values.[9] Ogbu and Fordham argue that black students and other "nonvoluntary minorities" (e.g., Chicanos, Puerto Ricans, Native Americans, and others whose groups have been dominated by white European culture) come to equate academic success with "acting white." For these researchers, such perceptions lead to the devaluation of academic pursuits and the adoption of self-defeating behaviors that inhibit possibilities for academic success. In this framework, the few students who aspire to achieve academically must pay a heavy price for success. Black students who perform at high levels may be ostracized by their peers as traitors and sellouts and may be forced to choose between maintaining ties with their peers or achieving success in school.[10] This would explain why middle-class minority students like Joaquín might underperform academically despite their social and economic advantages. (See "Understanding 'Acting White': What Educators Need to Know" by Michael Sadowski, following this chapter.)

My own research challenges Ogbu and Fordham's "acting white" thesis. While carrying out research among high school students in Northern California, I discovered that some high-achieving minority students are ostracized by their peers, but others learn how to succeed in both worlds by adopting multiple identities (as I did). Still others actively and deliberately challenge racial stereotypes and seek to redefine their racial identities by showing that it is possible to do well in school and be proud of who they are.

Claude Steele's work on the effects of racial stereotypes on academic performance helps provide a compelling explanation for the identity-achievement paradox. Through his research on student attitudes toward testing, Steele (twin brother of the more conservative Shelby) has shown that students are highly susceptible to prevailing stereotypes related to intellectual ability.[11] According to Steele, when "stereotype threats" are operative, they lower the confidence of vulnerable students and negatively affect their performance on standardized tests. Steele writes, "Ironically, their susceptibility to this threat derives not from internal doubts about their ability but from their identification with the domain and the resulting concern they have about being stereotyped in it."[12] According to Steele, the debilitating effects of stereotypes can extend beyond particular episodes of testing and can have an effect on overall academic performance.

RACE IN THE SCHOOL CONTEXT

Stereotypes and Expectations

As Steele's research illustrates, in the United States we have deeply embedded stereotypes that connect racial identity to academic ability, and children become aware of these stereotypes as they grow up in the school context. Simply put, there are often strong assumptions made that if you're white you'll do better in school than if you're black, or if you're Asian you'll do better in school than if you're Latino. These kinds of stereotypes affect both teachers' expectations of students and students' expectations of themselves.

One of the groups most affected by these stereotypes is Asian Americans. There is a perception in many schools that Asians are naturally academically gifted, especially in math. This stereotype is based on the following notions: (1) that Asians are inherently smart (either for genetic or cultural reasons); (2) that they have a strong work ethic; (3) that they are passive and deferential toward authority; and (4) that unlike other minorities, they don't complain about discrimination. These perceptions make up what is often called the model minority stereotype. (See "Model Minorities and Perpetual Foreigners" by Stacey J. Lee, pp. 75–83.)

One of my former students, Julian Ledesma of the University of California–Berkeley, has done research on the model minority stereotype at a high school in Oakland. He started his work by interviewing various teachers and students about who they believed were "the smartest kids." In nearly every case, those he asked reported that the Asians were the smartest students. Even Asian students who were doing poorly in school reported that Asians were the smartest. The surprising thing about their responses to this question was that the average grade point average for Asians at the school was 1.8.

One reason for the gross misconception at this school was that Asians were overrepresented in the honors courses and were among the students with the highest ranks in their class. Yet these successful students were not representative of Asians as a whole at the school. Overall, Asian students were dropping out in high numbers and not doing well academically. The school where Ledesma did his research also had a considerable gang problem among Asians. Yet, because the stereotype is so powerful, students and teachers at the school were more likely to regard the majority of Asian students as the exceptions and the smaller numbers who were successful as the norm.

The stereotypical images we hold of certain groups are powerful in influencing what people see and expect of students. Unless educators consciously try to undermine and work against these kinds of stereotypes, they often act on them unconsciously. Our assumptions related to race are so deeply entrenched that it is virtually impossible for us not to hold them unless we take conscious and deliberate action. (See the commentary by Beverly Daniel Tatum, "Opening the Dialogue about Race at School," pp. 47–50.)

Sorting Practices and "Normal" Racial Separation

Beyond these stereotypes, the sorting practices that go on in schools also send important messages to students about the meaning of racial categories. For example, in many schools students in the remedial classes are disproportionately black and brown, and students often draw conclusions about the relationship between race and academic ability based on these patterns. They might say to themselves, "Well, I guess the kids in these 'slow' classes are not as smart as those in the honors classes." They also notice that the students who are most likely to be punished, suspended, and expelled are the darker students.

In addition to reinforcing stereotypes, grouping practices, which teachers and administrators often say are not based on race but on ability or behavior, often have the effect of reinforcing racial separation. Unless the adults in a school are conscious of how this separation influences their own perceptions and those of students, over time this separation may be regarded as normal. For example, black students may assume that, because there are no black students in advanced or honors courses, they cannot excel academically. Of course, black students can distinguish themselves in sports, because there are numerous examples of black individuals who do. Similarly, white students may assume that they should not seek academic assistance from tutorial programs, especially if those programs primarily serve black or brown students. When these kinds of norms associated with race take on a static and determining quality, they can be very difficult to counteract.

Students who receive a lot of support and encouragement at home may be more likely to cross over and work against these separations. But, as my wife and I found for a time with Joaquín, middle-class African American parents who try to encourage their kids to excel in school often find this can't be done because the peer pressure against crossing these boundaries is too great.

The racial separation we see in schools might also be considered an element of the "hidden curriculum," an unspoken set of rules that "teaches" certain students what they can and cannot do because of who they are. There are aspects of this hidden curriculum that are not being taught by the adults; students are teaching it to each other. No adult goes onto the playground and says, "I don't want the boys and girls to play together." The girls and boys do that themselves, and it's a rare child who crosses over. Why? Because those who violate gender norms are often ostracized by their peers. The girls who play with the boys become known as tomboys, and the boys who play with the girls become known as sissies. Although the children are sanctioning each other without instruction from adults, they are engaging in behavior that has been learned from adults—not explicitly, but implicitly. Adults can reinforce narrow gender roles by promoting certain activities, such as highly physical sports for boys and dance for girls.

In many schools there may not be explicit messages about race, but students receive implicit messages about race all the time that inform what they think it means to be a member of a particular racial group. For example, children receive messages about beauty standards. Who are the favored students and what are their characteristics? Who are the people who get into trouble a lot and what are their characteristics? Much of the time preferential (or nonpreferential) treatment is very much related to race. In addition, when students see black students overrepresented on the basketball team but underrepresented in Advanced Placement courses, or Latino students overrepresented among those who've gotten into trouble but underrepresented among those receiving awards, they get a clear sense about the meaning of race. The hidden curriculum related to race presents racial patterns as normal and effectively reinforces racial stereotypes. When it is operative it can completely undermine efforts to raise student achievement because students may believe that altering racial patterns simply is not possible.

Too often educators assume that, because of the choices black students make about such things as whom to socialize with or which classes to take, they are anti-intellectual.[13] However, the vast majority of black students I meet express a strong desire to do well in school. The younger students don't arrive at school with an anti-intellectual orientation. To the degree that such an orientation develops, it develops in school, and from their seeing these patterns and racial hierarchies as permanent. Because a great deal of this behavior plays out in schools, educators can do something about it.

WHAT *CAN* EDUCATORS DO?

Understanding and debunking racial stereotypes, breaking down racial separations, and challenging the hidden curriculum are tasks not just for teachers, but for principals, administrators, and entire school communities. In addition, there are a number of things educators can do to support their students' positive racial identity development.

First, educators can make sure that students are not segregating themselves by sitting in racially defined groups in the classroom. For teachers, this can be as simple as mixing students and assigning them seats. Or, if work groups are created, students can be assigned to groups in ways that ensure that students of different backgrounds have an opportunity to work together. This approach to race mixing is often far more effective than holding an abstract conversation about tolerance or diversity. By working together, students are more likely to form friendships naturally, and as they gain familiarity with one another they may be more willing to break racial norms. If teachers let students choose, they will more than likely choose those they perceive to be "their own kind."

Second, educators can encourage students to pursue things that are not traditionally associated with members of their group. If students of color are encouraged by adults to join the debating team or the science club, to play music in the band, or to enroll in advanced courses, it will be possible for greater numbers to challenge racial norms. Extracurricular activities in particular can serve a very important role in this regard and give young people a chance to get to know each other in situations that are not racially loaded. As is true for work groups, in the course of playing soccer or writing for the newspaper, students can become friends. Research on extracurricular activities has shown that sports, music, theater, and other activities can play an important role in building connections among young people and breaking down the very insidious links between racial identity and academic achievement.[14]

Third, teachers can find ways to incorporate information related to the history and culture of students into the curriculum. This is important in helping students understand what it means to be who they are, an essential aspect of the identity formation process for adolescents. Literature also can be very effective in this regard because it can help students to identify and empathize with people from different backgrounds. Field trips and out-of-class experiences that provide students with opportunities to learn about the experiences of others can also help expand their horizons.

Finally, an effective teacher who is able to inspire students by getting to know them can actually do a great deal to overcome anti-academic tendencies. They can do this by getting students to believe in themselves, by getting them to learn how to work hard and persist, and by getting them to dream, plan for the future, and set goals. When you talk to students who have been successful, they speak over and over again about the role that significant adults have played at various points in their lives.[15] They talk about how these adults helped them recognize their own potential, and how they opened doors that the students previously did not know existed.

I believe there are many young people who are crying out for supportive relationships with caring adults. Differences in race, gender, or sexual orientation need not limit a teacher's ability to make a connection with a young person. In my own work with students and schools I have generally found kids to be the least prejudiced of all people. They tend to respond well to caring adults regardless of what they look like. However, they can also tell if the adults who work with them are sincere or are acting out of guilt and faked concern.

Today, most social scientists recognize race as a social rather than a biological construct. It is seen as a political category created largely for the purpose of justifying exploitation and oppression.[16] For many adults and kids, especially those of mixed heritage, the categories often do not even correspond to who they think they are. Rather than being a source of strength, the acquisition of racial identities may be a tremendous burden.

For many years to come, race will undoubtedly continue to be a significant source of demarcation within the U.S. population. For many of us it will continue to shape where we live, pray, go to school, and socialize. We cannot simply wish away the existence of race or racism, but we can take steps to lessen the ways in which the categories trap and confine us. As educators who should be committed to helping young people realize their intellectual potential as they make their way toward adulthood, we have a responsibility to help them find ways to expand their notions of identity related to race and, in so doing, help them discover all that they may become.

NOTES

1. Beverly Daniel Tatum, "Talking about Race, Learning about Racism: The Application of Racial Identity Development Theory in the Classroom," *Harvard Educational Review* 62, no. 1 (1992): 1–24; William E. Cross, *Shades of Black: Diversity in African American Identity* (Philadelphia: Temple University Press, 1991); Jean S. Phinney, "Ethnic Identity in

Adolescents and Adults: Review of Research," *Psychological Bulletin* 108, no. 3 (1991): 499–514.

2. Barry Troyna and Bruce Carrington, *Education, Racism and Reform* (London: Routledge, 1990).

3. Pedro Noguera and Miranda Bliss, *A Four-Year Evaluation Study of Youth Together* (Oakland, CA: Arts, Resources and Curriculum, 2001).

4. Erik H. Erikson, *Identity: Youth and Crisis* (New York: W. W. Norton, 1968).

5. Troyna and Carrington, *Education, Racism and Reform*.

6. Pedro Noguera, "The Role of Social Capital in the Transformation of Urban Schools," in Susan Saegert, J. Philip Thompson, and Mark R. Warren (eds.), *Social Capital and Poor Communities* (New York: Russell Sage Foundation, 2001).

7. Gary Orfield and Susan Eaton, *Dismantling Desegregation* (New York: New Press, 1996).

8. Belinda Williams, "Closing the Achievement Gap," in Milli Pierce and Deborah L. Stapleton (eds.), *The 21st-Century Principal: Current Issues in Leadership and Policy* (Cambridge, MA: Harvard Education Press, 2003); Pedro Noguera and Antwi Akom, "Disparities Demystified," *The Nation*, June 5, 2000.

9. John Ogbu, "Opportunity Structure, Cultural Boundaries, and Literacy," in Judith A. Langer (ed.), *Language, Literacy, and Culture: Issues of Society and Schooling* (Norwood, NJ: Ablex Press, 1987); Signithia Fordham, *Blacked Out: Dilemmas of Race, Identity, and Success at Capital High* (Chicago: University of Chicago Press, 1996); Signithia Fordham and John Ogbu, "Black Students and School Success: Coping with the Burden of Acting White," *Urban Review* 18 (1986): 176–206.

10. Other researchers, such as Marcelo Suárez-Orozco of New York University, have argued that recent immigrant students of color are largely immune to the insidious association between race and achievement that traps students from domestic minority backgrounds. For so-called voluntary minorities (Mexican, Asian, African, or West Indian), schooling is more likely to be perceived as a pathway to social mobility, and for this reason they are also more likely to adopt behaviors that increase the likelihood of academic success.

11. Claude Steele, "A Threat in the Air: How Stereotypes Shape the Intellectual Identities and Performance of Women and African Americans," *American Psychologist* 52 (June 1997): 613–629.

12. Steele, "A Threat in the Air," 614.

13. John H. McWhorter, *Losing the Race: Self-Sabotage in Black America* (New York: New Press, 2000); Deborah Meier, *The Power of Their Ideas: Lessons for America from a Small School in Harlem* (Boston: Beacon Press, 1995).

14. Laurence Steinberg, *Beyond the Classroom: Why School Reform Has Failed and What Parents Need to Do* (New York: Simon & Schuster, 1996).

15. Patricia Phelan, Ann Locke Davidson, Hanh Cao Yu, *Adolescents' Worlds: Negotiating Family, Peers, and School* (New York: Teachers College Press, 1997); James M. McPartland and Saundra M. Nettles, "Using Community Adults as Advocates or Mentors for At-Risk Middle School Students: A Two-Year Evaluation of Project RAISE," *American Journal of Education* 99, no. 4 (August 1991): 568–586.

16. Michael Omi and Howard Winant, *Racial Formation in the United States* (New York: Routledge, 1986); Reginald Horseman, *Race and Manifest Destiny* (Cambridge, MA: Harvard University Press, 1981).

Research feature

Understanding "Acting White": What Educators Need to Know

MICHAEL SADOWSKI

> Go into any inner-city neighborhood, and folks will tell you that government alone can't teach our kids to learn. They know that parents have to teach, that children can't achieve unless we raise their expectations and turn off the television sets and eradicate the slander that says a black youth with a book is acting white.
>
> —*Barack Obama, 2004 Democratic National Convention keynote address, Boston*

In a finding that has puzzled researchers for decades, black[1] students, on average, score lower on most measures of academic achievement than their white and Asian American peers. These differences begin before kindergarten and continue through high school and beyond. They have been tracked over decades (some narrowing and widening trends notwithstanding) and exist even when researchers compare students from similar socioeconomic backgrounds. Similar patterns of underachievement have been found among Latino students, but these have been studied far less extensively.

As is often the case when an educational phenomenon defies simple explanation, ideologues and politicians have attempted to account for what is commonly called "the achievement gap" with a variety of theories, most of which have little or no empirical basis. Researchers Christopher Jencks and Meredith Phillips, editors of the anthology *The Black-White Test Score Gap*, report that these "explanations" have included genetic differences among racial groups, the "decline of the family" (the notion that if there were simply more two-parent households the achievement gap would disappear), and the "culture of poverty," the idea that many communities of color hold persistent cultural attitudes that stand in the way of their upward mobility. [2]

Thankfully, virtually all reputable education researchers have rejected these theories, yet the puzzle of black and Latino underachievement remains largely unsolved. One highly regarded theory that gained prominence in the 1980s has taken hold not only in academia and K-12 schooling but in popular culture as well: the theory that students of color reject academic achievement because they perceive it as "acting white." Barack Obama referred to this perception in his 2004 keynote address at the Democratic National Convention, and, as one might predict, it has not escaped becoming politicized on both the left and the right, as it has moved from the pages of academic journals to the popular media and into people's living rooms.

For these reasons, I teach about acting white theory in my teacher education classes because I believe it is critically important for educators to be aware not only of the popularized and somewhat diluted version of the original theory, but also the ways in which more recent research has qualified the theory or called it into question. Only with this kind of complex understanding can educators use their knowledge of the acting white theory effectively, in ways that will ultimately benefit their students.

FORDHAM AND OGBU: DEFINING "ACTING WHITE"

In 1986, Signithia Fordham and the late John Ogbu published an article in the journal *Urban Review* that has been widely cited and has opened new lines of education research over the past two decades.[3] Fordham and Ogbu conducted a study among students at a predominantly black Washington, D.C., high school and based their work on social theory about the ways in which "subordinate minorities" in the United States develop their identities and attitudes toward the dominant white culture:

> [S]ubordinate minorities regard certain forms of behavior and certain activities or events, symbols, and meanings as not appropriate for them because those behaviors, events, symbols, and meanings are characteristic of white Americans. . . . To behave in the manner defined as falling within a white cultural frame of reference is to "act white" and is negatively sanctioned.[4]

According to Fordham and Ogbu, schooling is a central component of white-dominated culture in which performance criteria, evaluation, and rewards have largely been determined and controlled by whites. They argue that many black students perceive schooling as a "subtractive process"— that is, it attempts to erase aspects of their culture and to force them to assimilate into a white-dominated context while not offering them the same rewards available to white students.

As a result, Fordham and Ogbu say, many black students and peer groups reject academic achievement as "acting white." In addition, the researchers argue that black students are forced to develop strategies to negotiate between racial group loyalty and academic achievement. These strategies include not trying as hard as they could, skipping school or classes, "clowning" (joking around to appear less interested in academics than they really are), maintaining a low profile (not raising one's hand or demonstrating good academic performance publicly), and adopting a "split personality"— for example, behaving one way with their teachers and another way with their peers. Fordham and Ogbu call the need to negotiate this tension "the burden of acting white," a distraction from and deterrent to academic achievement, and conclude:

> [T]he academic learning and performance problems of black children arise not only from a limited opportunity structure and black people's responses to it, but also from the way black people attempt to cope with the burden of acting white.[5]

THE USE AND ABUSE OF ACTING WHITE THEORY

Fordham and Ogbu's article created a stir in education research circles when it was first published, but the discussion of acting white theory also reached the popular consciousness soon thereafter, as evidenced by the publication of a 1992 article in *Time* magazine called "The Hidden Hurdle," by Sophronia Scott Gregory. A subheading to the article's main title proclaims, "Talented black students find that one of the most insidious obstacles to achievement comes from a surprising source: their own peers." Later in the piece, Gregory adds, "It is a truism to say the problem most often begins at home. When parents are not able to transmit the value of achievement, the ever present peer group fills the gap."[6]

Whether Gregory intended it to or not, the language of this article demonstrates how acting white theory can be used as a political tool, placing the blame for black student underachievement on the students themselves and their families, rather than suggesting that educators or policymakers assume any responsibility. A 2003 column by Neal Boortz in the conservative web journal *WorldNetDaily* exemplifies this way of thinking more explicitly:

One of the most crippling race-related problems we have in this country has little to do with white bigotry, prejudice, or racism. It's the anti-achievement mentality that pervades black culture. . .

Boortz also writes:

While it is justifiably demanded of whites that they examine their prejudices and feelings toward black Americans, there seems to be no eagerness on the part of black Americans to examine the aspects of their cultures that hold them back from a full participation in our economy.[7]

Boortz argues here that there is an "anti-achievement mentality" among black Americans that "holds them back" and "has little to do with white bigotry, prejudice, or racism"—and presumably is therefore the responsibility of black Americans to solve.

Recent education research into the acting white phenomenon, however, has found that the acting white notion is far from universal among students of color, that many black and Latino students want to and do succeed academically, and that educators can do a great deal to influence students' attitudes and academic self-perceptions:

- Using data from the National Education Longitudinal Study, which included more than 17,500 students, researchers Philip J. Cook and Jens Ludwig found no evidence that black students felt alienated from school or that high-achieving students of any racial group were more likely to be unpopular than other students.[8]
- In a 2002 survey of more than 34,000 students attending mostly suburban and small-city high schools, Harvard University researcher Ronald F. Ferguson found that black and Latino students were significantly *more* likely than their white peers to say their friends believe it is very important to study hard and get good grades.[9]
- In another study of students in the Cleveland suburb of Shaker Heights, Ohio, Ferguson found that all segments of the student population, regardless of race, reported some anti-academic peer pressures. Ferguson also found in the Shaker Heights study that black students, when controlling for academic course level, spent just as much time on homework as white students, and he found virtually no significant differences between black and white students in terms of anti-academic peer attitudes.[10]
- Similarly, a series of three studies by North Carolina researchers Karolyn Tyson, William J. Darity, Jr., and Domini Castellino found that both black and white students reported some anti-achievement sentiment

among their peers, but it did not appear to be race-specific. They also note that less than one-third of high-achieving black students in one study said they feel pressure against academic achievement from their black peers, and among eleven North Carolina schools studied, perceptions equating academic achievement with acting white appeared to be a significant factor only in one high school where very few minority students took advanced classes relative to the student population. Thus, the North Carolina researchers do not dismiss the acting white phenomenon but conclude that it is context-dependent.[11] As Darity, quoted in a 2005 *Harvard Education Letter* article, explains:

> Our position is not a claim that it [the acting white phenomenon] never occurs, but that it occurs contextually. . . . In cases where the vast majority of students in advanced classes are white, students tend to view these classes as belonging to the white students. But this phenomenon is less likely to occur . . . in schools where students of color have a history of participation in advanced classes.[12]

- Finally, Darity and his colleagues report in their latest study that among 65 high-achieving black tenth graders, 27 had been identified as gifted and talented in elementary and/or middle school. According to Darity, this suggests a sort of "anointment effect," whereby students are identified as high-achieving in the early grades, incorporate this "anointment" into their self-perceptions, and act on these positive self-perceptions by continuing to achieve.[13]

WHAT IT MEANS FOR EDUCATORS

While much of this later research on issues related to the acting white phenomenon has geographic and other limitations, collectively it carries strong implications for teachers and administrators. Among the most important findings that have emerged across various studies:

1. Despite widespread concern about an "achievement gap," many black and Latino students are high achievers.
2. Black and Latino students are just as likely as white and Asian American students, *if not more so*, to believe that academic achievement is important and to want to succeed.
3. Perceptions of academic achievement as acting white are far from universal among black and Latino students.

4. The acting white phenomenon is highly context-dependent and is at least as much a function of school culture as it is a function of peer culture or oppositional belief systems within communities of color.

Perhaps most important, this research suggests that it is within the power of educators to change the cultures of their schools and classrooms and, in turn, the orientation that some students of color have to their learning experiences. The North Carolina researchers' findings about gifted and talented designation, for example, suggest that students develop strong perceptions of their academic ability, whether positive or negative, in the early elementary grades. So one way educators can work to change both school cultures and students' self-perceptions is to expand access to high-level curriculum such as gifted and talented programs in the early grades. Similarly, if only a small percentage of black and Latino students in a high school historically have taken part in advanced curriculum, then expanding access to that curriculum can help to dispel the notion, as Darity puts it, that these classes "belong to the white students." In the ideal scenario, of course, these kinds of curricular experiences would belong to *everyone*; that is, all students would have access to the kinds of enriching opportunities that mark the best gifted and talented programs in the earlier grades and advanced curriculum at the high school level.

There is still much to learn about students' perceptions and how these influence the ways in which they realize (or do not realize) their potential as academic achievers. But one thing is clear: facile, overly politicized explanations that focus only on students' oppositional attitudes to achievement, while failing to account for the deeper structural elements in schools and society that support these beliefs, will only lead to "solutions" that perpetuate the status quo and continue to leave many children behind.[14]

NOTES

1. I use "black" rather than "African American" in this chapter because it is the term used in the majority of research cited.
2. Christopher Jencks and Meredith Phillips (eds.), *The Black-White Test Score Gap* (Washington, DC: Brookings Institution Press, 1998).
3. Signithia Fordham and John Ogbu, "Black Students and School Success: Coping with the Burden of Acting White," *Urban Review* 18, no. 1 (1986): 176–206.
4. Fordham and Ogbu, "Black Students and School Success," p. 181.
5. Fordham and Ogbu, "Black Students and School Success," p. 201.
6. Sophronia Scott Gregory, "The Hidden Hurdle," *Time* 139, no. 11 (1992): 44–46.

7. Neal Boortz, "Charges of Racism," *WorldNetDaily.* Posted August 5, 2003, at worldnet-daily.com

8. Philip J. Cook and Jens Ludwig, "The Burden of Acting White: Do Black Adolescents Disparage Academic Achievement?" in Christopher Jencks and Meredith Phillips (eds.), *The Black-White Test Score Gap* (Washington, DC: Brookings Institution Press, 1998).

9. Ronald F. Ferguson, "What *Doesn't* Meet the Eye: Understanding and Addressing Racial Disparities in High-Achieving Urban Schools," *North Central Regional Education Laboratory (NCREL) Policy Issues* 13 (December 2002).

10. Ronald F. Ferguson, "A Diagnostic Analysis of Black-White GPA Disparities in Shaker Heights, Ohio," in Diane Ravitch (ed.), *Brookings Papers on Education 2001* (Washington, DC: Brookings Institution Press, 2001).

11. Karolyn Tyson, William J. Darity, and Domini Castellino, "It's Not 'a Black Thing': Understanding the Burden of Acting White and Other Dilemmas of High Achievement," *American Sociological Review* 70, no. 4 (2005): 582–605.

12. Michael Sadowski, "Beyond the Gap: What Educators and Researchers Are Learning from High-Achieving African American and Latino Students," *Harvard Education Letter* 21, no. 1 (2005): 1–4.

13. Sadowski, "Beyond the Gap."

14. An earlier version of this piece appeared in the Bard College Master of Arts in Teaching Program publication, *Field Notes.*

Profile

Listening to Minority Students: One District's Approach to Closing the Achievement Gap

THOMAS FOWLER-FINN[1]

> When we were presented the information describing the minority student achievement gap, we felt that we were stereotyped. We felt less human.
> —*High school senior, Fort Wayne (Ind.) Community Schools*

This young woman was one of a large group of African American and other minority students learning for the first time that students of color and lower-income students perform at dramatically lower levels than their peers by a variety of measures: state standardized tests, college entrance exams, grades, attendance and graduation rates, and others. The news that such a wide achievement gap exists hit hard at their identities. For some, the feelings of being "stereotyped" and "less human" led to anger, discouragement, and an undermining of self-confidence. For others more resilient, these feelings ignited determination and action.

As part of an ongoing effort to close the achievement gap between white students and students of color in the Fort Wayne Community Schools, minority students participated in workshops with district staff in which they revealed their personal perspectives and committed to leading projects in school and the community.[2] Through these discussions with African American and Latino high school students, we learned important lessons about how they saw themselves in the school environment and how these self-perceptions were bound up in their academic achievement. The following is a snapshot of some of these lessons.

COMPLEX MOTIVATIONS

Roderick Sleet, an African American high school senior at the time he participated in our project (later an engineering student at Tennessee State), viewed himself as a streetwise kid who did well in school due to strong family support, but he worried about his friends. Rod felt that he and his African American peers were often not treated respectfully by teachers and feared that some of his peers would be tempted to seek the most expedient routes to short-term gratification. Rod was resilient, however, taking as a challenge events and issues that might have discouraged others. When he was a junior he entered an Advanced Placement class, and the teacher looked up at him and asked, "Are you sure you're in the right class?" He became determined to be an outstanding student to prove his worth to himself as well as to this teacher. But Rod felt that many teachers do not encourage students of color to see the value in learning and worried that, without such encouragement, his friends might not make it:

> When asked, "Why do we need to learn this?" teachers should not tell their students that it is to get a good job and earn a lot of money. I'm an urban kid, and as soon as you find other ways to earn money in the city, school is out the door. I absolutely hate it when a teacher says that, because I know if the wrong person hears that then they're going to say, "If the only reason to come to school is to earn money, I can find money other places and get it faster, so what's school for?" Tell students that the reason to go to school is to please themselves. Most teachers think that [telling kids about jobs and money] is a motivator, but it is a downplayer because it is making school secondary to money. And it isn't like that. You should get educated for yourself.

Rod's comments illustrate how educators' assumptions about minority students (in this case, that they are only interested in making money) can send a message that we think very little of them as human beings. These kinds of assumptions also fail to take into account the wide range of factors that motivate these students in school. The students we heard from in our workshops based their definitions of success on their own conduct, current performance versus past performance, the respect and recognition they received from others, how well they met obligations, and how they were doing in relation to family members and friends. Their identities were connected to all these factors, and for some they were also connected to their religion or the strong sense of a higher power. All of these things can serve as motivators. If we assume that the only thing an urban minority teen wants out of life is a financial payoff, we may close off an opportunity to inspire them to learn.

Regardless of the mixed grades earned by the group of students we spoke with (some were A and B students, while others earned mostly Cs, Ds, and Fs), we found that all but a few students saw themselves as successful. Still, we noted differences in the ways the higher- and lower-achieving students viewed their success. Students who earned As and Bs connected their success to classwork and saw connections between good school performance and future plans and goals. For students with lower grades, these connections were much less clear. One student said, "I don't get straight Fs, so I think I'm a little successful." Another student equated success, in part, to "not getting into trouble," and one felt successful because "I am happy [about] where I am at in life." These lower-achieving students also were far more likely to point to class size, the presence of "troublemakers" in their classes, poor teachers, and other factors as obstacles to their success. Unlike their higher-achieving peers, they did not connect success in school with their own agency, nor did they internalize the ramifications of grades and standardized tests on their future aspirations. The markers these students used as criteria for success were therefore not consistent with the results-oriented focus currently being demanded of students and educators in the name of higher standards all over the country. Although the self-acceptance of these lower-achieving students is heartening on one level, it is also cause for concern. Today, simply graduating from high school, even though you may be the first in your family to do so, is inadequate and will ensure a future with fewer options and closed doors.

FROM ALIENATION TO COMMUNITY

> This workshop really did a lot for me and helped me understand what I must do to achieve my goals. It helped me to express the way I feel about our society and to know that I am not alone [in] the way I see people and things.
>
> —*Minority achievement workshop participant*

The minority students we spoke with wanted very much to be a part of school life but felt trepidation about getting connected. Many told us, both in the workshops and in student school climate surveys we conducted, that they had experienced too many rejections and too much subtle disrespect from teachers, administrators, staff, and their fellow students. The student's comment excerpted above also reveals that minority students can see themselves as alone in the struggle.

This is not to say that the students do not wish to see themselves as part of the larger community; in fact, they yearn for such connection. The students we spoke with wanted to be active members of the school as contributors and valued citizens. As our workshop participants indicated in their final reflections:

> I've learned that I can improve myself as a student and as a person by working with others to improve the minority student gap.

> Since last year's meeting, I have learned that I need to be more committed to the growth and development of others.

> I've learned that helping others brings joy and improvement to others and myself.

> This is an experience that I will remember. I plan to take all that I have learned and make an effort to change things at my school.

In addition to wanting to make a contribution to the school community, many students were motivated to close the achievement gap, in the words of one, "because it [the gap] makes me as an African American look bad." The data on the performance of minority students served as an awakening that drew very strong reactions, including some defensiveness. It hurt many to hear about the gap because it attacked their self-esteem; some felt threatened by it because it seemed to confirm societal messages they received through personal experience with discrimination.

The plans students outlined to close the gap included roles for teachers, other minority students, and—as some participants noted pointedly—majority students. After all, they argued, there were plenty of white students with poor grades, too. Moreover, the participants reasoned that we all need to take responsibility for the entire learning community.

One of the greatest challenges facing school systems and teachers today is giving state standards and testing requirements meaning on a personal level for urban minority students. This is an enormous task, because it demands that we understand our students better. The perspectives and self-perceptions of high school students are key contributors to their academic achievement. Without a better understanding of the thoughts and feelings of our students and a school culture informed by and responsive to their perspectives, the most skilled teaching of an aligned, accountability-based curriculum will fall far short of student achievement goals. Closing the achievement gap is as dependent on closing "perception gaps," "caring gaps," and "culture gaps" as it is on any other factors. If we are prepared to listen, minority students can teach educators a lot about these gaps and how to close them.

NOTES

1 Thomas Fowler-Finn, former superintendent of the Fort Wayne (IN) Community Schools, is now superintendent of schools in Cambridge, Massachusetts.

2 Other aspects of the district's concerted effort to improve minority students' achievement and connection to school included student surveys, staff development, mentoring programs for incoming freshmen, and an analysis of discipline referrals at district schools.

Commentary

Opening the Dialogue about Race at School

BEVERLY DANIEL TATUM

Psychologist Beverly Daniel Tatum, president of Spelman College and the author of Why Are All the Black Kids Sitting Together in the Cafeteria?, Can We Talk about Race?, *and several other titles, has worked with schools for many years on developing ways to support the positive identity development of students of color. The first step in any such effort, Tatum says, is to open the dialogue about race and racism among teachers, school leaders, and other members of the community. In the following commentary, based on an interview, Tatum offers suggestions on how to begin this difficult and often painful conversation.*

WHY TALK ABOUT RACE?

In my presentations to students and educators, I often ask participants to think about an early race-related memory. I ask them to remember how old they were at the time the incident occurred and what feelings were associated with it. Everyone raises a hand; they all can think of something. Most people report an incident that happened during their childhood, perhaps as young as age three, but usually somewhere around five, six, or seven, in the early elementary years. In talking about the feelings associated with these memories, people often report emotions such as fear, embarrassment, anger, disappointment, and humiliation. Strong words come out. Then I ask, "Did you discuss it with anyone?" Very few people say that they did.

When young children are upset they usually talk about their experiences, so it is somewhat puzzling that a person would have an experience that she or he remembers years later, one with a negative emotion attached to it, yet not discuss it. When I ask why they didn't tell anyone, participants often respond by saying something like, "Maybe I tried to, but I was silenced" or "I had already picked up that I wasn't supposed to talk about it."

Most of us have had experiences that have been shaped in some way by racism, yet there's not much dialogue about it. In fact, there seems to be active socialization encouraging us *not* to talk about it. We use a lot of energy not talking about it, energy that would be better used interrupting it. A long time ago, James Baldwin wrote that not every problem that's recognized can be solved, but you can't solve a problem until it's recognized. If we acknowledge that we need to address issues of race and racism in order to support the positive identity development of students of color, first we have to be able to talk about them.

BEGINNING THE CONVERSATION

Opening the dialogue about race at school begins with creating a safe climate for discussion. People are not going to take the kind of psychological risks they need to take to explore these issues deeply unless they feel a sense of safety and confidentiality. People need to know that "we're all in this together, learning." They need to know that no one is blaming anyone else. It's all about working together to interrupt a system that was in place long before any of us showed up on the planet. It's not our fault, but we all have responsibilities.

A good place to start the dialogue is with colleagues who are interested. Sometimes people want to start with mandatory professional development training, and that is not necessarily a bad idea. It's great to send a clear message that this discussion is something that the leaders of the institution or the school district are supportive of and think is important. At the beginning, however, there are usually people whose life experiences or work with particular students have inspired them to think about these issues. If you start with these people, you can help them become fluent in their ability to talk about the issues in ways that engage others.

When I advocate this approach, some people say, "You're just preaching to the choir." That may be true, but I always reply that the choir needs rehearsal. When you work with the choir and they sing really well, other people are inspired to join them. If you start with the hard-core folks, those who really don't want to talk about the problem, don't want to think about it, and will do whatever they can to prevent you from doing so, you probably won't get very far.

Sometimes students are eager to address issues of race—and you might have a program for them as well. But if you don't also have a program for faculty, the students may get ahead of the faculty in terms of their comfort level and willingness to engage in the conversation. When that happens, faculty who haven't thought enough about these issues may shut down the conversation in ways that are very frustrating for the students.

OVERCOMING THE OBSTACLES

One of the challenges to talking about race in school is that most schools have a largely white teaching population. A lot of people will shut down around the topic because they feel as though they're going to be blamed, made to feel guilty, attacked, or otherwise maligned. There can be a lot of discomfort generated by these conversations. People struggle with language. What words can we use? The pressure to feel politically correct can be a part of it. There might be adults, parents as well as staff members, who think this conversation is inappropriate.

Sometimes people think that by talking about race they will create a problem where there is none. Someone will say something like, "Race relations have been very harmonious here. Why stir that pot?" Sometimes you hear this from parents of color, particularly in mostly white environments where there are few children of color. You might have a parent who will say, "My child is fine. She's doing fine. She has friends. She's getting along. I don't want you to rock that boat." They may think that to talk about these issues will generate discomfort for the student where it doesn't currently exist. In those situations, there may be more discomfort than the parent knows. The child doesn't necessarily have to be called names or be treated in a hostile way, but just the fact of being in a token position can be very uncomfortable for that child. Trying to figure out how to support a child's positive identity development under those circumstances is something that a parent may not have experience doing.

Sometimes teachers or school leaders will decide to open a school dialogue about race because there's been a very public problem, such as student protests or racist language written in the school newspaper. An incident has occurred, and the principal responds by saying, "We need to have this conversation." One of the dangers to this kind of reactive response is that there's a risk of not sustaining it long enough. The prevailing attitude might be, "We needed to respond, we responded, and now we don't have to talk about it anymore."

There is always the risk of discomfort when raising these issues, but one of the things you learn from doing it is that the discomfort often starts to subside. Sometimes what seems like fear can change to excitement. "You mean everyone can talk about that elephant in the room?" Once people are able to talk about what they've known was there all along, it's such a relief that it feels energizing. When you get to a point in the conversation where people start to feel the benefits of it, it's extremely powerful.

Unfortunately, what often happens instead is that people stop the dialogue before they get to that point. I sometimes use the analogy of treating an ear infection. When your child has an ear infection, you go to the doctor, they give you a two-week dose of antibiotics, and they tell you to give it to the child until it's gone. After a few days it seems that the ear infection has subsided—the child feels fine. She doesn't like the taste of the medicine and it's not very pleasant to keep administering it for fourteen days, but if you don't the bacteria that are being contained by the medicine won't be completely killed off. If you stop three or four days into treating the infection, maybe you've wounded it, but it will come back—and when it comes back, it comes back stronger.

Schools that have a race-related incident often want to respond to it. This response may make things a little bit better for a short period of time, but in that process you might also generate some long-term problems unless you give people the tools to work through it, process it, and start thinking about action strategies so that they feel they can do something about it. If you don't do those things, sooner or later there will be a new incident, just like there will be another ear infection.

At that point, not only is there a problem, but people don't want to go to another workshop. It's important to tell people right up front that this work is going to be hard, but it does get easier. If you can push through the discomfort, sustain yourself, and get to the next level, you can start to make meaningful progress.

CHAPTER THREE

Adolescents from Immigrant Families
Relationships and Adaptation in School

CAROLA SUÁREZ-OROZCO, DESIRÉE BAOLIAN QIN,
AND RAMONA FRUJA AMTHOR

Today, one out of every five children entering a classroom in the United States is either an immigrant or the child of an immigrant; by 2040 it is projected that the ratio will be one out of every three. Arriving from hundreds of countries, immigrant children are a highly diverse population with substantially different experiences and adaptation challenges before and after migration. Some are the children of highly educated professional parents, while others have parents who are illiterate, low-skilled, and struggling in the lowest-paid sectors of the service economy. Some have received schooling in exemplary educational systems, while others arrive from educational systems that are in shambles. Some are documented migrants, while others are in a documentation limbo. Some arrive in well-established immigrant-receiving communities with dense support networks that ease entry, while others move from one migrant setting to another.

For children from immigrant families, educational outcomes play a key role in future social and economic mobility. This is particularly the case in today's segmented labor market, which limits the opportunities of those who have low levels of formal education.[1] In fact, today's immigrant youth tend to follow a path that is considerably different from the one that was expected of earlier waves of immigrants, namely that they would be assimilated progressively, as if in a "straight-line," into the mainstream. This understanding of assimilation was based on the assumption that immigrants would go through an irreversible generational process, albeit at different speeds and in varying stages, by which their differences would be diminished and their paths would ultimately converge toward an allegedly uniform, mainstream "American" way of living. While some immigrants still integrate with relative ease, it is important to look at the different trajectories of integration available to today's immigrants, which depend on factors such as national origin, socioeconomic status, family resources, and the way they are received in the United States.[2] Depending on the social, economic, and educational contexts in which they live and attend school both before and after arriving in the United States, today's immigrant youth are more likely than their past counterparts to integrate into widely different segments of society.[3]

In this chapter, we examine the challenges facing immigrant students and those from recently immigrated families and review different patterns in their educational adaptation, which we define as involving both their academic performance and their school experiences and engagement. We also present data from the Longitudinal Immigrant Student Adaptation (LISA) study on the educational engagement of immigrant students. We pay special attention to how immigrant students navigate and adapt to the social worlds of school and how their adaptation may lead to diverse educational outcomes.

THE LIFE EXPERIENCES OF IMMIGRANT STUDENTS

Educators have long recognized that students' lives outside of school influence their social and academic engagement in the classroom. By any measure, immigration is one of the most stressful events individuals can undergo, removing them from their predictable contexts—community ties, jobs, customs, and (often) language. Stripped of many of their significant relationships—extended family members, best friends, neighbors—immigrants are often disoriented and feel a keen sense of loss.[4] For children and adolescents, immigration can be a transformative process with profound implications, one in which they go through a constellation of changes that have a lasting impact on their development.

First, in the process of immigration, separation occurs at very high rates in immigrant families,[5] generating challenges and problems even after reunification. Often one or more children are left in the country of origin with a loving caretaker for an extended period of time, while one or both parents move to the United States first. In this case, the children are likely to become attached to that caretaker, and when they finally join their parents in the United States, while happy about the prospect of "regaining" them, these youth may lose sustaining contact with their caretakers back home. Moreover, after reunification with their parent or parents in the new country, immigrant children must get reacquainted with their own family; they often find themselves entering new familial configurations that may include stepparents, stepsiblings, and siblings born in the United States that they have never met. This can create relational challenges and difficulties as the youth learn to adapt to new dynamics of authority, family loyalty, and expression of affection.[6]

Second, although some immigrant youth come from families with well-educated parents holding professional positions before and after migration, a large number face the myriad challenges associated with poverty. Compared with their nonimmigrant counterparts, noncitizen immigrant children are more likely to live in poverty[7] and crowded housing conditions[8] and are more than three times as likely to have no health insurance.[9] Poverty limits opportunities and frequently coexists with a variety of other factors that are associated with risk in adolescence, such as single-parenthood, residence in violent neighborhoods saturated with gang activity and drug trade, and segregated, overcrowded, and understaffed schools.[10] Indeed, where immigrant families settle strongly shapes the experiences and adaptation of children.[11] Children from immigrant families who settle in segregated and impoverished urban settings, where there are few opportunities to participate in the formal economy and virtually no systematic contact with the middle class, are at risk for profound cultural and linguistic isolation from the mainstream. Segregated and poor neighborhoods are more likely to have dysfunctional schools characterized by distrust among students, teachers, and administration, low academic expectations, and the ever-present fear of violence. Such settings undermine wellbeing and students' ability to sustain academic engagement.[12] Moreover, children raised in poverty are more vulnerable to an array of psychological distresses including anxiety, depression, and difficulty concentrating and/or sleeping.

Third, immigrant children face the unique challenges of learning a new culture and negotiating different cultural contexts and expectations. Cultural practices are first learned in childhood as part of socially shared repertoires that make the flow of life predictable. This social flow changes dramatically following migration; without a sense of cultural competence, control, and belonging, immigrants often feel disoriented. Since schools are significant sites of cultural socialization for immigrant youth, young people typically come into contact with the new culture more intimately and intensely than their parents do. In schools, they meet teachers—often members of the dominant culture—as well as children from other backgrounds. As a result of their greater exposure to the new culture in schools as well as in the media, youth frequently learn the new language and culture more quickly than their parents.[13] This can be particularly true in situations where the parents work in low-status jobs with other coethnics, as is the case with many poorer immigrants who may have less formal education or lower English-language skills.

Maria,[14] for example, vividly remembers going to the bank with her godmother, who was making a living cleaning houses in wealthier neighborhoods. The woman's English was clearly accented and her vocabulary more limited, since most of her work was done alone and she communicated mainly with her family in her native language. She was nonetheless able to communicate in English and initiated a bank transaction with the clerk. When he responded in a soft voice, the godmother asked him to repeat the information, but the clerk immediately turned to Maria and repeated it to her instead. "He thought my godmother did not speak English well enough for him to repeat, so he just wanted to talk to me," Maria says. "I felt bad for her, because she did try to learn, and I just told the clerk that she understands him but could not hear him well. It also made me angry because I felt he did not show her respect." Narratives like this abound in immigrant families, as the youth become intermediaries between their parents or guardians and the host culture. The resulting frustrations are also common, as youth feel at times in charge of defending their own caregivers from the negative perceptions and judgments of those with whom they interact.

The relatively high speed of the child's absorption into the new culture can thus create opportunities but also predicaments and tensions. As educators, it is important that we understand these multiple aspects of acculturation, while not idealizing or pathologizing immigrant adolescents' experiences. Indeed, a unique challenge faced by many immigrant youth is the need to live in different, often conflicting worlds that come with very different expectations.[15] They are constantly exposed to two sets of norms—those of the country of origin and those of the receiving society. Most immigrant parents move to and stay in the United States because they want their children to have a good education and a bright future, which necessitates their learning English and acculturating to what are considered mainstream cultural norms and values. The gap between children's and parents' acculturation, however, can lead to increasing conflicts and alienation at home.[16] For example, messages children receive in school that stress the importance of personal freedom and independence are likely to conflict with the hierarchical structures that characterize parent-child relations in many immigrant families.[17]

Something as simple as an evening out with friends causes tension in Marc's family, as his mother comments on the differences between such socializing in the United States and what they know from previous experience. "He would go meet friends in the evening," his mother says, "and just when I would think it was time for him to come home for the night, he would call me and say that the group decided to see a movie. At that hour of the night?!" As she tells of her frustration with her teenage son's ideas about what is acceptable, the mother seems to attribute these clashes of opinion more to cultural differences than to generational ones. For immigrant youth, how they negotiate different and often conflicting expectations plays an important role in their adaptation and development, both during adolescence and beyond.

For refugee and undocumented immigrant youth, the process of adaptation may be even more challenging. Many refugees and asylum seekers experience harrowing situations, including war and trauma in their native lands, before migrating.[18] Undocumented immigrants can encounter a variety of dangers at the border including heat exhaustion, drowning, rape, and other forms of violence.[19] These experiences can lead to severe posttraumatic symptoms as well as feelings that range from mild sadness to depression.[20] Boys who have experienced trauma tend to exhibit greater levels of anger and depression than girls, but these symptoms usually decline over time. Girls who have had traumatic experiences associated with immigration, while they do better academically than boys on average, report more psychosomatic complaints the longer they are in their new homeland.[21]

Anne Makepeace's award-winning film *Rain in a Dry Land*[22] documents the hopes and challenges of resettlement for Somali Bantu refugees who spent more than a decade in a Kenyan refugee camp before receiving refugee status and immigrating to the United States. The older children, who have never been officially educated but, due to their age, enter high school upon arrival in the United States, face challenges that range from the basic expectations of classroom behavior to the insurmountable content difficulties of algebra and decontextualized U.S. history. Ali, an optimistic adolescent, told his interviewer that when he was in the Kenyan camp he wanted to be a doctor in the United States. Once he was in the United States, however, Ali's mother suffered from depression and his father struggled with learning the language and finding work, both of which had a profound effect on Ali. Eventually, he dropped out of high school, got married, and continued to have difficulty finding long-term employment. Although these narratives are testimonies to the extraordinary resilience of individuals, they are also a call to consider the tremendous obstacles these young people face in the process of adaptation in a new society.

Finally, undocumented students are particularly at risk as a result of their unstable legal status. Once settled, they may continue to experience fear and anxiety about being apprehended, being again separated from their parents, and being deported. Such psychological duress can take its toll on their academic performance and engagement in school. In addition, undocumented students with dreams of graduating from high school and going on to college may find that their legal status stands in the way of their access to post-secondary education.[23] When immigrant adolescents know this reality while still in high school, it can affect their engagement with learning. For immigrant students who view high school mainly as an intermediate requirement toward higher education, those who know they will be unable to take that further step may get discouraged and feel that doing well at this stage is little more than an aimless endeavor.

EDUCATIONAL ADAPTATION AND SUCCESS

The popular media often highlight impressive and endearing stories of immigrant youth who succeed against the odds,[24] and there are those in our society who tend to interpret the experiences of other immigrant students from the same perspective. A number of recent studies indeed suggest that many immigrant-origin youth are successfully navigating the American educational system, faring as well as or better than their native peers and maintaining positive attitudes toward schoolwork.[25] Other studies, however, point to problems in the educational adaptation of immigrant youth.[26] Many immigrant students struggle academically, leaving school without having acquired the tools they need to function effectively in the highly competitive, knowledge-intensive U.S. economy,[27] where limited education severely impedes social mobility over time.[28] In particular, students who immigrate as adolescents often experience a more difficult adaptation than younger immigrant students, given that the transitions of adolescence and young adulthood are combined with the challenges of migration.[29] As such, it is crucial that educators recognize the complexity of immigrant adolescents' educational adaptation, considering that outcomes can vary significantly depending on multiple factors such as generational status, language proficiency, length of residence in the United States, gender, country of origin, access to support systems, and the attitudes and reception they encounter in their new contexts.

Studies that have followed immigrant youth over time suggest that 1.5- and second-generation adolescents are best able to take full advantage of schooling in their family's new country. To clarify, first-generation youth are born abroad, where they spend their childhoods and receive the foundations of their education. Members of the 1.5 generation are born abroad but arrive in their new homeland prior to the age of twelve, exposing them to the new country's schools and culture during their formative years. Second-generation youth are born in the new country to foreign-born parents. In terms of these groups' comparative educational advantages and disadvantages, first-generation students benefit from immigrant optimism[30] and a dual frame of reference[31]—that is, immigrants tend to compare their current circumstances with those they left behind and thus tend to be more optimistic and hopeful even though their situations may not be ideal. Compared with native-born students, however, newcomer students tend to struggle more with English, particularly academic English. Research has shown that English proficiency that enables quality engagement with academic subjects takes up to seven years to acquire, even when a student's English appears functional under other circumstances.[32]

The second generation and beyond, being born in the new land, no longer have comparative points of reference to the other culture, but they have the advantage of full citizenship and more consistent exposure to English, facilitating both fluency and eased curricular access.[33] This language advantage of the second generation also plays out in students' social interactions in school, since first-generation adolescents are more likely to report language barriers in their interactions with native-born peers. In the words of one adolescent, who immigrated at age fifteen to be reunited with his parents, "The moment you open your mouth, they'll know you are not one of their own."

For third generation students and beyond, recent research shows that length of residence often correlates with declining academic engagement and performance. This is a counterintuitive finding, since one might assume that the longer immigrants have been in the new country, the better they and their offspring will adapt. The new research in this area, however, suggests

that factors such as racism, poverty, anti-immigrant sentiment, and acculturation to anti-academic peer norms may each play a role in diminishing
the academic achievement and school engagement of young people who are
of the third generation and beyond.

Gender is another important factor to consider in understanding immigrant students' educational experiences. There is mounting evidence of
a gender gap in educational outcomes such that boys lag behind girls in
academic settings across ethnic groups. A number of factors contribute to
immigrant girls' outperforming immigrant boys in school. First, researchers have documented a gender-role shift after immigration to the United
States within many immigrant communities. Parents are more likely to support girls' education here than in many countries of origin because they
perceive that their daughters' education and future job opportunities are
closely linked to the family's sense of "making it" in the United States.[34]
Second, ethnographic research has consistently shown that across ethnic
groups, when regulating their children's activities outside the home, immigrant parents usually place much stricter controls on their daughters than
their sons.[35] This parental monitoring, though restrictive by mainstream
standards, may result in unanticipated benefits to girls' schooling by mini-
mizing their exposure to violence and toxic environments, particularly in
inner-city contexts.[36] Third, some researchers have found that immigrant
girls have more positive attitudes toward school than boys.[37] These positive attitudes may stem from immigrant girls' view of school as a liberating
social space where they are free from their parents' heavy monitoring and an
image of education as "empowerment against tradition." From these girls'
perspective, a good education may give them more leverage in future schooling and/or marriage.[38]

Finally, immigrant girls are less likely to perceive and internalize racism from the dominant society and are less likely than boys to develop an
"oppositional relationship" with the educational system. Unfortunately,
classrooms all too often replicate societal biases both about "cultures" and
about gendered behaviors. One teacher who participated in a recent study
noted that before she started teaching she received "cultural awareness
training" about the Mexican community: "They told me that Latino boys
are aggressive and really, really, really, macho and very hard to teach. And
they taught me that the girls are pure sweetness." When asked if she thought
these "insights" were true, she responded, "Well, yes." Many immigrant
boys in the same study indeed reported hostile and racist attitudes among
their teachers and administrators and, as a result, did not feel strongly con-

nected to their teachers. Many boys appear to respond to these largely nega-tive interactions with teachers by effectively "checking out" of the academic process.[39]

Besides gender and generational status, the ways in which immigrant youth are received in the new society—particularly its schools—play a very important role in educational adaptation. In cases where racial and eth-nic inequalities between immigrant and native populations are highly struc-tured, such as for Algerians and Moroccans in France, Koreans in Japan, or Mexicans in California, social disparagement often permeates the experi-ence of minority youth.[40] Members of these groups are not only effectively locked out of the opportunity structure (through segregated and inferior schools and, later, work opportunities available only in the least desirable sectors of the economy) but are also the objects of stereotypes associated with inferiority, sloth, and violence. Facing such charged attitudes in their surroundings, socially disparaged youth may come to experience the insti-tutions of the dominant society (e.g., school) as enemy territory where the inequality of the larger society is reproduced and reinforced. While nearly all immigrant and racial minority groups face structural obstacles, not all groups experience the same attitudes of social disparagement across genera-tions. Furthermore, some immigrant groups elicit more negative attitudes than others do—in the United States, for example, immigrants of Asian ori-gin are often seen more favorably than Afro-Caribbeans or Latinos, con-tinually walking the line between being perceived as "perpetual foreigners" and "model minorities" or "honorary whites."[41] (See "Model Minorities and Perpetual Foreigners: The Impact of Stereotyping on Asian American Students" by Stacey J. Lee on pp. 75–83.)

RELATIONSHIPS AND ENGAGEMENT:
TWO RELATED FACTORS IN IMMIGRANT STUDENTS' SUCCESS

From the time individual immigrants and their families arrive in their new country, social supports provide them with tangible aid under different cir-cumstances of need (such as babysitting or making a loan), as well as guid-ance and advice (including job information and housing leads). These sup-ports are particularly critical for immigrant newcomers, for whom the new norms and networks they encounter can initially be quite disorienting. Rela-tionships can also serve a critical function in maintaining and enhancing self-esteem, providing a sense of acceptance, approval, and belonging. For many immigrant students, social relations are also critical in initiating and sustaining academic motivation.[42] Immigrant students are typically motivated to achieve for their families, whom they often perceive as having sacrificed a great deal so that they themselves might have better opportunities.

In addition to nonacademic support through family, ethnic networks, religious institutions, and other community-based organizations, school-based supportive relationships are key to immigrant students' academic *engagement*.[43] According to a significant body of research, engagement—the extent to which students are connected to what they are learning, how they are learning it, and whom they are learning with—appears to play a central role in how well both native-born and immigrant youth do in school.[44]

Engagement occurs along a continuum and through a dynamic interplay of a variety of dimensions, all of which contribute significantly to academic performance. Highly engaged students are actively involved in their education, consistently completing the tasks required to perform well. Marginally engaged students may be doing "good enough" academic work, but they are not reaching their full academic potential. Further down this continuum, there may be a significant gap between students' intellectual potential and their academic achievement. In cases of more extreme disengagement, lack of interest in academics, erratic class attendance, and inadequate assignment completion can lead to multiple course failures that often foreshadow dropping out of school.[45] Moreover, academic disengagement may not be immediate, but may occur over time in response to the accruing difficulties associated with various community, school, and family circumstances, and the consequent adjustments and compromises students must make in response to them.

While all students face various challenges that might threaten their academic engagement, research suggests that the circumstances affecting immigrant adolescents—such factors as their previous migration experiences and the complex processes associated with adaptation outlined previously—can result in specific risks to their academic engagement. In the sections that follow, we consider three dimensions of academic engagement—cognitive, behavioral, and relational—as they relate to immigrant adolescents and their experiences in school. To exemplify these dimensions and their significance for academic success, we offer data from the Longitudinal Immigrant Student Adaptation (LISA) Study, led by Carola Suárez-Orozco and Marcelo M. Suárez-Orozco. This was a five-year longitudinal study of the educational adaptation of recent immigrant students from China, Mexico, the Dominican Republic, Haiti, and Central America. The study followed a sample of approximately 400 recently-arrived immigrant students from

1997 to 2002, representing more than fifty schools in the Boston and San Francisco areas.[46]

Cognitive engagement

Cognitive engagement refers to the extent to which students are engrossed and intellectually involved in what they are learning. Seventeen-year-old Rosa, from Mexico, for example, says "[I like] physics and calculus. It's interesting to me how planes lose altitude and how bridges are constructed." Rodney, a sixteen-year-old from Haiti, reports being fully cognitively engaged around scientific inquiry: "During the science fair, I did a project on looking at the effect of water on substances such as sugar and salt that I found really interesting." Another student, Yadira, from the Dominican Republic, talks about reading in an English class "a book called *A Taste of Salt* about a Haitian kid." She adds, "I did a project on the book that was creative and original that I really liked." Cognitive engagement, therefore, is the antithesis of the adolescent student lament of being bored in school. While cognitive engagement does not have a direct impact on grades and achievement test scores, it does strongly predict whether or not students exert effort in their schoolwork.[47]

Behavioral engagement

Behavioral engagement reflects students' participation and effort in academic tasks. The components of this element include students' expending their best effort in completing class work and homework, turning in assignments on time, paying attention in class, and attendance.[48] Teachers often report that they find newcomer immigrant students to be more behaviorally engaged in their studies than nonimmigrant students; they attribute this engagement to the immigrants' dual frame of reference. As one teacher says:

> Immigrant students seem to be more motivated to do well because they look at it as an opportunity that they are going to make the most out of. But sometimes students who are second generation, or who are native born, are not as motivated . . . [and] take things for granted. [49]

Although behavioral engagement may appear to depend on individual students themselves and on their choice to invest or not invest in their education, it is in fact part of a complex interplay among such elements as personal inclinations, previous experiences, school environment, peer culture, teacher motivation, and even an understanding on the student's part of the socioeconomic consequences of her or his efforts. Moreover, in the case of some refugee students—or even those who simply do not speak English upon arrival—behavioral engagement is much more difficult to sustain than it is for other students, and a student's disengaged or possibly even disruptive class behavior can be misunderstood as lack of interest or disrespect. It is thus important that educators not attribute immigrant students' differing investment in academic tasks too readily to individual factors when other issues might be involved.

Relational engagement

Relational engagement is the extent to which students feel connected to their teachers, peers, and others at school. Successful adaptation among immigrant students appears to be linked to the quality of relationships they forge in their school settings.[50] Indeed, social support at school has been implicated in the academic adaptation of all students, and immigrant students appear to be no exception.[51] Social relations provide a variety of protective functions—a sense of belonging, emotional support, tangible assistance and information, guidance, role modeling, and positive feedback.[52] Research suggests that relationships in school play a particularly crucial role in promoting socially competent behavior in the classroom and fostering academic engagement and achievement.[53]

As sixteen-year-old Dominican student Yunisa explains, "When you come here, you don't know English. Your friends help you with English, with classes, and with showing you the school." Hence, for Yunisa and other immigrant students like her, peers can act as "vital conduits"[54] of information to disoriented newcomer students. Dario, a fourteen-year-old Dominican boy, echoes and elaborates on Yunisa's comments, adding that peers can serve as buffers against the violence and drugs that are of special threat to boys in the low-income communities in which so many immigrants live:

> Other students from my country gave me courage to come to school because at the beginning I didn't like to go to school. I found it strange and different. When I missed school, they called to give me the new homework assignment. They would tell me who not to hang around with and they would tell me not to get into bad things like gangs and marijuana.[55]

Peers, then, can moderate the effects of school-related risks such as drugs and violence and provide support and relief from anxiety.[56] In the absence of such negative circumstances, they can act as providers of vital transition information in the new school environment and, by valuing certain academic outcomes and modeling specific academic behaviors, help to establish positive "norms" of academic engagement.[57] The findings from this longitudinal study show that relational engagement among immigrant students increases over time and that girls tend to report more school-based supportive relationships than boys. These findings resonate with the overall pattern that immigrant girls do better academically than immigrant boys.

Connections with teachers, counselors, coaches, and other supportive adults in the school are important to the academic and social adaptation of adolescents in general[58] and appear to be particularly important for immigrant adolescents.[59] Dario elaborates on the supportive role of teachers:

> [Some] teachers treat us well and watch out for our safety. When I came here, I didn't speak English and I didn't know how things were here. But a teacher helped me out and would explain things to me in Spanish.[60]

Thus, because newcomer immigrant youth undergo profound shifts in their sense of self and are struggling to negotiate changing circumstances in relationships with their parents and peers,[61] positive school relationships can help bridge the gap between home and school cultures and create important linguistic and cultural connections to the new society.[62] Supportive relationships with caring adults in the school context also provide emotional sustenance and practical help and advice for newcomers, sometimes sparking active participation in subject areas that may have traditionally held little interest for them. Conversely, students may lose interest in a subject if they perceive little interest in their progress on the part of the teacher. A sixteen-year-old student who started attending school in the United States shortly after immigrating, for example, says he became less engaged in his math work when he realized that the teacher only checked the answers to problems and not students' process work, even though the teacher knew that students could easily copy the answers from the back of the book. Our findings thus lend empirical support to what parents and educators have long observed—that students' motivation and effort in school are strongly associated with their connection to their teachers.

IMPLICATIONS FOR EDUCATORS

Our data suggest that efforts to understand and bolster immigrant students' cognitive, behavioral, and relational engagement are likely to yield important academic results, and that teacher practices to bolster engagement in one area will likely have ripple effects across the spectrum. Practices that enrich school-based supportive relationships with both peers and adults—for example, fostering nurturing, safe learning environments, creating advisory groups, and grouping students in small, multi-year cohorts—clearly have the potential to enhance both behavioral and cognitive engagement as well.

Teacher-student relationships are, of course, a two-way street; they also depend on how the two parties involved perceive each other. Not surprisingly, teachers tend to treat students whom they perceive positively in a more nurturing and supportive manner. This teacher epitomizes a sentiment we heard frequently during our interviews:

> The thing I really love about teaching immigrant children is [that they] respect adults, teachers and parents, and older people in general. When they come here, they still have respect for authority figures like teachers and principals. They listen to you when you need to talk to them, and if you get serious about it they will respond to that.[63]

The reverse of this scenario, however, is also evident in relationships between some immigrant students and their teachers. In cases where students do not perceive a genuine, invested interest on the part of their teachers, their level of engagement may decrease and the students may disidentify with teachers and with school. This situation may make teachers uneasy. While many educators genuinely wish they could meet the needs of all their students, at the same time they may justifiably feel anxious at the prospect of becoming overwhelmed by the details of all their students' lives and of meaningfully engaging with the diverse array of adolescents in their classrooms.

Of course, a teacher cannot possibly know all the intricate details of her or his students' histories, experiences of transition, and cultures. Immigrant adolescents themselves often recognize the magnitude of the teacher's task and are not expecting the impossible. Pedagogy that is sensitive to students' cultural backgrounds and needs and demonstrates respect for their cultural heritages is necessary for enhancing their cognitive and behavioral engagement, yet having experienced the difficult process of transition—including the need to learn a new language and new systems of interaction—perhaps the things immigrant students long for the most are basic respect, warmth, and a genuine interest in them as people.[64] Teachers can express this interest through close attention to their progress as learners and through thoughtful, sincere efforts to improve their academic engagement in every way possible. Reaching out relationally to students is the first step and will pay off in huge learning dividends.

NOTES

1. Herbert J. Gans, "Second-Generation Decline: Scenarios for the Economic and Ethnic Futures of the Post-1965 American Immigrants," *Ethnic and Racial Studies* 15 (April 1992): 173–192; Angela B. Ginorio and Michelle Huston, *Si, se puede! Yes, we can!* (Washington, DC: American Association of University Women, 2001).
2. Rubén G. Rumbaut, "Immigration Research in the United States: Social Origins and Future Orientations," *American Behavioral Scientist* 42, no. 9 (1999): 1285–1301.
3. Alejandro Portes and Min Zhou, "The New Second Generation: Segmented Assimilation and Its Variants," *Annals of the American Academy of Political and Social Sciences* 530 (1993): 74–96.
4. Carola Suárez-Orozco, "Identities Under Siege: Immigration Stress and Social Mirroring among the Children of Immigrants," in Antonius C. G. M. Robben and Marcelo M. Suárez-Orozco (eds.), *Cultures Under Siege: Social Violence & Trauma* (Cambridge, England: Cambridge University Press, 2000), 194–226; Carola Suárez-Orozco and Marcelo M. Suárez-Orozco, *Children of Immigration* (Cambridge, MA: Harvard University Press, 2001).
5. Carola Suárez-Orozco, Irina L. G. Todorova, and Josephine Louie, "Making Up For Lost Time: The Experience of Separation and Reunification among Immigrant Families," *Family Process* 41, no. 4 (2002): 625–643.
6. Celia Jaes Falicov, "Ambiguous Loss: Risk and Resilience in Latino Immigrant Families," in Marcelo M. Suárez-Orozco and Mariela Páez (eds.), *Latinos: Remaking America* (Berkeley, CA and Cambridge, MA: University of California Press and David Rockefeller Center for Latin American Studies, 2002).
7. Ron Haskins, Mark Greenberg, and Shawn Fremstad, "Federal Policy for Immigrant Children: Room for Common Ground?" *The Future of Children* 14, no. 2 (2004).
8. Nancy McArdle and Kelly S. Mikelson, "The New Immigrants: Demographic and Housing Characteristics," Working Paper W94-1 (Cambridge, MA: Joint Center for Housing Studies of Harvard University, 1994).
9. Olveen Carrasquillo, Angeles I. Carrasquillo, and Steven Shea, "Health Insurance Coverage of Immigrants Living in the United States: Differences by Citizenship Status and Country of Origin," *American Journal of Public Health* 90, no. 6 (2000): 917–923.
10. Min Zhou, "Growing Up American: The Challenge Confronting Immigrant Children and Children of Immigrants," *Annual Review of Sociology* 23 (1997): 63–95.
11. Portes and Zhou, "The New Second Generation."
12. Mary C. Waters, *Black Identities: West Indian Immigrant Dreams and American Realities* (Cambridge, MA: Harvard University Press, 1999).
13. Lily Wong Fillmore, "When Learning a Second Language Means Losing the First," in Marcelo M. Suárez-Orozco, Carola Suárez-Orozco, and Desirée Baolian Qin (eds.), *The New Immigration: An Interdisciplinary Reader* (New York: Routledge, 2005).
14. All student names used in this chapter are pseudonyms. Except where indicated, all students, teachers, and parents quoted were either interviewed by one of this chapter's authors or participated in a research study in which one or more of the authors were involved.
15. Cynthia Garcia Coll and Katherine Magnuson, "The Psychological Experience of Immigration: A Developmental Perspective," in Alan Booth, Ann C. Crouter, and Nancy Lan-

dale (eds.), *Immigration and the Family: Research and Policy on U.S. Immigrants* (Mahwah, NJ: Lawrence Erlbaum Associates, 1997).

16. Desirée Baolian Qin, "Our Child Does Not Talk to Us Anymore: Alienation in Immigrant Chinese Families," *Anthropology and Education Quarterly* 37 (2006): 162–179.

17. Betty Lee Sung, *The Adjustment Experience of Chinese Immigrant Children in New York City* (Staten Island, NY: Center for Migration Studies, 1987); Zhou, "Growing Up American."

18. Marcelo M. Suárez-Orozco, *Central American Refugees and U.S. High Schools: A Psychosocial Study of Motivation and Achievement* (Palo Alto, CA: Stanford University Press, 1989).

19. Pierrette Hondagneu-Sotelo, "Families on the Frontier: From Braceros in the Fields, to Braceras in the Home." In Marcelo M. Suárez-Orozco and Mariela Páez (eds.), *Latinos: Remaking America* (Berkeley, CA and Cambridge, MA: University of California Press and David Rockefeller Center for Latin American Studies, 2002).

20. Vamik D. Volkan, "Immigration and Refugees: A Psychodynamic Perspective," *Mind and Human Interaction* 4, no. 2 (1993): 63–69; Joseph Westermeyer and Karen Wahmanholm, "Refugee Children," in Roberta J. Apfel and Bennett Simon (eds.), *Minefields in Their Hearts: The Mental Health of Children in War and Communal Violence* (New Haven: Yale University Press, 1996), 75–103.

21. Carola Suárez-Orozco and Desirée Baolian Qin, "Gendered Perspectives in Psychology: Immigrant Origin Youth," Special Issue on Gender and Migration of *International Migration Review* 40, no. 1 (2006): 165–198.

22. Anne Makepeace (director), *Rain in a Dry Land*, Anne Makepeace Productions, Inc., and the Independent Television Service (ITVS), in association with American Documentary/P.O.V. and the Center for Independent Documentary, 2006.

23. Hinda Seif, "'Wise Up!' Undocumented Latino Youth, Mexican-American Legislators, and the Struggle for Higher Education Access," *Latino Studies* 2, no. 2 (2004): 210–230.

24. See, for example, the film *Spellbound* (2002, directed by Jeffrey Blitz), where native-born and immigrant youth participating in the National Spelling Bee are followed through the preparation process, demonstrating commendable dedication but different levels and types of support.

25. Carola Suárez-Orozco and Marcelo M. Suárez-Orozco, *Transformations: Immigration, Family Life, and Achievement Motivation among Latino Adolescents* (Palo Alto, CA: Stanford Universit y Press, 1995).

26. Alejandro Portes and Rubén G. Rumbaut, *Legacies: The Stories of the Immigrant Second Generation* (Berkeley, CA, and New York: University of California Press and Russell Sage Foundation, 2001).

27. Richard Murnane, *Teaching the New Basic Skills: Principles for Educating Children to Thrive in a Changing Economy* (New York: Martin Kessler Books/Free Press, 1996).

28. Portes and Zhou, "The New Second Generation."

29. Margaret Beale Spenser and Sanford M. Dornbusch, "Challenges in Studying Minority Youths," in Shirley S. Feldman and Glen R. Elliott (eds.), *At the Threshold: The Developing Adolescent* (Cambridge, MA: Harvard University Press, 1990), 123–146.

30. Grace Kao and Marta Tienda, "Optimism and Achievement: The Educational Performance of Immigrant Youth," *Social Science Quarterly* 76, no. 1 (1995): 1–19.

31. John U. Ogbu, "Immigrant and Involuntary Minorities in Comparative Perspective," in Margaret A. Gibson and John U. Ogbu (eds.), *Minority Status and Schooling: A Comparative Study of Immigrant and Involuntary Minorities* (New York: Garland Press, 1991), 3–36.

32. Aida Walqui, *Access and Engagement: Program Design and Instructional Approaches for Immigrant Students in Secondary School* (McHenry, IL: Delta Systems, 2000).

33. Carola Suárez-Orozco and Marcelo M. Suárez-Orozco, *Children of Immigration* (Cambridge, MA: Harvard University Press, 2001).

34. Shamita Das Dasgupta, "Gender Roles and Cultural Continuity in the Asian Indian Immigrant Community in the U.S." *Sex Roles* 38, no. 11–12 (1998): 953–974; Min Zhou, *Chinatown* (Philadelphia: Temple University Press, 1992).

35. Stacey J. Lee, "Exploring and Transforming the Landscape of Gender and Sexuality: Hmong American Teenaged Girls," *Race, Gender & Class* 8, no. 1 (2001): 35–46; Loukia K. Sarroub, "The Sojourner Experience of Yemeni American High School Students: An Ethnographic Portrait," *Harvard Educational Review* 71, no. 3 (2001): 390–415.

36. Robert C. Smith, "Gender, Ethnicity, and Race in School and Work Outcomes of Second-Generation Mexican Americans," in Marcelo M. Suárez-Orozco and Mariela M. Páez (eds.), *Latinos: Remaking America* (Berkeley, CA and Cambridge, MA: University of California Press and David Rockefeller Center for Latin American Studies, 2002), 110–125.

37. Mary Waters, "The Intersection of Gender, Race, and Ethnicity in Identity Development of Caribbean American Teens," in Bonnie J. Ross Leadbeater and Niobe Way (eds.), *Urban Girls: Resisting Stereotypes, Creating Identities* (New York University Press, 1996), 65–84.

38. Trica Danielle Keaton, "Muslim Girls and the 'Other France': An Examination of Identity Construction," *Social Identities* 5, no. 1 (1999): 47–64.

39. Carola Suárez-Orozco and Desirée Baolian Qin-Hilliard, "The Cultural Psychology of Academic Engagement: Immigrant Boys' Experiences in U.S. Schools," in Niobe Way and Judy Chu (eds.), *Adolescent Boys: Exploring Diverse Cultures of Boyhood* (New York University Press, 2004).

40. Kay Deaux, *To Be an Immigrant* (New York: Russell Sage Foundation, 2006); Carola Suárez-Orozco, "Identities Under Siege: Immigration Stress and Social Mirroring Among the Children of Immigrants," in Antonius C. G. M. Robben and Marcelo M. Suárez-Orozco (eds.), *Cultures Under Siege: Social Violence and Trauma* (Cambridge, England: Cambridge University Press, 2000), 194–226.

41. Mia Tuan, *Forever Foreigners or Honorary Whites? The Asian Ethnic Experience Today* (New Brunswick, NJ: Rutgers University Press, 1998).

42. C. Suárez-Orozco and M. M. Suárez-Orozco, *Transformations.*

43. Carola Suárez-Orozco, Allison Pimentel, and Margary Martin, "The Significance of Relationships: Academic Engagement and Achievement among Newcomer Immigrant Youth," *Teachers College Record,* in press.

44. Margaret A. Gibson, Patricia Gándara, and Jill Peterson Koyama (eds.), *School Connections: U.S. Mexican Youth, Peers, and School Achievement* (New York: Teachers College Press, 2004); Gilberto Q. Conchas, *The Color of Success: Race and High-Achieving Urban Youth* (Albany: State University of New York Press, 2005); Jennifer A. Fredricks, Phyllis C. Blumenfeld, and Alison H. Paris, "School Engagement: Potential of the Concept, State

of the Evidence," *Review of Educational Research* 74, no. 1 (2004): 54–109; Charles R. Greenwood, Betty T. Horton, and Cheryl A. Utley, "Academic Engagement: Current Perspectives in Research and Practice," *School Psychology Review* 31, no. 3 (2002): 328–349; National Research Council, *Engaging Schools: Fostering High School Students' Motivation to Learn* (Washington, DC: National Academies Press, 2004); Laurence Steinberg, Bradford B. Brown, and Sanford Dornbusch, *Beyond the Classroom: Why School Reform Has Failed and What Parents Need to Do* (New York: Simon and Schuster, 1996); Carola Suárez-Orozco, Marcelo M. Suárez-Orozco, and Irina Todorova, *Learning a New Land: Immigrant Students in American Society* (Cambridge, MA: Harvard University Press, 2008).

45. Russell W. Rumberger, "Why Students Drop Out of School," in Gary Orfield (ed.), *Dropouts in America: Confronting the Graduation Rate Crisis* (Cambridge, MA: Harvard Education Press, 2004).

46. For more information on the LISA study, see C. Suárez-Orozco, M. M. Suárez-Orozco, and Todorova, *Learning a New Land.*

47. C. Suárez-Orozco, M. M. Suárez-Orozco, and Todorova, *Learning a New Land.*

48. Anthony S. Bryk and Barbara Schneider, "Trust in Schools: A Core Resource for School Reform," *Educational Leadership* 60, no. 6 (2003): 40–44; Ricardo D. Stanton-Salazar, "Social Capital among Working-Class Minority Students," in Margaret A. Gibson, Patricia Gándara, and Jill Koyama Peterson (eds.), *School Connections: U.S. Mexican Youth, Peers, and School Achievement* (New York: Teachers College Press, 2004); C. Suárez-Orozco, M. M. Suárez-Orozco, and Todorova, *Learning a New Land.*

49. C. Suárez-Orozco, M. M. Suárez-Orozco, and Todorova, *Learning a New Land.*

50. Anna M. Cauce, Robert D. Felmer, and Judith Primavera, "Social Support in High-Risk Adolescents: Structural Components and Adaptive Impact," *American Journal of Community Psychology* 104 (1982): 417–428; Eric F. Dubow, John Tisak, David Causey, Ann Hryshko, and Graham Reid, "A Two-Year Longitudinal Study of Stressful Life Events, Social Support, and Social Problem-Solving Skills: Contributions to Children's Behavioral and Academic Adjustment," *Child Development* 62, no. 3 (1991): 583–599; Mary J. Levitt and Kathryn R. Wentzel, "Social Influences and School Adjustment: Commentary," *Educational Psychologist* 34, no. 1 (1999): 59–69.

51. Portes and Rumbaut, *Legacies*; Min Zhou and Carl I. Bankston, *Growing Up American: How Vietnamese Children Adapt to Life in the United States* (New York: Russell Sage Foundation, 1998).

52. Sidney Cobb, "Social Support as a Moderator of Life Stress," *Psychosomatic Medicine* 385 (1976): 300–314; Irwin G. Sarason, Barbara R. Sarason, and Gregory R. Pierce, "Social Support: The Search for Theory," *Journal of Social and Clinical Psychology* 9 (1990): 133–147.

53. Fredricks, Blumenfeld, and Paris, "School Engagement."

54. Ricardo D. Stanton-Salazar, *Manufacturing Hope and Despair: The School and Kin Support Networks of U.S.-Mexican Youth* (New York: Teachers College Press, 2001).

55. Suárez-Orozco, Pimentel, and Martin, "The Significance of Relationships."

56. Gibson, Gándara, and Koyama, *School Connections*; Hope M. Hill and Serge Madhere, "Exposure to Community Violence and African American Children: A Multidimensional Model of Risks and Resources," *Journal of Community Psychology* 24 (1996): 26–43.

57. Thomas J. Berndt, "Friends' Influence on Students' Adjustment to School," *Educational Psychologist* 341 (1999): 15–28; John U. Ogbu and Herbert D. Simons, "Voluntary and Involuntary Minorities: A Cultural-Ecological Theory of School Performance with Some Implications for Education," *Anthropology and Education Quarterly* 29 (1999): 155–188; Steinberg, Brown, and Dornbusch, *Beyond the Classroom*.

58. Stephen F. Hamilton and Nancy Darling, "Mentors in Adolescents' Lives," in Klaus Hurrelmann and Stephen F. Hamilton (eds.), *Social Problems and Social Contexts in Adolescence: Perspectives across Boundaries* (New York: Aldine D. Gruyter, 1996), 199–215; Robert C. Pianta, *Enhancing Relationships between Children and Teachers* (Washington, DC: American Psychological Association, 1999); Robert W. Roeser and Jacquelynne S. Eccles, "Adolescents' Perception of Middle School: Relation to Longitudinal Changes in Academic and Psychological Adjustment," *Journal of Research on Adolescence* 8, no. 1 (1998): 123–158.

59. Jennifer Roffman, Carola Suárez-Orozco, and Jean E. Rhodes, "Facilitating Positive Development in Immigrant Youth: The Role of Mentors and Community Organizations," in Francisco A. Villarruel, Daniel F. Perkins, Lynne M. Borden, and Joanne G. Keith (eds.), *Community Youth Development: Practice, Policy, and Research* (Thousand Oaks, CA: Sage, 2003).

60. Suárez-Orozco, Pimentel, and Martin, "The Significance of Relationships."

61. Jean E. Rhodes, *Stand by Me: The Risks and Rewards of Youth Mentoring Relationships* (Cambridge, MA: Harvard University Press, 2002).

62. Jean A. Baker, "Teacher-Student Interaction in Urban At-Risk Classrooms: Differential Behavior, Relationship Quality, and Student Satisfaction with School," *Elementary School Journal* 1001 (1999): 57–70; Rumberger, "Why Students Drop Out"; Margaret C. Wang, Geneva D. Haertel, and Herbert J. Wahlberg, "What Influences Learning? A Content Analysis of Review Literature," *Journal of Educational Research* 84 (1994): 30–43.

63. Suárez-Orozco, Pimentel, and Martin, "The Significance of Relationships."

64. Anna Kirova, "Loneliness in Immigrant Children: Implications for Classroom Practice," *Childhood Education* 77, no. 5 (2001): 260–267.

Profile

"Desde entonces, soy Chicana":
A Mexican Immigrant Student Resists Subtractive Schooling

ANGELA VALENZUELA

In a three-year study of immigrant and non-immigrant youth attending Seguín High School (a pseudonym), an overcrowded, segregated, inner-city school in Houston, Texas, I observed the existence of powerful pressures for immigrants to rapidly assimilate, or "Americanize." I explore this pattern in my book, *Subtractive Schooling: U.S.-Mexican Youth and the Politics of Caring*.[1] There I argue that the Americanization of immigrant students' identities results from the way the curriculum at Seguín High School is organized—and not organized. Specifically, the educational process fails to promote bilingualism, biculturalism, and biliteracy. Instead, schooling is more about subtracting than adding these competencies and, in so doing, compromises the achievement of immigrant and non-immigrant youth alike.

Most of the youth I interviewed for the study were members of the "1.5 generation," those who had emigrated from Mexico at an early age but who, for the major part of their young lives, had a U.S. schooling experience and were thus similar in many respects to their more acculturated, U.S.-born Mexican American peers. I conclude that recent immigrants' rush to claim a new identity renders them marginal not only with respect to the academic mainstream, but also with respect to their families' social identities.

The rapid assimilation of first-generation immigrant youth is often a sign of maladjustment, because identity "choices" are based on a disaffirmation of the self and of the family's social identity. While I observed this pattern, however, I also observed that some students are able both to assimilate and to learn to value the cultural assets that they bring to the schooling context. Nelda was one such student from whom we can learn a great deal.

NELDA

I first encountered Nelda, an eleventh grader, through her English teacher, an Anglo female, who insisted that I meet her. The teacher found Nelda to be a phenomenal student because she had arrived in the United States only three years earlier (in eighth grade) and was already a high achiever. Nelda was virtually fluent in English and blended in well socially with the other students in the class. The teacher was most impressed with the fact that, except for a "very mild" accent, Nelda seemed little different from "the others" (i.e., U.S.-born youth) in the way she carried herself. Explaining to Nelda my interest as a researcher, the teacher prepared her for my morning visit to her class.

When I arrived, the students were busy working at their desks. Nelda saw me and, after a nod from the teacher, stepped out into the hall with me, where we talked for the greater part of the 50-minute period. Our conversation began with questions about her background. The entire conversation took place in English, with Nelda occasionally asking me to translate certain words for her.

Nelda said that she was from the interior of Mexico but had lived for several years in Matamoros, Tamaulipas, which is adjacent to the city of Brownsville at Texas' southernmost border. She explained that her family was lured to the U.S.-Mexico border by the availability of industrial jobs. The pay was still low, however, and to make ends meet her mother crossed the border daily into Brownsville, where she worked as a cleaning woman in various homes. Nelda's family lived in Matamoros for five years, where Nelda and her younger sister had the opportunity to attend *secundaria* (middle school). An English-language course was offered at the school one year, but the instruction was very poor. Nevertheless, Nelda appreciated the opportunity to plow through the assigned book for the course. The family's continuing economic struggles ultimately drove her father to seek better-paying construction jobs in Houston. Her mother still works cleaning homes.

I next asked Nelda which subjects she liked the most in school. This question sparked an immediate intellectual exchange. Nelda began by saying that she has always been interested in history, but especially Mexican and Mexican American history. She said that she had always wondered if the relationship between Mexico and the United States parallels that between Anglos and Mexicans in Texas. "Well, what do you think?" I asked. "I think it is very similar," she said. She went on to explain very articulately that Mexico is a poor country compared to the United States and that Mexican Americans are poor compared to Anglos, "though they are richer here than they are in Mexico." Already the budding scholar, Nelda said that she wanted to read and study more to find out why this parallel exists. Nelda also said that she would love to attend college and continue with her interest in history.

I then asked Nelda whether her parents were educated, where her interest in history came from, and how she acquired native-like fluency in English in such a short period of time. She told me that her father had attained a *secundaria* level of schooling, while her mother had received no more than a primary education: "They both had to work to support their families. Life is very hard in Mexico."

Regarding her interest in history and her facility with English, Nelda explained that living on the border and having a lot of exposure to Chicanas/os, hearing the English language, and reading books in English influenced both her thinking and her language fluency. Her mother's experiences as a cleaning woman were pivotal. She explained that in Brownsville her mother worked for many years for a middle-class Mexican American woman. The woman frequently gave Nelda's mother books in English as gifts, which were soon passed on to Nelda. Nelda said she welcomed the opportunity, dictionary in hand, to improve her literacy in English. She recalled reading such authors as Isabel Allende and Laura Esquivel in English. Most important, however, was her discovery of Rodolfo Acuña's book, *Occupied America*, which provides a historical perspective on the taking of the southwestern lands formerly owned by the Mexican government.[2] *"Desde entonces, soy Chicana,"* she said. ("Since then, I am Chicana.") Interestingly, this was the only complete sentence she said in Spanish during any of our interviews.*

Given the vexed relationship between immigrants and Mexican Americans, her comment about being Chicana stunned me at the time. The actual terms *Chicana* and *Chicano* were rarely used as self-identifiers by Mexican American students at Seguín, much less by immigrant females. U.S.-born students prefer to refer to themselves as Mexican Americans, Mexicans, or Hispanics. Our hallway discussion was thus more enlightening for me than

*In her use of the term *Chicana*, Nelda identifies herself not only with her own biculturalism (which began with her experience living along the U.S.-Mexico border) but also with the Chicano movement ideology of seeking social justice and a right to self-determination for Mexican Americans.

for her, though I did jot down on a piece of paper some additional readings that I thought she could locate in the public library.

Nelda said she often talked with her parents at home about how possible it was for Mexican Americans to become middle class. Although she was exposed to a lot of criticism about Chicanas/os, even in her own family, Nelda felt that through reading history she had come to see their struggles as her own. Nelda further explained that while she will always consider herself Mexican, she sees herself as different from other Mexicans who "look down" on Chicanos. Thus, she manages the dual identities of Mexican and Chicana without seeing any conflict between the two.

THE EXCEPTION OR THE RULE?

Nelda's case strongly suggests the role that ideology can play in mediating the assimilation of adolescents. Armed with excellent literacy skills and empowering historical knowledge, Nelda demonstrated the capacity both to achieve and to blend in within her social milieu. I later wondered why she was not placed in the honors or magnet level of the curriculum. I speculated that, like the vast majority of immigrant students, she had been tracked into regular-level courses during her first year in middle school.

While living on the border and being exposed to Chicanas/os were contributing factors, these are arguably not sufficient for any immigrant to assimilate as rapidly as Nelda seems to have done. Such contexts abound wherever Mexicans and Mexican Americans are concentrated, yet rapid assimilation within a three-year period is nevertheless exceptional. Clearly, Nelda's passion for history and her desire to understand more fully the sources of both Mexicans' and Chicanas/os' oppression was gripping. The fact that she bore at least some of the emblems of Americanized speech, dress, and interpersonal skills is a side note to a more central awakening within her that helps explain her rapid transformation into a Chicana against the historical and institutional odds of her doing so.

Although it is impressive that Nelda was able to arrive at an in-depth understanding of the Mexican American experience, it is unfortunate that she represents the exception rather than the rule. Indirectly, her case embodies an implicit critique of the more general pattern of subtractive schooling, wherein a child's opportunity to develop her or his existing knowledge base is virtually nonexistent. Most significantly, Nelda's case reveals how schools can support a positive sense of identity for immigrant students in ways that are "additive" and empowering. When immigrant youth, and indeed all Mexican American youth, are allowed to maintain their cultural identities— even if that means deliberately exploring the distinct challenges they can expect to face as bicultural people—they can develop an enhanced sense of efficacy and personal control over their futures and reap immense psychic, social, emotional, and academic benefits.

NOTES

1. Angela Valenzuela, *Subtractive Schooling: U.S.-Mexican Youth and the Politics of Caring* (Albany: State University of New York Press, 1999).
2. Rodolfo Acuña, *Occupied America: A History of Chicanos*, 3rd ed. (New York: Harper-Collins, 1988).

CHAPTER FOUR

Model Minorities and Perpetual Foreigners

The Impact of Stereotyping on Asian American Students

STACEY J. LEE

> The [whites] will have stereotypes, like we're smart, . . . and some-
> times you tend to be what they expect you to be and you just lose
> your identity . . . lose being yourself.
> —*High-achieving Asian American high school student*

Like other people of color in the United States, Asian Americans live under
the burden of racial stereotypes that structure their experiences and identities. Stereotypical images of Asian Americans include those of the valedictorian, the violin prodigy, the computer science whiz, the martial arts expert,
the greedy merchant, the gang member, and the bad driver. However, the
two most powerful and persistent stereotypes of Asian Americans are those
of the foreigner and the model minority.

The foreigner stereotype casts Asian Americans as perpetual foreigners
regardless of the length of time they or their families have been in the United
States.[1] The model minority stereotype depicts them as an exceedingly hardworking and successful group that has achieved the American Dream and
no longer experiences any barriers to success.[2] These two stereotypes have
been prevalent since the 1960s, and many of the current stereotypical beliefs
about Asian Americans are variations on these two recurrent themes. For

example, the valedictorian and violin prodigy are specific expressions of the model minority stereotype, and the gang member and bad driver are based on society's image of Asian Americans as perpetual foreigners.

As microcosms of American society, schools are places where the foreigner and model minority stereotypes are, unfortunately, alive and well among students and educators. As illustrated by numerous studies I have conducted with Asian American youth, these stereotypes can have a tremendous impact on these adolescents' self-concept, academic choices, and relationships with others in the school environment.[3]

THE PERPETUAL FOREIGNER STEREOTYPE IN SOCIETY AND IN SCHOOLS

The image of the perpetual foreigner is perhaps the oldest stereotype of Asian Americans. While European American ethnics are accepted as "real" Americans soon after their arrival in the United States, Asian Americans are often viewed as outsiders.[4] Third-, fourth-, and even fifth-generation Asian Americans find that they are not seen as authentic Americans.[5] As sociologist Mia Tuan explains in her book *Forever Foreigners or Honorary Whites? The Asian Ethnic Experience Today*, "While white ethnics must actively assert their ethnic uniqueness if they wish this to feature prominently in their interactions with others, Asian ethnics are assumed to be foreign unless proven otherwise."[6]

To the extent that schools mirror the larger society, Asian American students are strongly affected by the perpetual foreigner stereotype. The Eurocentric curriculum that pervades most schools reinforces this stereotype through its silence around Asian American history.[7] Moreover, when the history or the literature of Asian Americans is taught in schools, it is usually relegated to the periphery of the curriculum, thereby marking Asian American issues as being somehow distinct from "mainstream American" concerns. Superficial approaches to multicultural education, such as programs that focus on Asian holidays and foods, represent another attempt to include Asian American issues in school curriculum, but the token approach with which many are implemented often serves merely to perpetuate the foreigner stereotype.

The image of Asian Americans as perpetual foreigners also informs the way many teachers view their Asian American students. In my research, I have found that teachers typically refer to students of Asian descent as

"Asian" and not as "Asian American" or "American."[8] Although teachers may not intentionally be excluding Asian Americans from the category American, their language reveals an implicit assumption that the categories Asian and American are mutually exclusive. Also, the foreigner stereotype influences teachers' expectations of Asian American students as learners. For example, some teachers automatically assume that Asian American students will do better in math and science than in classes that require strong verbal skills. Other research suggests that some teachers equate accents (i.e., sounding foreign) with low cognitive abilities.[9]

In addition, the foreigner stereotype informs the way non–Asian American students view their Asian American peers. During moments of interracial conflict between students, this stereotype can emerge in full force, such as when non–Asian American students tell Asian American youth to "go back to where they came from" or use fake Asian accents to mock them.[10] Through this kind of behavior, non–Asian American youth send their peers a clear message: they are outsiders in their own schools.

INTERNALIZING—AND RESISTING—THE PERPETUAL FOREIGNER STEREOTYPE

Given the tremendous power of the perpetual foreigner stereotype in schools and society, many Asian American youth have internalized the belief that they are not real Americans. In fact, research suggests that many Asian American students view white people as the only real or authentic Americans.[11] A consistent finding in my studies has been that Asian American students reserve the term *American* for whites and refer to all other groups by their specific races. When asked to describe an American, for example, many Asian American youth will describe a blond-haired, blue-eyed person.[12] Even Asian American students born in the United States are reluctant to use the term *American* to describe themselves because they know that others do not see them that way.[13]

Along with the belief that they are in some way foreign, many Asian American youth have internalized the notion that this foreignness makes them inferior to real (i.e., white) Americans. These students hate qualities they understand to be associated with Asianness (i.e., foreignness). In an effort to distance themselves from these stigmatized images, some Asian American youth may reject things that they understand are perceived to be foreign, such as their names or languages. One Asian American student attending a large high school in the Northeast, for example, explained that he changed his name to an "American" one because he was tired of people making a joke of his name. "People make rhymes like 'fee fi fo fum,'" he explained. "I hate it."[14] Unfortunately, this student has learned that he cannot keep his Asian name and be accepted as American. He and other Asian Americans are forced to reject central aspects of their identities because Asianness and Americanness are seen as mutually exclusive.

Asian American students also have been found to go to great lengths to downplay physical traits that are associated with being Asian. Some girls and young women, for example, wear green or blue contact lenses in order to mask their Asianness and to emulate what they believe are white, "American" standards of beauty. One student explained that popular culture had influenced her ideas about beauty standards. She said, "Watching MTV affected the way I acted very much. I think I wanted to be more Americanized. I changed my hair color. I got colored contact lenses."[15]

In addition to self-perceptions, the foreigner stereotype affects relationships among Asian American students themselves. In an effort to distance themselves from the stigma of foreignness, some U.S.-born Asian youth reject their non–U.S.-born peers, calling them such derogatory terms as *fobs* or *fobbies* (from the initials F.O.B. for "fresh off the boat") or mocking them for not being Americanized. One U.S.-born student at a high school in the Midwest expressed this disdain as follows: "Fobs don't care about clothes. . . . They dress in out-of-date 1980s-style clothes."[16] This student went on to explain that U.S.-born students were "into clothes and cars." By asserting the difference between themselves and non–U.S.-born youth, the American-born students are attempting to claim their rightful status as Americans, but they are unfortunately also reflecting their internalization of racist stereotypes.

The stigma associated with the foreigner stereotype also affects students' participation in classes. Students with Asian accents are often afraid to speak in class for fear that their non-Asian peers will mock the way they talk. Even Asian American students who speak accent-free English are often quiet in classes because they have internalized the belief that their experiences are not valid. One student explained her silence in class by saying, "I don't really have much to say. The American kids have had a lot of really interesting experiences. Lots of them have been to Europe and stuff."[17] Significantly, this student uses the term *American* to refer only to white students. Although she was born in the United States, she clearly has internalized the idea that she is not fully American in the same way most of her classmates are.

THE MODEL MINORITY STEREOTYPE

According to the model minority stereotype, Asian Americans have achieved academic, social, and economic success through hard work and adherence to Asian cultural norms. Unlike many stereotypes, the model minority designation seems at first to be positive and even flattering. A close examination of this stereotype, however, reveals its damaging effects both for Asian Americans and for other people of color. First, the stereotype denies the fact that some Asian Americans continue to struggle against structural and other barriers. Second, it has been used as a political weapon against other marginalized groups of color.

Many of the early articles that perpetuated the model minority stereotype several decades ago explicitly compared Asian Americans, who were described as hardworking and successful, with other racial minorities, who were often depicted as lazy welfare cheats. An example of such an article appeared in a December 1966 issue of *U.S. News & World Report*. The authors praised Chinese Americans for "moving ahead on their own—with no help from anyone" and chastised those who "proposed that hundreds of billions be spent to uplift Negroes and other minorities."[18] Asian Americans were considered good citizens precisely because the dominant culture saw them as a passive, quiet minority who did not challenge the status quo. By contrast, African Americans and other racial minorities were cast as loud and demanding complainers who were looking for a handout. In short, adherents to the model minority stereotype used examples of Asian American success to support their claim that equal opportunity existed for all races and that groups who fail have only themselves to blame.

Teachers and other education professionals commonly evaluate Asian American students according to the standards of the model minority. While there is evidence that Asian Americans do well academically as a group, this lumping together of numerous Asian ethnic groups hides the variation in academic achievement across groups and among individuals.[19] Students able to live up to the standards are held up as examples for others to follow, and those unable to meet them are deemed failed or substandard Asians. In my research on Hmong American students at a high school in the Midwest, I found that educators identified many Southeast Asian American students as failing to achieve model minority performance.[20] "An East Asian student might be number three in the class, going to Yale, but the Southeast Asians aren't very motivated," one counselor said.[21] Here, the "success" of East Asian American (i.e., model minority) students is used against the Southeast Asian American youth to cast the latter as underachievers.

Like the perpetual foreigner stereotype, the notion of the model minority also affects interracial relationships. At a high school in a large northeastern city, I found educators who used the model minority stereotype against African Americans and other groups of color.[22] In response to evidence that black students were the most likely population to drop out or experience failure at Academic High School (a pseudonym), teachers and administrators pointed to the success of Asian American students as "proof" that the system was not racist. In comparing the aspirations of the school's Asian American and African American students, one counselor said, "Asians like U. of P. [University of Pennsylvania], M.I.T., Princeton. They tend to go to good schools. . . . I wish our blacks would take advantage of things instead of sticking to sports and entertainment."[23]

The model minority stereotype also influences perceptions about race among Asian American students. Those who believe the stereotype are likely to assume that they are the superior minority. At Academic High I found that Asian American students who internalized this stereotype often held overtly racist attitudes toward their African American peers.[24] Conversely, the stereotype also led African American students to resent their Asian American counterparts. One African American student explained, "A lot of people I know don't like Asian people because they are intimidated by their intelligence. They say, 'They [Asians] came over here and they bought everything and now look at them in school.'"[25] According to this student's description, his peers see Asian Americans as excellent students (i.e., model minorities), but also as greedy people who go into black neighborhoods and take over businesses. Like many of the Asian American students at Academic High, the majority of African American students believed that the interests of Asian Americans and the interests of African Americans were at odds.

THE IMPACT OF THE MODEL MINORITY STEREOTYPE ON ASIAN AMERICAN IDENTITY

The model minority stereotype places a lot of pressure on Asian American students to do well in school. At Academic High, I found that both high-

and low-achieving students experienced a great deal of anxiety over their ability to achieve to model minority standards.[26] Some low-achieving Asian American students were so ashamed about their academic struggles that they hid their difficulties from teachers and peers. Many high achievers lived in fear that they were not doing well enough. One high-achieving student remarked:

> The [whites] will have stereotypes, like we're smart. . . . They are so wrong; not everyone is smart. They expect you to be this and that, and when you're not . . . [shakes her head]. And sometimes you tend to be what they expect you to be and you just lose your identity . . . just lose being your-self. [You] become part of what . . . what someone else want[s] you to be. And it's really awkward, too! When you get bad grades, people look at you really strangely because you are sort of distorting the way they see an Asian. It makes you feel really awkward if you don't fit the stereotype.[27]

As this student's comments illustrate, the model minority stereotype shapes not only the way others perceive Asian American students but also these youths' perceptions of themselves.

On the other hand, some Asian American students resist the model minor-ity stereotype entirely because they fear that it marks them as being "nerdy" or "uncool." Male students may fear that being cast as a model minority makes them appear unmasculine. Sometimes these young men exhibit ste-reotypically masculine traits in order to reject the nerd image of the model minority. Unfortunately, these young men often believe that they must resist school in order to appear manly. One young man at Academic High who affected a sort of hypermasculinity in response to the model minority stereo-type explained, "I'm not a wimp. I can defend myself. A lot of Asians can't fight, so they have to go around in gangs. They're small—you know Asian guys." Although this student succeeded at not being seen as a nerd, his atti-tude toward schooling earned him a place at the bottom of his graduating class.

CONCLUSIONS AND RECOMMENDATIONS

Both the perpetual foreigner stereotype and the model minority stereotype impose limitations on Asian American students that negatively affect their schooling experiences. The perpetual foreigner stereotype excludes Asian Americans from their rightful place as Americans and marks them as inferior to white Americans. The model minority stereotype denies problems within Asian American communities, ignores the continuing inequality faced by Asian Americans, and reinforces the myth of equal opportunity.[28]

Although schools currently play an active role in perpetuating these and other stereotypes, they also contain the seeds of potential change. Schools can make curricular changes that disrupt and challenge these stereotypes. In literature classes, for example, students can read autobiographies and works of fiction by Asian American authors in order to see which stereotypes are confirmed or challenged by the stories. By teaching the long and complex history of Asian Americans in this country, schools can combat the stereotype of Asian Americans as perpetual foreigners. Information about the historical roots of the foreigner and model minority stereotypes and about the political uses of these stereotypes can be incorporated into discussions of American history. Finally, students need a truly multicultural curriculum that challenges the idea that Asianness and Americanness are mutually exclusive categories. These changes, though seemingly small, could represent, for both Asian American students and the larger school community, the first steps toward broader and more encompassing change.

NOTES

1. Mia Tuan, *Forever Foreigners or Honorary Whites? The Asian Ethnic Experience Today* (New Brunswick, NJ: Rutgers University Press, 1998).
2. Stacey J. Lee, *Unraveling the "Model-Minority" Stereotype: Listening to Asian American Youth* (New York: Teachers College Press, 1996); Keith Osajima, "Asian Americans as the Model Minority: An Analysis of the Popular Press Image in the 1960s and 1980s," in Gary Y. Okihiro, Shirley Hune, Arthur A. Hansen, and John M. Liu (eds.), *Reflections on Shattered Windows: Promises and Prospects for Asian American Studies* (Pullman: Washington State University Press, 1988), 165–174; Robert H. Suzuki, "Education and the Socialization of Asian Americans: A Revisionist Analysis of the 'Model Minority' Thesis," *Amerasia Journal* 4 (1977): 23–51.
3. See *Unraveling the "Model-Minority" Stereotype* and other works by Stacey J. Lee: "More Than 'Model Minorities' or 'Delinquents': A Look at Hmong American High School Students," *Harvard Educational Review* 71, no. 3 (Fall 2001): 505–528; "Learning 'America': Hmong American High School Students," *Education and Urban Society* 34, no. 2 (2002): 233–245.
4. Tuan, *Forever Foreigners*.
5. Tuan, *Forever Foreigners*.
6. Tuan, *Forever Foreigners*, 137.
7. Ronald Takaki, *Strangers From a Different Shore: A History of Asian Americans* (New York: Penguin Books, 1989).

8. Lee, *Unraveling*.
9. A. Lin Goodwin and Maritza B. MacDonald, "Educating the Rainbow: Authentic Assessment and Authentic Practice for Diverse Classrooms," in A. Lin Goodwin (ed.), *Assessment for Equity and Inclusion: Embracing All Our Children* (New York: Routledge, 1997), 211–228.
10. A. Lin Goodwin, *Growing Up Asian in America: A Search for Self* (Greenwich, CT: Information Age Publishing, 2003); Lee, *Unraveling*.
11. Lee, *Unraveling* and "More Than 'Model Minorities'"; Laurie Olsen, *Made in America: Immigrant Students in Our Public Schools* (New York: New Press, 1997).
12. Lee, *Unraveling* and "Learning 'America.'"
13. Lee, *Unraveling*.
14. Lee, *Unraveling*, 46.
15. Stacey J. Lee and Sabina Vaught, "You Can Never Be Too Rich or Too Thin: Popular Culture and the Americanization of Asian American Women," *Journal of Negro Education* 72, no. 4 (2003): 457–466.
16. Lee, "More Than 'Model Minorities,'" 51.
17. Lee, "Learning 'America,'" 243.
18. "Success Story of One Minority Group in the U.S," *U.S. News & World Report*, December 23, 1966, 73–78.
19. Valerie O. Pang, "Asian American Children: A Diverse Population," in Donald T. Nakanishi and Tina Y. Nishida (eds.), *The Asian American Experience: A Source Book for Teachers and Students* (New York: Routledge, 1995); Wendy Walker-Moffat, *The Other Side of the Asian American Success Story* (San Francisco: Jossey-Bass, 1995).
20. Lee, "Learning 'America'"; Walker-Moffat, *The Other Side*.
21. Lee "Learning 'America,'" 523.
22. Lee, *Unraveling*.
23. Lee, *Unraveling*, 78.
24. Lee, *Unraveling*.
25. Lee, *Unraveling*, 99.
26. Lee, *Unraveling*.
27. Lee, *Unraveling*, 59.
28. Osajima, "Asian Americans."

CHAPTER FIVE

"Who am I as a learner?"

Would Girls and Boys Tend to Answer Differently?

MICHELLE GALLEY

So many theories about why boys and girls achieve academically at different levels have been put forth in recent years that some have dubbed the verbal jousting the "gender war" in education. First schools were shortchanging girls; then it was the boys who were getting left behind. Even as some arguments grew heated, it was clear that educators needed to do more to address gender differences. But what exactly? How do gender differences play out in the emerging identities of adolescents, and how do these differences affect them both as people and as learners?

The answers to these questions are almost too numerous to count and can vary greatly, depending on whom you ask. Carol Gilligan's groundbreaking book, *In a Different Voice: Psychological Theory and Women's Development*, fired what some saw as the first shots in this gender war when it was published in 1982.[1] At a time when many in the feminist movement were insisting that there are no differences between men and women, Gilligan, a longtime faculty member of the Harvard Graduate School of Education and now a professor at New York University, theorized that there are important psychological differences between the sexes. In subsequent work Gilligan expanded her exploration of these differences and focused specifically on how they play out for adolescent girls. She found in her research that as girls entered their preteen years they became unsure of themselves, even if they were previously daring, perceptive, and outspoken in the ways they communicated and acted. They became more focused on what they were "supposed to do," even if that differed from what they knew was right. Gilligan theorized that in order to maintain relationships with others—often those they were expected to please, including teachers and boys—adolescent girls would sacrifice "relationship" with themselves.[2]

More shots were fired on the education front when the American Association of University Women (AAUW) issued the influential—and highly controversial—report entitled *How Schools Shortchange Girls: The AAUW Report, A Study of Major Findings on Girls and Education.* The report claimed that schools were geared more toward educating boys than girls. It also said the books schools used were male oriented and had more male role models and central characters; in essence, they were more supportive of boys' identities than girls'. In addition, the report noted that teachers called on boys more often and suggested that girls were taught to view themselves as less capable of working in the highest-paying professions. Girls were discouraged from taking courses that could eventually lead to lucrative jobs, the researchers charged. They believed that the "glass ceiling" women faced in the job market was also found in classrooms across the country.[3]

Not long after that report was released, research showed that girls were scoring lower on math and science standardized tests. Those test scores were used as further evidence that boys were being better served in schools. More recently, however, girls have started to close the gap in scores on these tests. Recent results show that as high school seniors, girls are trailing boys by an average of only two points on the National Assessment of Educational Progress (NAEP) mathematics test, and boys hold statistically significant advantages in only two of the four math content areas tested. Even more impressively, girls significantly outperform boys on all aspects of the NAEP reading tests, with twelfth-grade females in 2005 scoring thirteen points higher overall than their male counterparts (a significantly wider gender gap than in 1992).[4] These trends are not unique to the United States; in many countries around the world, girls score significantly higher than boys on language arts tests.[5] Moreover, girls in the United States now have higher school grade-point averages than boys and obtain bachelor's degrees in greater numbers.[6]

Partly fueled by such developments, the gender war has shifted fronts in the past decade or so to include concerns about boys. Perhaps the best-known writer about the difficulties boys face in school and elsewhere in their lives is William Pollack of Harvard University, who cites the disproportionate number of boys in special education as one piece of evidence that schools are not as "boy friendly" as they could be.[7] (Males make up about two-thirds of the special education population in U.S. public schools.) According to Pollack, the curriculum in most schools is set up in a way that is friendlier to girls than boys. Boys have a natural learning tempo that is more action oriented and hands-on than girls', Pollack says, but because most curricula require students to work independently and quietly, many boys end up feeling like failures.

While these theories and research findings may seem difficult to reconcile, one fact seems to emerge from all of them: There are differences between boys and girls in school. As the research suggests, many of these differences may be related to the ways boys and girls see themselves as learners, what might be called their "learner identities." There are, of course, countless exceptions that remind us of the need to put such generalities in perspective. (Pollack, for example, would never argue that all boys' learning styles are ill served by schools.) Still, it is important for educators to consider some of the patterns that researchers have observed in the different learner identities of boys and girls. This will help teachers and administrators envision classroom environments that might yield the greatest success for both.

A BIOLOGICAL BASIS?

By the time young people reach adolescence they have had years of educational experiences influenced both by biological factors and by the ways society socializes boys and girls. According to Michael Gurian, author of the book *Boys and Girls Learn Differently*, many of the differences in the ways boys and girls develop as learners can be traced back to their brain functions.[8] Girls' brains mature earlier than boys', Gurian says, which is why they are, on average, able to read earlier and speak with better grammar. He notes that girls are also able to hear, smell, and feel tactile sensations better; have better overall verbal abilities; and are better able to control their impulses than boys because of differences in the ways their brains are wired. According to Gurian, those differences result in girls being less likely to take risks and cause boys to be more likely to show a tendency toward aggressive behavior, both of which greatly affect how they see themselves and interact with others in the school context. (See "'I am not insane; I am angry,'" by Michael S. Kimmel, pp. 99–110, and "Male Adolescent Identity and the Roots of Aggression: A Conversation with James Garbarino," pp. 111–115, in this volume.)

On the other hand, because the male brain tends to have better development in the right hemisphere, boys have more advanced spatial abilities on average, according to a study by researchers at the University of Chicago.[9] The Chicago researchers found that differences in girls' and boys' spatial abilities show up by age four and one-half and are manifest in tasks such as interpreting graphs and maps and in understanding geography. In addition, boys tend to rely on nonverbal communication, which Gurian says has enormous ramifications for them in an education system that relies so heavily on conversation and words.

These factors and a host of others are bound to have an effect on how children view themselves as learners: the extent to which they connect to and like school, how they see their place in the social environment with both teachers and peers, and whether they believe they are "good at" certain subjects or tasks. Because teenagers spend so much of their time together at school, Gurian notes that outside the family, school is the primary identity development system for adolescents: "By the time we turn fifteen, we've expanded the palette or canvas of our identity development well outside our parents."[10]

DIFFERENT VIEWS OF SUCCESS AND FAILURE

One difference in boys' and girls' identities as learners is reflected in the way they view success and failure, according to research by psychologist Janice Streitmatter of the University of Arizona. Boys, Streitmatter says, tend to see failure as something that is caused by external factors and is unstable, "that there is some reason other than themselves that caused the failure." For example, to explain why he performed poorly on an exam, a boy might say that his teacher wrote a bad test, that he was unlucky, or that he was just having a bad day. The cause of his failure has relatively little to do with his actions and is more tied to the education system or factors beyond his control. However, when adolescent boys succeed, they have more of a tendency to identify that success as internal and stable. They say things like, "Of course I aced that test. I knew the material." In other words, boys have a relatively easy time taking credit for their victories. Such an orientation toward success may also be consistent with the way Pollack says boys are socialized in our culture "to present to the world an image of male toughness, stoicism, and strength," whether that image represents their true feelings or not.[11]

Girls, on the other hand, seem to have the opposite orientation, says Streitmatter. When girls do well on a test—particularly in math and science—they tend to report that maybe the exam was easy or that they just got lucky that day. And if they don't do well they say that they have never been good at that subject, or that it is just very difficult for them. Streitmatter notes, "Even girls who are in upper-level math classes, like Advanced Placement geometry, tend to hold to this pattern." And, although the causes are hard to pinpoint, these findings seem to support Gilligan's data showing that girls become unsure of themselves in adolescence, particularly in male-dominated domains (as math and science traditionally have been).

What kind of learner we become can be influenced by how we view ourselves in relation to our educational achievements and challenges. If we think that we are just random victims of bad tests when we fail, for example, we might be less invested in our learning. Therefore, teachers may need to help some boys understand that failure is often just as much a result of their own doing as success (or, as Pollack's work suggests, that it is okay to admit when material is difficult for them and to seek help). On the other hand, seeing success as something random could be just as damaging, so it is vital for girls to take ownership of their successes and learn to appreciate when they have performed well.

SEEING SCHOOL AS RELEVANT

Boys' and girls' identities as learners are also revealed in the degree to which they see school as relevant to their everyday lives. Research has found that boys in particular can have a difficult time finding practical uses for school, especially in the subjects of reading and writing. And, as any observant teacher can tell you, a student who sees course content as irrelevant to "real life" is one who is more reluctant to learn.

In the book *Reading Don't Fix No Chevys: Literacy in the Lives of Young Men*, researchers Michael W. Smith and Jeffrey D. Wilhelm describe their study of the reading habits of forty-nine boys from different academic, ethnic, and socioeconomic backgrounds. Smith and Wilhelm found that even though many of the boys they interviewed valued school, they rejected reading because they saw it as something they had to do for no immediately apparent reason. Even when teachers told them that they needed to pass their classes in order to go to college, for example, the boys still failed to see the importance of that because college, to them, was far off in the future. What mattered most to them was what was happening right then and there. When the boys talked about the experiences with reading that they enjoyed, these were connected to their lives in some concrete way. One boy complained to the researchers that his girlfriend read romances. When asked what was wrong with that, the boy replied, "You can't fix a toilet when you're done."[12]

Smith and Wilhelm also found that the boys tended to look for a sense of "flow" in their activities. The state of flow, originally conceived by psychologist Mihaly Csikszentmihalyi, is one "in which people are so involved in an activity that nothing else seems to matter."[13] Csikszentmihalyi used eight principles to define that experience, which Smith and Wilhelm have combined into four: a sense of control and competence, a challenge that requires an appropriate level of skill, clear goals and feedback, and a focus on the immediate experience.

Most of the boys Smith and Wilhelm studied experienced flow outside of school, often when they were playing video games. This was in part because they felt like they had control over the activity and its outcome, the researchers note. In school, however, many of the boys reported that they never felt in control and that this alienated them from their studies. For example, some felt they never really mastered one activity before they were asked to move on to another one. Wilhelm says that "the very structure of school is contradictory to the elements of flow" and that this circumstance has an effect on the way boys see themselves in connection to learning.

MAKING CONNECTIONS DIFFERENTLY

The girl reading the romance novel in the earlier anecdote was obviously not expecting it to have a practical, immediate application. Researchers have noted that girls are generally able to stick to subjects for longer periods of time and are less distracted from them than boys. They also are far less likely than boys to be diagnosed with attention-deficit/hyperactivity disorder (AD/HD). Girls are therefore more willing to be patient with a lesson even if it doesn't pertain to their everyday lives or seem to give them immediate benefits. This focus seems to give girls at least one kind of edge in school.

But there may be other aspects of schooling that run counter to girls' identities as learners, say researchers Frances A. Maher and Janie Victoria Ward, in their book *Gender and Teaching*.[14] They say the teaching styles prevalent in too many schools are based on competition, thus making them less conducive to girls' success. "Pedagogies built on competitive hand waving silence the quieter students, particularly the girls," Maher and Ward write, because often it is boys who do most of the hand waving.[15] Girls are also able to garner more information and make more connections from discussion than from trying to find the absolute right answer, they note.

Not only do girls have the problem of trying to make their way through a competitive school environment, but entering puberty also pulls them in a different direction. For example, Gilligan has found that the pressures of trying to succeed academically by speaking up, but also trying to be attractive to boys by staying quiet, can cause girls to silence themselves in school. Citing Gilligan, Maher and Ward note, "Beginning with puberty, girls 'fall silent' as they try to meet the contradictory expectations of pleasing others, accommodating male standards for female attractiveness and docility, and yet succeeding academically."[16]

Interestingly, however, even in some single-sex classrooms girls still remain relatively quiet. Kathryn Herr, a professor at Montclair State University, studied 1,100 students—boys and girls—who were being educated in single-sex classrooms at a public middle school in Long Beach, California. In many of the girls-only classes, just a few of the girls spoke up and took leadership roles, says Herr. Some teachers thought these classes were successful because there were no disruptions. But "a quiet classroom is not necessarily the ideal, and we can't equate that with an equitable education," Herr says. Perhaps the pressure of still being in the same school and, thus, the same social setting as boys caused the girls to stay silent in class. Or perhaps the teaching methods used in those classes did not encourage group discussion. Whatever the reason, it is obvious that just excluding young men did not in and of itself cause girls to speak out more.

While taking boys out of the classroom may not have done much to bring out the voices of girls, teaching boys separately did seem to have some benefits, Herr found. The boys she studied who were educated in single-sex classes felt that they could take more risks in class and in making friends. They reported that it felt like a release to be in classes without girls and said that they asked questions they might not have felt comfortable asking if girls had been in the room. Thus, boys were better able to express their learner identities, including being able to speak freely and take risks, in classes that did not include girls.

A WORD OF CAUTION

Of course, as every teacher knows, each student is an individual. Although there are many similarities that researchers have observed among students with certain defining characteristics, such as gender, it is dangerous to oversimplify the issue. Not all boys are alike, nor are all girls alike. Wilhelm and Smith claim that the battle lines in the gender war are misdrawn because there are boys and girls on both sides. They write, "Though people often must necessarily think in generalizations and categories, these are always too simple. Many girls excel in math; many boys love to read. We categorize for the sake of argument, clarity, and for ease of thinking, but sometimes our categories cause problems and keep us from seeing the students before us."[17]

While it is important to note that young women are generally less likely than boys to speak up in class and tend to perform better than boys in reading and writing, that does not mean that every adolescent girl fits into that category. Such assumptions would surely fail those girls who need extra help with literacy skills and falsely define the ones who are natural leaders. Likewise, researchers note that boys tend to respond better to hands-on learning opportunities and perform better in science and mathematics. That does not mean, however, that in science and math classes one should assume that every boy will perform well. Finally, the fact that boys in Herr's study felt freer to take risks does not mean that single-sex classes are a panacea or that they enable all boys and girls to express themselves fully as learners in school.

A struggling student needs extra attention, regardless of gender. What this research tells us, however, is that if a student is not achieving to her or his full potential, educators might consider the ways in which issues related to gender may play a part.

NOTES

1. Carol Gilligan, *In a Different Voice: Psychological Theory and Women's Development* (Cambridge, MA: Harvard University Press, 1982).
2. One of several works in which Gilligan reports these findings is a book she coauthored with Lyn Mikel Brown, *Meeting at the Crossroads: Women's Psychology and Girls' Development* (Cambridge, MA: Harvard University Press, 1992).
3. American Association of University Women, *How Schools Shortchange Girls: The AAUW Report. A Study of Major Findings on Girls and Education,* research by the Wellesley College Center for Research on Women (Washington, DC: AAUW Educational Foundation, 1992).
4. National Center for Education Statistics (NCES), *The Nation's Report Card: 12th Grade Reading and Mathematics 2005, National Assessment of Educational Progress* (Washington, DC: NCES, 2007).
5. Organisation for Economic Co-operation and Development (OECD), *Knowledge and Skills for Life: First Results from PISA 2000* (Paris: OECD, 2001).
6. Donghun Cho, "The Role of High School Performance in Explaining Women's Rising College Enrollment," *Economics of Education Review* 26, no. 4 (2007): 450–462.

7. William Pollack, *Real Boys: Rescuing Our Sons from the Myths of Boyhood* (New York: Random House/Owl Books, 1998/1999).

8. Michael Gurian, *Boys and Girls Learn Differently! A Guide for Teachers and Parents* (San Francisco: Jossey-Bass, 2001).

9. Susan Levine, Janellen Huttenlocher, Amy Taylor, and Adela Langrock, "Early Sex Differences in Spatial Skill," *Journal of Developmental Psychology* 35, no. 4 (November 2002): 940–949.

10. Quotations in this chapter are from interviews with the researchers, except where noted.

11. Pollack, *Real Boys,* xxii.

12. Michael W. Smith and Jeffrey D. Wilhelm, *Reading Don't Fix No Chevys: Literacy in the Lives of Young Men* (Portsmouth, NH: Heinemann, 2002).

13. Smith and Wilhelm, *Reading*, 28.

14. Frances A. Maher and Janie Victoria Ward, *Gender and Teaching* (Mahwah, NJ: Lawrence Erlbaum Associates, 2002).

15. Maher and Ward, *Gender and Teaching*, 93.

16. Maher and Ward, *Gender and Teaching*, 93.

17. Smith and Wilhelm, *Reading*, 9.

Research feature

"Getting the message across":[1]
Adolescent Girls and Note Writing

THERESA SQUIRES COLLINS

School is the place where the personal meets the academic. Obviously course work is of paramount importance in an adolescent's school life, but because middle and high schools are also places where girls develop into young women, the impact of the hundreds of social interactions they have during the course of any day cannot be ignored. Many girls make space for their friendships and for other concerns in their busy school lives by writing notes to each other in classes.

In studying the note writing practices of adolescent girls as a teacher-researcher in the 1990s, I came to develop an appreciation for this activity, which most teachers and other adults find frivolous, as one that helps girls navigate the academic and social changes vital to their developing sense of self at this important juncture in their lives. Adolescent boys, too, write notes occasionally, though the purpose of their writing is almost always in response to a note received from a girl acquaintance or girlfriend.

Many researchers in the latter part of the twentieth century lamented what they saw as the neglect of the adolescent female.[2] Girls, they wrote, were silencing themselves, drowning in a girl-hating culture, and generally being forgotten in schools. By contrast, the twenty-first century has seen a new crop of writers classify girls in a different way based on the allegedly aggressive social habits they exhibit at school. Books such as Rachel Simmons' *Odd Girl Out: The Hidden Culture of Aggression in Girls* and Rosalind Wiseman's *Queen Bees and Wannabees: Helping Your Daughter Survive Cliques, Gossip, Boyfriends, and Other Realities of Adolescence* are written primarily for parents, with suggestions as to what they can do to help their daughters negotiate the minefield of potential social attacks in school. There are even how-to books for girls, such as *Mean Chicks, Cliques, and Dirty Tricks: A Real Girl's Guide to Getting Through the Day with Smarts and Style* by Erika V. Shearin Karres. All seek to assist girls with the real concerns of school cliques and conflicts, using the very vocabulary that so divides girls from one another and that perpetuates a vision of girls as a bunch of "chicks," "queen bees," "snobs," and "name droppers." Instead of silenced and forgotten wallflowers, these writers see overly aggressive young women manipulating each other for social status. These conflicting views of girls give us reason to step back from overly simplistic characterizations of their behavior and experiences and examine what girls themselves are communicating to each other over the course of the school day.

DO GIRLS *STILL* WRITE NOTES?

As we approach the close of the first decade of the twenty-first century, technology has provided girls with a myriad of ways to connect with friends and has expanded social networks. The rise of "cyberbullying" is a disturbing trend, and the lack of privacy and control over material shared online is at times terrifying. Kids' jockeying for social position becomes a community event in spaces like Facebook or online blogs, where the story of a girl's life can be written by a virtual community. All of these advances raise the question of whether the world of online communication is a benefit or detriment to girls. In spite of instant messaging, "texting," and online chat rooms where girls can go to communicate with friends, the practice of writing and passing notes in class is alive and well; it may even be a last site where girls have near complete control over what they say and to whom the message is delivered.

Then as now, many of the girls who talked to me about writing notes admitted that they feel compelled to write a note to a friend as soon as they have finished reading one, but few believed that writing notes interfered with their class work. Instead, many felt that writing a note alleviated the social tension they were experiencing and allowed them to reclaim focus. In this way, girls negotiate the reality of how social and academic life are intertwined at school. As one of my respondents explained, "If your mind's not there [in class], it'll do no good to try and concentrate—write it [the note] and get back to class with the conflict off your mind; at least you know that the person will know your feelings and then you can do your work." Another concurred, "Either way, it's on your mind, so you might as well write about it and get it off."[3] In a recent conversation with middle school girls at the Francis W. Parker School in Chicago, one girl added, "I'll pretend like I'm listening in history class, but then I'll write a note on the note cards I'm supposed to be using for class." Others use their assignment note-books or take advantage of desks set up for group work so that "I can just move a note with my elbow to get my friend to see that I've written some-thing in the margins of my paper."

Note writing, in addition to freeing up cognitive space, can help girls discover the primacy of relationships as they make sense of who they are and what's important to them. Notes from friends are, as one of my respon-dents said, a "casual reminder of everyday life . . . little things that most people wouldn't think of but that make you feel good when you read them in a note." For example, in a note to her friend Kate about planning a dis-ruptive "revolution" in French class, Jessica writes a friendly postscript: "Sorry, but I have to break the military talk to inform you that you look cute today." The note is simultaneously mischievous and supportive, sub-versive and sweet, and is, as in most cases, concerned with the maintenance of the friendship. As Zoe explains, "Notes are just fun, they make you feel like people want to talk to you."

Conversely, notes can also be a place where girls work out their feelings about the difficult life transitions that take place as they mature, including friendships that have run their course. This kind of conflict is illustrated in the following excerpt from one respondent's note to a longtime friend:

> For me I entirely believe that absence makes the heart grow fonder and I want to be able to say that that was true in our case. Time and timing is everything to me. And I need time because now is not our time. Also, I think you need to figure out why you are after my friendship and many other ones and figure out if the reasons are valid. Also, please figure out what would actually make you truly happy and work to achieve that. . . . Whatever happens I will always love you, I will never forget you, and I hope that I never can say, "I don't know Kat anymore."

Notes also can be an outlet where girls discover different parts of them-selves. They may draw on artistic sensibilities, experiment with emergent voices, play with conventions of style, and defy the oppressions of the class-room. For example, as girls compose letters to one another, they sometimes use writing techniques that are more sophisticated than any they've used in a required paper; their notes can contain passages that are vivid and heart-breaking as well as virulent and hilarious. One girl in my study prided her-self on her "Technicolor notes," written in several colors of ink and enjoyed for their cleverness by friends throughout the day. In their middle school history class, girls from Francis Parker School make "big signs with messages on them," which they hold up, placard style, behind a teacher's turned back. "Getting the message across" takes on an entirely new meaning in classes when girls actually fly folded note cards across the classroom, risking the ire of the teacher while catching a buzz of excitement, the eye of their classmates, and the attention of the girl who safely receives and reads the note. Another group of girls I interviewed created an elaborate cartoon/story series in their notes that chronicled the trials and tribulations of a beleaguered high school girl. And, in a particularly poetic exchange, two eighth grade friends gave each other—without comment or explanation of subject matter—photographs they had taken. Each girl then took her photo, pasted it into a notebook, and wrote a poem in response. The resulting two books of their original poetry, they said, reflected their creativity as well as "where we were mentally that year."

NOTE WRITING AS IDENTITY DEVELOPMENT

Adolescent girls' notes reveal that, in very significant ways, they are coping together with stresses and issues that are central to their middle and high school experience. This is not to say that notes take care of every emotional and social need that girls have or that girls do not need caring adults in their lives to assist with difficult times. Still, note writing shows girls' spirit, independence, and solidarity in the face of the difficult transition of adolescence.

Girls obviously do not think about their identity development in the same way that adult theorists do, but their notes reveal that they *are* thinking about more than gossip. The act of note writing is prevalent within classrooms—almost so ubiquitous that it becomes invisible. As frustrating as note writing can be for the teacher trying to keep everyone focused on a lesson, we need to take seriously the things girls do independently in school to help them navigate through the minefield of cliques, tests, passing periods, and social traumas. The fact that girls are still taking the time to write in light of all of the technology at their disposal indicates a lingering need to connect in a very personal and physical way. Notes don't vanish with a keystroke, and somehow the immediacy of a handwritten letter seems to provide girls with a sense of reality and permanence that the Internet or text-messaging simply do not.

"They are our food," remarked a girl I interviewed. Notes give their readers "a chance to know that someone was thinking about you that day," as one student put it. They praise good grades, a goal scored, or a date made, and in so doing they help girls foster one another's positive self-esteem. They are the arbiters of disagreements between friends and enemies alike, and they are sometimes coded in case they fall into enemy hands. Despite adults' tendency to dismiss them as a distraction, these messages written on 8½ × 11-inch notebook paper, an old Spanish assignment, a math worksheet, or a history note card are binding missives that chronicle some of an adolescent girl's most meaningful thoughts, feelings, and relationships in the context of the school day.

NOTES

1. Many thanks to the girls at the Francis W. Parker School, whose comments during our conversation about notes inspired the new title, which in the first edition of *Adolescents at School* was "Writing Their Way Through."

2. American Association of University Women, *How Schools Shortchange Girls: The AAUW Report. A Study of Major Findings on Girls and Education*, research by Wellesley College Center for Research on Women (Washington, DC: AAUW Educational Foundation, 1992); Peggy Orenstein, *Schoolgirls: Young Women, Self-Esteem, and the Confidence Gap* (New York: Doubleday, 1994); Mary Pipher, *Reviving Ophelia* (New York: Putnam, 1994); Myra Sadker and David Sadker, *Failing at Fairness: How America's Schools Cheat Girls* (New York: Charles Scribner's Sons, 1994).

3. Some quotations from interviews and notes come from an ethnographic study I completed for my master's thesis, *Handwritten with Care: A Study of Girls' Notewriting in School* (Evanston, IL: Northwestern University, 1998), for which I conducted group interviews and collected, read, and categorized more than 2,000 notes. Others come from an October 2007 conversation with middle school girls at the Francis W. Parker School in Chicago.

CHAPTER SIX

"I am not insane; I am angry"[1]

Adolescent Masculinity, Homophobia, and Violence

MICHAEL S. KIMMEL

Violence in our nation's schools has emerged as one of our most gripping social problems. All over the country, Americans are asking why some young people open fire apparently randomly, killing or wounding other students and their teachers. Are these adolescents emotionally disturbed? Are they held in the thrall of media-generated violence—in video games, the Internet, rock or rap music? Are their parents to blame? Our shock and concern, and the wrenching anguish of parents who fear that their children may not be safe in their own schools, demand serious policy discussions. And such discussions demand serious inquiry into the causes of school violence.

As several recent events have made clear, it isn't just high schools where these shootings are taking place. In the deadliest college campus shooting in U.S. history on April 16, 2007, Seung-Hui Cho shot and killed thirty-two students and faculty members at Virginia Polytechnic Institute (Virginia Tech) before turning the gun on himself. In the fall of that same year, students were shot at Delaware State University, and a shooting was thwarted at St. John's University in New York. Then in February 2008, six students were killed and fifteen were injured when a former student opened fire, then took his own life in a lecture hall at Northern Illinois University.

This spate of college shootings follows a longer wave of high school violence that took place in the preceding two and a half decades. In November 2000, the FBI released its report of all twenty-eight cases of school shootings that had occurred in the United States since 1982.[2] The report noted that these cases—where a young student opens fire, apparently randomly, and shoots teachers and other students—were the only type of school violence that had increased since 1980.[3] This document was preceded by two government studies, the Surgeon General's *Report on Youth Violence* and the Bureau of Justice Statistics' *Indicators of School Crime and Safety 2000*, and followed quickly by a major study of bullying behaviors.[4] Clearly questions about safety and school violence have been of pressing national concern for some time.

All the studies on these school shootings, however, concentrated on identifying potential antecedents of school violence—for example media influence, drug and alcohol behavior, Internet usage, and family dynamics and structure. They paid little or no attention to the fact that *all* the shootings were committed by boys. This uniformity cut across all other differences among the shooters: some came from intact families, others from single-parent homes; some boys had acted violently in the past, others were quiet and inconspicuous; some boys also expressed rage at their parents (two killed their parents the same morning), and others seemed to live in happy families.

For a contrast, imagine what these studies would have examined had it been *girls* who had committed all the shootings: Wouldn't gender be the *only* story? The single greatest risk factor in school violence is masculinity. The analytic blindness of previous work runs even deeper than gender. All but two of the twenty-eight school shootings profiled in the FBI report were committed by white boys who lived in suburbs or rural areas. As a result, the public has assumed that these boys were deviants, their aberrant behavior explainable by some psychopathological factor.

While this is no doubt true, at least in part—the boys who committed these terrible acts probably did have serious psychological problems—such a framing also masks the way race and class play a significant role in school violence. Again, imagine if all the school shooters had been poor African American boys in inner-city schools. It is unlikely that our search for causes would have pathologized the boys as much as the culture of poverty or the "normality" of violence among inner-city youth.

Still, most students—white or nonwhite, male or female—are not violent, schools are predominantly safe, and school shootings are aberrations. As a public, we seem concerned with school shootings because the story is not one of simply "when children kill" but is often specifically about when suburban, predominantly white boys kill.

ASKING THE RIGHT QUESTIONS

Figure 1 shows a map of the United States marked with sites of the twenty-eight school shootings tracked in the FBI report. It's immediately apparent that these shootings didn't occur uniformly or evenly in the United States, which makes one skeptical of uniform cultural explanations such as violent video games, musical tastes, the Internet, or television and movies. Of these shootings, all but one (in Chicago) were in rural or suburban schools. All but two (in Chicago and Virginia Beach) were committed by white boys. In addition, 20 of the 28 school shootings took place in what have come to be called "red states" (those states that voted for George W. Bush in both 2000 and 2004). Among the other shootings, one was in suburban Oregon; one was in rural (eastern) Washington; two were in Southern California; one was in rural and another in suburban Pennsylvania; and one was in rural New Mexico.

Of course, all of this does not suggest that rural and suburban whites who vote Republican are responsible for school violence. But it does suggest that school violence has been unevenly distributed, and that understanding it requires that we look locally at the factors that accompany political affiliation. We need to look at local "gun culture" (percentage of homes owning firearms, gun registrations, NRA memberships) and at local gender culture and school cultures—attitudes about gender nonconformity, tolerance of bullying, and teacher attitudes. We need to focus less on the form of school violence—documenting its prevalence and presenting a demographic profile of the shooters—and more on the *content* of the shootings, asking questions instead about family dynamics and composition, psychological problems and pathologies, local school cultures and hierarchies, peer interactions, prevailing gender ideologies, and the interactions among academics, adolescence, and gender identity.

What we have ignored is a striking consistency in the stories that have emerged about the boys who did commit the violence: All had stories of being constantly bullied, beaten up, and, most significantly for this analysis, "gay baited." All had stories of being mercilessly and constantly teased, picked on, and threatened. And, most strikingly, it was *not* because they

FIGURE I   *Sites of Documented School Shootings in the United States, 1982–2001*

were gay (none of them was gay as far as we can tell), but because they were *different* from the other boys—shy, bookish, an honor student, a "geek," or a "nerd." Theirs are stories of "cultural marginalization" based on criteria for adequate gender performance—specifically the enactment of codes of masculinity. (By contrast, boys in inner-city schools are structurally marginalized by racism and income inequality; their violence will often take a different form.)

The next section of this chapter reports some preliminary findings from an investigation of these issues. I locate the causes of school violence in the constellation of adolescent masculinity, homophobia, and other gender-related factors that may help us understand—and prevent—school violence before it occurs.[5]

TAKING AWAY THEIR MANHOOD

Before beginning any inquiry, it's often helpful to ask an expert. When confronted about his homophobic lyrics, the rap star Eminem once offered the following explanation. Calling someone a "faggot" was not a slur on his sexuality, but on his gender: "The lowest degrading thing that you can say to a man when you're battling him is to call him a faggot and try to take away his manhood. Call him a sissy. Call him a punk. 'Faggot' to me just means taking away your manhood."[6]

In this rationalization, Eminem, perhaps unwittingly, addresses the central connection between gender and sexuality, and particularly the association of gender nonconformity with homosexuality. Homophobia is far less about the irrational fear of gay people, or the fear that one might actually be gay or have gay tendencies, and more about the fear that *heterosexuals* have that others might (mis)perceive them as gay.[7] The terror that others will see one as gay, as a failed man—the fear I call homophobia—underlies a significant amount of men's violence. Put another way, homophobia might be called "the hate that makes men straight."

There is much at stake for boys during adolescence, and heterosexual boys engage in a variety of evasive strategies to ensure that no one gets "the wrong idea" about them. These strategies range from the seemingly comic (though telling)—such as two young boys occupying three movie seats by placing their coats on the seat between them—to the truly tragic, such as engaging in homophobic violence, bullying, threatening other boys, excessive risk taking (drunk or aggressive driving), and even sexual predation and assault. The impact of homophobia is felt not only by gay and lesbian students, but also by heterosexuals who are targeted by their peers with constant harassment, bullying, and gay-baiting. In many cases, gay-baiting is "misdirected" at heterosexual youth who may be somewhat gender nonconforming.

As we have examined all available media reports of the high school shootings, a striking picture emerges: in the overwhelming majority of these cases there were also reports that the boys were teased and bullied mercilessly by classmates, that they were constantly called "faggot," "homo," and "queer." For example, young Andy Williams, who shot several classmates in Santee, California, was described as "shy" and was "constantly picked on" by others in school. (They stole his clothes, his money, and his food, beat him up regularly, and locked him in his locker, among other daily taunts and humiliations.)[8] Classmates described Gary Scott Pennington, who killed his teacher and a custodian in Grayson, Kentucky, as a "nerd" and a "loner" who was constantly teased for being smart and wearing glasses.[9] Barry Loukaitis, who killed his algebra teacher and two other students in Moses Lake,

Washington, was an honor student who especially loved math; he was also constantly teased and bullied and described as a "shy nerd."[10] And Evan Ramsay, who killed one student and the high school principal in Bethel, Alaska, was also an honor student who was teased for wearing glasses and having acne.[11]

Fourteen-year-old Michael Carneal was a shy and frail freshman at Heath High School in Paducah, Kentucky, barely 5 feet tall, weighing 110 pounds. He wore thick glasses and played in the school band. He felt alienated, pushed around, and picked on. He was said to be very upset when students called him a "faggot" and almost cried when the school gossip sheet labeled him as gay. On Thanksgiving Day, he stole two shotguns, two semiautomatic rifles, a pistol, and 700 rounds of ammunition, and after a weekend of showing them off to his classmates, brought them to school hoping that they would bring him some instant recognition. "I just wanted the guys to think I was cool," he said. When the cool guys ignored him, he opened fire on a morning prayer circle, killing three classmates and wounding five others. Now serving a life sentence in prison, Carneal told psychiatrists weighing his sanity, "People respect me now."[12]

At Columbine High School, site of the nation's most infamous school shooting in 1999, this connection was not lost on Evan Todd, a 255-pound defensive lineman on the Columbine football team, an exemplar of the jock culture that Dylan Klebold and Eric Harris found to be such an interminable torment. "Columbine is a clean, good place, except for those rejects," Todd said. "Sure we teased them. But what do you expect with kids who come to school with weird hairdos and horns on their hats? It's not just jocks; the whole school's disgusted with them. They're a bunch of homos. . . . If you want to get rid of someone, usually you tease 'em. So the whole school would call them homos."[13] In the videotape made the night before the shootings, Harris said, "People constantly make fun of my face, my hair, my shirts." Klebold added, "I'm going to kill you all. You've been giving us shit for years."

What Klebold said he had been receiving for years apparently included constant gay-baiting, being called "queer," "faggot," "homo," being pushed into lockers, grabbed in hallways, mimicked and ridiculed with homophobic slurs. For some boys, high school is an interminable torment, a constant homophobic gauntlet, and they may respond by becoming withdrawn and sullen, using drugs or alcohol, becoming depressed or suicidal, or acting out in a blaze of overcompensating, violent "glory."[14] The prevalence of bullying, teasing, and marginalization among boys who eventually go on to commit mass killings is staggering. (See "Still in the Shadows?" by Michael Sadowski, pp. 117–135, in this volume.)

My hypothesis about these high school shootings is decidedly *not* that gay and lesbian youth are more likely to open fire on their fellow students. In fact, from all available evidence, none of the shooters was gay. But homophobia—being constantly threatened and bullied *as if they were* gay, as well as the homophobic desire to make sure that others knew that they were not gay—seems to have played a significant and understudied role in these school shootings.

Still, several key questions remain. I've already suggested that the first question to ask is why boys? But more than this, why white boys? Failure to see race while looking at gender often causes us to miss the real story. We know that African American boys face a multitude of challenges in schools—from racial stereotypes to formal and informal tracking systems, low expectations, and underachievement. But they do not plan and execute random and arbitrary mass shootings. And this is particularly interesting, since the dynamics of the classroom and academic achievement have different valences for African American girls and African American boys. In their fascinating ethnographies of two inner-city public high schools, both Signithia Fordham and Ann Ferguson discuss these differences. When African American girls do well in school, their friends accuse them of "acting white." But when African American boys do well in school, their friends accuse them of "acting like girls."[15]

Perhaps cultural marginalization works itself out differently for subordinates and superordinates, the privileged and the unprivileged. Even if they are silenced or lose their voice, subordinates—women, gays and lesbians, students of color—can tap into a collective narrative repertoire of resistance, "the ongoing narrative of the struggle for racial equality." White boys who are bullied are supposed to be real men, supposed to be able to embody independence, invulnerability, manly stoicism. The cultural marginalization of the boys who committed school shootings extended to feelings that they had no other recourse. They felt they had no other friends to validate their fragile and threatened identities; they felt that school authorities and parents would be unresponsive to their plight; and they had no access to other methods of self-affirmation.

DANGEROUS INTERSECTIONS OF RACE AND MASCULINITY: THE VIRGINIA TECH SHOOTING

When examining questions of race and gender, the case of Seung-Hui Cho is particularly instructive. Following the Virginia Tech shootings, commentators and pundits immediately made one of two claims (though some tried to make both). On the one hand, some offered a hyperindividuated psychological profile of a mentally ill person with access to guns. Others instantly rushed to stereotypes about Asians, especially Asian Americans in predominantly white educational enclaves, where the pressure to excel can be significant.

Once again, neither perspective saw gender—specifically, how Cho's experience of both his psychological distress and his ethnicity were filtered through the prism of masculinity. In his videotape, Cho expressed a sort of *aggrieved entitlement* that is largely framed through gender identity—a sense that explosive rage about his victimization was an appropriate way to express his emotions and that revenge against his tormentors was thus legitimate, justified. (Psychologist William Pollack has said that boys in our culture are taught to view anger as the one "OK male emotion."[16]) Cho was mentally ill, yes. But he was not just a madman, and he did not just get mad.

In addition, the profile of Cho that has emerged from news accounts suggests less overt bullying than many of the high school shooters experienced, but he was certainly teased and dismissed (and, arguably, emasculated) as a social nonentity within the Virginia Tech community. Awkward socially, Cho seemed to feel that he never fit in. He had no friends or girlfriends, rarely (if ever) spoke with his dorm mates, and maintained near-invisibility on campus. His web screen name was a question mark, further illustrating the extent to which he felt invisible. No one seems to have actually known him, although his professors in the English department said they thought he was strange and possibly dangerous.

His marginalization also appeared to be cultural and class-based, not entirely the result of his obvious, overdetermined psychiatric problems. His videotape raged against the "brats" and "snobs" at Virginia Tech, who weren't even satisfied with their "gold necklaces" and "Mercedes." The nature of the teasing he endured was not overtly based in homophobia, as far as we know, but some of it certainly had a racist component and attacked Cho's masculinity. The few times he had mustered the courage to actually speak in class, his tormentors told him to "go back to China." (Cho was Korean-American; his parents owned and operated a dry cleaning shop, and he felt his marginalization had a class and race basis.)

Finally, Cho's marginalization seems to have been based on a deep alienation from some of the more hypermasculine aspects of campus culture. Few campuses are as awash in school spirit as Virginia Tech: the campus is festooned with maroon and orange everywhere, and the branding of the campus sports teams through collegiate paraphernalia and widely proclaimed pride in "Hokie Nation" is prevalent.

But what if one doesn't feel oneself to be much of a citizen in "Hokie Nation?" What if one isn't much interested in football, or in sports-themed, beer-soaked weekend party extravaganzas (or perhaps isn't invited to partake in them)? It's possible that to the marginalized, "Hokie Nation" doesn't feel inclusive and embracing, but alien and coercive. If one is not a citizen in Hokie Nation, one does not exist. And perhaps, for someone like Cho, if *I* don't exist, then *you* have no right to exist either.[17]

WHY NOT OTHER BOYS?

There have to be some reasons why school shootings take place where they do and why these boys, and not others, become perpetrators. Obviously some boys—many boys—are picked on, bullied, and gay-baited in schools across the country on a daily, routine basis, and much of this taunting continues into college. How do they cope? What strategies do they use to maintain their composure, their self-esteem, and their sense of themselves as men?

David, who was interviewed by *Time* magazine during his sophomore year at the University of Rhode Island, said the bullying he experienced started when he was thirteen: "At first I tried to brush it off. But it got worse. I got beat up every day and couldn't take it. I'd fake being sick. My grades slipped." His parents tried to intervene with school officials, but the attacks continued. David's thoughts got darker:

> I felt, "What did I do to deserve this?" I wanted revenge. I never sat down and planned anything—I personally couldn't pick up a gun and kill someone, it's not who I am—but I will tell you I did want to hurt them. I wanted them to feel how bad I felt.[18]

But he didn't. Most boys who are bullied, harassed, and baited survive—as do their classmates. Several possible factors may help explain this. Perhaps there is a "charismatic adult" who makes a substantial difference in the life of the boy. Most often this is one or the other parent, but it can also be a teacher.

Perhaps the boy can develop an alternative pole around which he can experience and validate his identity. Bullying suggests that the boy is a failure at the one thing he knows he wants to be and is expected to be—a man. If there is something else that he does well—a private passion, music, art, someplace where he feels valued—he can develop a pocket of resistance.

Similarly, the structures of a boy's interactions can make a decisive difference. A male friend—particularly one who is not also a target, but one who seems to be successful at masculinity, can validate the boy's sense of himself as a man. As one male high school student commented, "If you go to school and people make fun of you every day, and you don't have a friend, it drives you to insanity."

But equally important may be the role of a female friend, a potential, if not actual "girlfriend." Five of the high school shooters had what they felt was serious girl trouble, especially rejection. It may be that the boys who are best able to resist the torments of incessant bullying, gay-baiting, and marginalization are those who have some girls among their friends, and perhaps even a girlfriend—that is, girls who can also validate their sense of masculinity (which other boys do as well) *as well as* their heterosexuality (which boys alone cannot do).

The successful demonstration of *heterosexual* masculinity requires not only successful performance for other men, but also some form of "sexual" success with women. (I put the word "sexual" in quotation marks because this doesn't necessarily mean actual sexual contact but rather a sexualized affirmation of one's masculinity by girls and women. If the girl is not a "girlfriend" she is at least a girl and a friend, and therefore a potential romantic and sexual partner; the boy can therefore assume some degree of heterosexual competence.)

These sorts of questions—the dynamics of local culture, the responsiveness of adults and institutions, and the dynamics of same-sex and cross-sex friendships—will enable us to understand both what factors led some boys to commit these terrible acts and what factors enable other boys to develop the resources of resistance to daily bullying and marginalization.

Take a walk down any hallway in any middle school or high school in America. The single most common put-down today is, "That's so gay." It is deployed constantly, casually, unconsciously. Boys hear it if they dare to try out for school band or orchestra, if they are shy or small, or physically weak and unathletic; if they are smart, wear glasses, or work hard in school. They hear it if they are seen to like girls too much, or if they are too much "like" girls. They hear it if their body language, their clothing, their musical preferences don't conform to the norms of their peers. They sometimes hear it beyond high school into college, and they often hear it not as an assessment of their present or future sexual orientation but as a commentary on their masculinity.

Eminem had at least this part right: Calling someone a "faggot" means questioning his manhood. And in this culture, when someone questions our manhood, we don't just get mad, we get even.

NOTES

1. Luke Woodham, age sixteen, perpetrator of school shooting in Pearl, Mississippi.
2. Mary Ellen O'Toole, *The School Shooter: A Threat Assessment Perspective* (Quantico, VA: National Center for the Analysis of Violent Crime, FBI Academy, 2000).
3. See Barry Glassner, "School Violence: The Fears, the Facts," *New York Times*, August 13, 1999, as well as Glassner's book, *The Culture of Fear* (New York: Basic Books, 1999).
4. Tonja R. Nansel, Mary Overpeck, Ramani Pilla, June Ruan, Bruce Simmons-Morton, and Peter Scheidt, "Bullying Behaviors among U.S. Youth: Prevalence and Association with Psychosocial Adjustment," *Journal of the American Medical Association* 285, no. 16 (2001): 2094–2100.
5. This research was conducted with Matt Mahler in the Department of Sociology at Stony Brook University.
6. Cited in Richard Kim, "Eminem—Bad Rap?" *The Nation*, March 5, 2001.
7. Michael S. Kimmel, "Masculinity as Homophobia: Fear, Shame and Silence in the Construction of Gender Identity," in Harry Brod and Michael Kaufman (eds.), *Theorizing Masculinities* (Newbury Park, CA: Sage, 1994).
8. Kristen Green and Bruce Lieberman, "Santana Gunman Targeted with Anti-Gay Epithets," *San Diego Union-Tribune*, March 10, 2001.
9. Jerry Buckley, "The Tragedy in Room 108," *U.S. News & World Report*, November 8, 1993.
10. "Did Taunts Lead to Killing?" *Minneapolis Star Tribune*, February 4, 1996.
11. Steve Fainaru, "Alaska Teen's Path to Murder," *Dallas Morning News*, December 4, 1998.
12. Jonah Blank, "The Kid No One Noticed," *U.S. News & World Report*, October 12, 1998.
13. Nancy Gibbs and Timothy Roche, "The Columbine Tapes," *Time*, December 20, 1999, 50–51.
14. Timothy Egan, "Patterns Emerging in Attacks at Schools," *New York Times*, June 15, 1998.

15. Signithia Fordham, *Blacked Out: Dilemmas of Race, Identity, and Success at Capital High* (Chicago: University of Chicago Press, 1996); Ann Ferguson, *Bad Boys: Public Schools in the Making of Black Masculinity* (Ann Arbor: University of Michigan Press, 2000).

16. William Pollack, *Real Boys: Rescuing Our Sons from the Myths of Boyhood* (New York: Random House/Owl Books, 1998/1999), 44.

17. Bob Herbert, "A Volatile Young Man, Humiliation, and a Gun," *New York Times*, April 19, 2007; Ben Agger, "Cho, Not Che? Positioning Blacksburg in the Political," *Fast Capitalism* 3.1 (2007), available at: www.uta.edu/huma/agger/fastcapitalism/3_1/agger.html

18. Robert Sullivan, "What Makes a Child Resilient?" *Time*, March 19, 2001, 35.

Interview

Male Adolescent Identity and the Roots of Aggression: A Conversation with James Garbarino

DARCIA HARRIS BOWMAN

James Garbarino has done extensive research into the issues that affect boys and men in contemporary society, including why a disturbing number of boys behave in ways that are aggressive and sometimes even violent. Garbarino is a professor of psychology at Loyola University in Chicago and former director of the Family Life Development Center at Cornell University. He also has authored or coauthored numerous books, including Lost Boys: Why Our Sons Turn Violent and How We Can Save Them *and, with Ellen deLara,* And Words Can Hurt Forever: How to Protect Adolescents from Bullying, Harassment, and Emotional Violence.

What has your work with violent boys taught you about the link between male adolescent identity and aggressive behavior?

I've learned that there's a culturewide problem, that the definition of male identity is wrapped up in three messages: that it's better to be mad than sad, that to be a man is to be powerful and strong, and that aggression is a legitimate way of responding to conflict and problems. Vulnerable and otherwise at-risk boys are likely to combine these three cultural themes with their own difficulties—family troubles, psychological problems, poverty—and are therefore at a high risk for aggressive or violent behavior.

What about boys who don't necessarily fall into this "at-risk" category?

These cultural principles apply to all boys, but most don't ever bring them all together in the form of extreme violence. Boys who don't have obvious social risk factors like poverty, exposure to racism, or family disruption may nonetheless be at high risk because they carry with them psychological troubles that predispose them to negative behavior. When that's coupled with the three cultural themes, they may act in aggressive or violent ways.

And, certainly, the average level of violence and aggression is higher for boys than it is for girls. Much of that is related to these cultural issues of identity. There are institutional forms of aggression that are particularly tied to male identity. An example would be in ice hockey, where they make rules for boys and men that give permission, even encouragement, for a high level of aggression, whereas rules for women in ice hockey preclude precisely that particular kind of behavior.

Are boys genetically hardwired for aggression and violence, or is such behavior solely an expression of how boys are socialized?

I think boys on average are predisposed genetically to patterns of behavior and arousal that make them more vulnerable to learning aggression if it's taught. The fact that boys are more physically aggressive than girls in virtually every culture in the world suggests that boys are more ready than girls to learn and demonstrate aggressive behavior.

But the fact that American girls are more aggressive than boys in some other societies would suggest that, while the average within a society may very well be a function of gender, the average across societies is mainly a matter of culture and experience. But will girls ever get to a point in America where they are as aggressive as boys? I, and I think most people, would be startled if that happened.

In your book Lost Boys: Why Our Sons Turn Violent and How We Can Save Them, *you use the term* progressive conformity *to describe how human behavior is a reflection of what is learned, encouraged, and rewarded in a given social context. What do boys learn about violence and aggression in the school setting, and how do these messages influence their behavior?*

A school, like any setting, is a social context, and that means it can either enhance or inhibit aggressive behavior. We've learned very clearly, for example, that to deal with the issue of bullies is not simply a matter of finding the bullies and stopping them, but also of recognizing that some social systems in schools tolerate and encourage bullying and others encourage less aggressive behavior. The same kid may be four times more likely to be an aggressive bully in one school than in another, and that speaks to the role of context and the validity of the principle of progressive conformity. Kids over time will to a large degree resemble what the setting rewards, models, and accepts. When it promotes positive character traits, most of the kids will fall into line with that. But when it tolerates aggression, that's particularly what the high-risk kids will do. I think the message is that being a male in a school doesn't make you a bully. Being a troubled male makes you more ready to take on the role of bully, but what the school offers has a lot to do with whether you will take on that role or not.

Who is the school bully? How does he view himself in relation to his peers, particularly the targets of his aggression, and what prompts his behavior?

There are several pathways to becoming a bully. One is this institutionalized form of bullying. You're a freshman, the seniors haze and bully you, and it becomes the cultural expectation that when you get to be a senior you'll do the same thing. Some boys will relish that role more than others. And all the usual factors that predispose kids to aggressive behavior generally—abuse or deprivation at home, for example—certainly predispose them to come to school and act aggressively. There's also a sort of generational passing on of bullying. Maybe half the kids involved in bullying at any one time have themselves been victims. So there is a violence-breeds-violence side to it as well.

And again, whether or not these predispositions and risk factors translate into bullying seems to depend on the school itself, and that may begin in elementary school. Take research by Shepard Kellum that looked at aggressive kids, particularly boys, who come into first grade and find a weak teacher who allows a chaotic classroom and the formation of aggressive peer groups. By sixth grade, those kids may be twenty times more aggressive than they would have been if they'd walked into first grade and found a strong teacher who took charge of the classroom and didn't allow chaos and the formation of aggressive peer groups.

There's always that social-system dimension to it, and that's really the thing people are least likely to get. They're more likely to see it as a problem of "aggressive individuals are bullies and vulnerable individuals are their victims." Certainly there are influences in that direction, but whether or not it actually happens depends much more on the social system, including the bystanders and what their norms are, what they support, and what they tolerate.

Are there social systems in schools that are particularly culpable when it comes to modeling or teaching aggression to boys, or perhaps some that are helpful in stemming the problem?

I think one important social system within the school is adult monitoring and control. When adults are in evidence throughout the school, that has a suppressing effect on aggression. Secondly, when the school models and rewards competition rather than cooperation, you're more likely to set loose the process of aggression. You see this in the classroom: the activities that are offered, the way academic rewards are structured. Also important is the way the adults in the school deal with issues of the various "isms"—sexism, racism, homophobia. If they give messages that these are acceptable ways to think about people, it is more likely to unleash phobias based on those things, or problems like sexual harassment.

What about the role of school athletics and other extracurricular activities?

I think extracurricular activities play several roles. The more widespread the participation, the more likely you'll get participation across cliques and groups. When diverse groups are involved in cooperative activities— winning a game, painting, performing a concert—that creates cooperative behavior and suppresses aggression.

Now, some of these activities have bullying built into them in the form of hazing. Certainly, there are many stories about how athletics have this problem. That may drive some kids out of these activities and the message becomes, once again, that the adults support bullying.

If the goal is to stem aggressive and violent behavior in boys and socialize them to be caring, considerate, and sensitive, what do schools and educators need to do?

Character education is fundamental to violence prevention, because the theme is "everybody in our school lives by some core values." It's not just "find the bullies and stop them." It's "we all live by the core values, and that makes bullying incompatible with the culture of our school." In addition to the usual meetings and discussion, this is translated into the adults being really on top of things and not tolerating certain behavior in the halls—and their actually being in the halls. A big issue is often that teachers stay in their classrooms during the changing of classes, so the halls become a no-man's land and the kids are on their own out there.

Character education also implies that adults will be responsive when kids or parents report incidents, that they won't simply say, "Look, there's nothing we can do, our hands are tied." So, it's partly an attitude, it's partly specific behaviors, and it's partly implementing programs so that when something happens, you don't just go to the bully and the victim, you go to everyone else who was there and say, "Why did you allow this to happen? Why didn't you make a statement here?"

Is there anything else specific teachers can do?

I think they can be very aware of the fact that the models they present through themselves, as well as in videos, films, and biographies, should show male strength as something other than aggression. Highlighting those qualities is a way of changing the culture in a school.

CHAPTER SEVEN

Still in the Shadows?

Lesbian, Gay, Bisexual, and Transgender Students in U.S. Schools*

MICHAEL SADOWSKI

The first day of seventh grade I started getting harassed. People, the older students, started calling me faggot in the hallways, and it just kind of trickled down so that—so that several people in every grade called me faggot in the hall and on the bus, people would throw things at me, throw things at me in the hall, they started pushing me. By eighth grade it got really bad. I got death threats, I got my gym clothes urinated on in the bathroom, I started skipping school *a lot*. . . . I—just had a horrible time, more and more harassment every day, like, it got to the point where it was *constant*, like all day, people would be saying things in class, between classes.
                    —*Daniel[1], gay student from Pennsylvania*

School's awesome. I love school. . . . Like, the freshmen are really open to that [my being bisexual], I guess. A lot of them are my friends and they just, like, respect me, and it's really cool. I appreciate that a lot.
                    —*Lindsey, bisexual student from Massachusetts[2]*

Adolescence is a time of tremendous personal growth and transition. Erik Erikson, the child and adolescent psychology pioneer whose work on identity is probably the most widely cited in the field, believed that people expe-

---

* This chapter contains explicit language describing incidents in which students in U.S. schools have been harassed for reasons associated with their sexual orientation and/or gender identity.

rience the central "crisis," or turning point, of identity development most acutely during adolescence. At this stage of life, young people strive to make sense of who they are within their culture and begin to envision future roles for themselves in the adult world.[3] A virtually universal aspect of this self-definition process is adolescents' keen awareness of how others, particularly their peers, perceive them. Indeed, any parent or teacher would likely echo Erikson's finding that adolescents are "morbidly, often curiously preoccupied with what they appear to be in the eyes of others as compared with what they feel they are."[4] As Daniel's and Lindsey's comments illustrate, peer responses to lesbian, gay, bisexual, and transgender (LGBT)[5] youth can range over a wide spectrum, from rejection, harassment, and even violence to acceptance, affirmation, and respect.

Daniel and Lindsey also demonstrate the powerful role school environments can play in the day-to-day experiences of sexual minority adolescents. For Daniel, being gay in middle and high school meant a barrage of harassment from which he was unable to escape until he left high school at the end of his junior year to attend college a year early. In the case of Lindsey, a freshman at a vocational-technical high school, friends, faculty, and administration make school a place where she can be out comfortably—and even have a girlfriend—without fear of any negative social repercussions.[6]

In the first edition of *Adolescents at School*, I included a chapter called "Growing Up in the Shadows" that focused primarily on the risks faced by LGBT students in U.S. schools. Since that chapter was first published in 2003, new studies have shed additional light on the school lives of LGBT youth, and cultural attitudes have evolved with regard to LGBT issues even in a relatively short time. (The growth, albeit slowly, of legally sanctioned same-sex unions and the increasing number of openly LGBT media stars and characters are two such examples.) Pointing to recent changes in adolescents' attitudes, a 2005 *Time* magazine cover story pronounced, "At many schools around the country it is now profoundly uncool to be seen as anti-gay."[7] While there is evidence to suggest that some peer and school cultures have become more accepting of LGBT students in recent years, current statistics on harassment as well as other risk factors affecting LGBT youth complicate the picture, showing patterns that are cause for continued concern.

This chapter, an update of "Growing Up in the Shadows," combines recent statistics on the school experiences of young people who identify themselves as lesbian, gay, bisexual, or transgender (and, for comparative purposes, their peers) with interview excerpts from a qualitative study I conducted with six other researchers at the Harvard Graduate School of Education on the family, school, and peer relationships of LGBT youth.[8] While the statistics outline the scope of issues such as homophobic harassment in school and other factors that affect LGBT students, the interview excerpts give voice to the numbers and illustrate how factors such as school environment, the availability of LGBT student groups, and supportive teachers and administrators (or the lack thereof) strongly influence what it means to be lesbian, gay, bisexual, or transgender in a middle or high school in the United States.

LGBT YOUTH: STILL AT RISK

Despite some improvements in recent years, statistical research shows that sexual minority youth are still at disproportionate risk for depression and substance abuse, as well as a number of other negative outcomes both in and out of the school environment.[9] The most disturbing finding about these young people continues to be the percentage who report suicidal thinking and behaviors. The most recently published data from the Massachusetts Youth Risk Behavior Survey (MYRBS), which includes the responses of more than 3,500 youth from randomly selected high schools around the state, indicates that, among the roughly 4 percent of students who identified themselves as lesbian, gay, or bisexual on the survey, one out of four (25%) reported having attempted suicide in the past year. This figure is an improvement over the 40 percent of sexual minority youth who reported a suicide attempt on the 2003 survey, but it is still more than four times the rate of reported suicide attempts for other students (5.7 percent).[10] Vermont's most recent Youth Risk Behavior Survey also found dramatically higher risk of suicide attempts for sexual minority youth: 27 percent of the students who identified themselves as lesbian, gay, bisexual, or questioning said they had attempted suicide in the previous twelve months, more than five times the percentage for heterosexual students.[11]

While it is obviously difficult for researchers to establish causal links between the experiences adolescents have in their school environments and risk factors such as depression, substance abuse, and suicide, there is evidence to suggest that school climates can contribute in powerful ways to these risks. Jason was one of several students I interviewed who linked the harassment they experienced in school with suicidal thoughts or behaviors:

I did a pill overdose of my medications I was on. Because I was at a school that I just really didn't feel safe at, and there were kids who were always picking on me and stuff and, I mean, it's the only, like, experience I had ever been in like that. . . . So, it was getting really hostile there and I knew that if, like, I was going to stay around at [the school], I'd probably end up, like, getting severely injured, or whatever. And then, like, probably kids would make fun of me because I couldn't stand up for myself. And just, like, I don't know. At the time it [suicide] seemed like the only and best thing to do.

Similarly, Daniel, the student quoted at the beginning of this chapter who experienced intense antigay harassment in middle and high school, told me, "Thoughts of suicide were running through my head since seventh grade—like every method of ending the harassment ran through my head." Daniel's suicide ideation reached a peak, he says, one afternoon after he had faced an unusually intense day of harassment at school:

We had a pistol in the closet and I knew right where it was, and the bullets were there too. I loaded it, I sat on the edge of my parents' bed, and I held it to my head for—probably [sighs], like, I don't know, it seemed like forever; it was probably like half an hour. And I was too afraid to shoot the gun because I was afraid of not dying, and I was afraid of like the physical pain—like I didn't want to lay there and suffer in case I didn't die instantly.

Daniel was fortunate enough to escape the harassment he experienced in middle and high school by enrolling in college early, in what would have been his senior year. Thankfully, Jason also was able to escape his hostile school environment by transferring to a vocational-technical high school in the same region (the same one Lindsey attends). Jason describes his new school as much more welcoming to LGBT students, a place "where you can't say things like 'fag' or you can't use, like, racial or sexuality slurs" and adds that he cannot imagine being suicidal again:

Like for me to be at that point, it really just doesn't make sense for me anymore. And I don't feel like I would ever be back at that place because I've been there once and I think I've been after, and I've seen that it can get better, and it is better. So I don't think I'd ever be down—back at that place anymore.

Nevertheless, the stories of both Jason and Daniel, as well as countless other students represented in the statistical studies and qualitative data, underscore the need for educators and others concerned about adolescents to take the elevated suicide risk of LGBT youth extremely seriously.

ANTI-LGBT LANGUAGE AND HARASSMENT

Unfortunately, not all students are able to escape hostile school environments, as Daniel and Jason did, by attending another school. And as recent data show, despite changes in some school cultures, homophobia and the language and harassment that accompany it are still rampant in many middle and high schools across the country. The most recently published survey by the Gay, Lesbian and Straight Education Network (GLSEN), taken among 1,732 students in grades 7-12 in 2005 and published in 2006, found that 75 percent heard homophobic slurs such as "fag," "faggot," or "dyke," either "frequently" or "often" in their schools. Even more pervasive, the survey respondents said, is the expression "that's so gay," a pejorative term used widely by adolescents to describe virtually anything perceived to be negative—a boring class, an ugly article of clothing, an unfair grade on a test. Eighty-nine percent of the youth GLSEN surveyed said they heard that expression (or the variant, "you're so gay") at school "frequently" or "often."[12] Earlier GLSEN studies, as well as research conducted by a number of other organizations, have yielded similar findings.[13]

At the very least, this kind of language contributes to an uncomfortable, if not hostile, environment for LGBT students or those who might be questioning their sexuality or gender identity. Many LGBT students, however, also experience such language in the form of verbal harassment targeted directly at them. Just under two-thirds (64%) of the youth GLSEN surveyed for its 2006 report (the vast majority of whom identified themselves as lesbian, gay, bisexual, or transgender) said they were victims of verbal harassment at school based on their sexual orientation, and roughly the same number said they felt unsafe at school for reasons associated with their sexual orientation. Physical violence against sexual minority youth appears to be somewhat less widespread than verbal harassment, but GLSEN's study found that about one-fourth of respondents (24%) had experienced physical harassment at school (being pushed or shoved) for reasons associated with their sexual orientation and that 10 percent reported having been physically assaulted. Moreover, 22 percent of the sample said they experienced cyberbullying, and 39 percent said they were harassed at school in sexual ways (for example, being the targets of sexual comments or taunts or being inappropriately touched by classmates).[14]

While verbal and physical harassment based on sexual orientation are slightly more common for boys than for girls, the past several GLSEN surveys suggest that lesbian and bisexual girls may be more likely than boys to experience harassment of a sexual nature.[15] The experiences of Kate, a lesbian student I interviewed who attended a suburban high school near Washington, D.C., illustrate how anti-LGBT harassment can take on disturbing physical and sexual overtones:

> People would push me into lockers or just mumble stuff at me under their breath. I once had pornography taped to my locker, like a girl giving a guy a blow job or something, and it said something on it like, "Learn how to do this," or something. I had a couple of the—the football players like corner me after school, you know, threatening to make me like dick.

GLSEN's survey also sheds light on how the risks students face based on their sexual orientation can intersect with other aspects of identity, such as race and gender. About 85 percent of students of color responding to the GLSEN survey said they have experienced at least some verbal harassment at school, and more than half of these said they have been harassed for reasons associated with both their race *and* their sexual orientation. Students who identify themselves as transgender—as not conforming to what society perceives to be their biological sex and/or to traditional binary categories of man/woman or boy/girl*—have some of the highest rates of harassment in the GLSEN sample: 93 percent said they've been verbally harassed, 55 percent said they've been physically harassed, and one-third said they've been physically assaulted at school.[16] As Matt, a transgender youth I interviewed, explains, students at the first high school he attended [before transferring to the same vocational-technical school that Jason and Lindsey attend] felt threatened by both his sexuality and his nontraditional gender expression even before he came out as transgender:

> I lost a lot of friends when I told, you know, them about my sexuality, and they were very derogatory, very, very—they would laugh at me behind my back and say stupid shit. It just was so bad that I just didn't want to be there anymore. Like I didn't really feel comfortable being there. I mean, I had four or five friends who stood up for me and accepted me, but to me, that wasn't really enough. I actually used to get harassed, too, for looking like a guy. People used to come up to me and say, "Are you a guy or

---

* Transgender identity thus generally includes, but is not limited to, people who might identify as transsexual.

a girl?" you know, and that really pissed me off at the time . . . (See "The Story of Matt, 'Transgender Superhero,'" following this chapter.)

While still a relatively understudied aspect of this research, there is also growing evidence that anti-LGBT harassment and other aspects of hostile school environments may have academic as well as emotional consequences for students. Both the Massachusetts and Vermont Youth Risk Behavior Surveys found that sexual minority students are about four times as likely as other students to stay home from school because they feel unsafe there (16% vs. 3.5% in the Massachusetts survey and 15% vs. 4% in Vermont), and 29 percent of students responding to GLSEN's latest survey said they've skipped school and/or classes for similar reasons. Moreover, GLSEN found that the LGBT students they surveyed who had experienced physical harassment had grade-point averages that were a half-grade (.5) lower on average than other students, and that students who had experienced verbal harassment had GPAs that were three-tenths of a point lower, on average. As Kevin Jennings, GLSEN's founder and former executive director has said, "How can you possibly focus on reading and writing skills when you're basically trying to survive every day?"[17]

A LACK OF REPRESENTATION

It's not even in the curriculum. It's like we're not even supposed to know about it. "That's so gay" is the only thing we ever hear about it.
—*Lauren M., as quoted in* Hatred in the Hallways[18]

If the language and harassment LGBT students experience make them feel painfully conspicuous at school, the curriculum they are studying may do just the opposite. Despite the fact that many students are aware of homosexuality—or at least the slurs that are associated with it—from the early elementary grades,[19] numerous studies have pointed to a lack of representation of anything having to do with LGBT people in school curricula. In GLSEN's latest survey, only 18 percent of students said they had studied anything related to LGBT issues or people in any of their classes, a statistic that has shown no significant change since GLSEN's 2001 survey and is consistent with the Human Rights Watch report *Hatred in the Hallways*, based on interviews with 140 youth and 130 educators and other adults in seven states, and several earlier studies.[20] Social studies/history was the subject area in which the greatest number of students in the GLSEN sample said they had studied LGBT issues, but this was still only 10 percent of the total sample. Even fewer, 7 percent, said they had been taught about LGBT people or issues in English, and just 5 percent said LGBT concerns were included in their health classes. As one high school junior who spoke at a public forum before the Massachusetts Governor's Commission on Gay and Lesbian Youth testified:

> The gay rights movement is not even mentioned during the civil rights chapter in my American history textbook. I have yet to read a book in English class with anything more than the implication of homosexuality, and in all my classes when we talk about discrimination, we stay to race issues between black and white communities. . . . With all these people in my life ignoring an issue that is a significant part of me, it is easy to feel that I don't matter.[21]

GLSEN also found that only about 19 percent of the students they surveyed said that LGBT issues were addressed in their textbooks. Access to information through library resources and the Internet was somewhat better, but still only 43 percent of students GLSEN surveyed said there were materials addressing LGBT concerns at the library, and just 44 percent could gain access to such information using the Internet at school. While Internet use for class work and independent projects is becoming more and more common in U.S. middle and high schools, many school systems use filters that block students' access to any websites that include words such as "gay," "lesbian," "bisexual," or "transgender," even if these are informational resources or educational sites specifically intended for youth (such as the GLSEN Students Resource Page).[22]

ADULT SUPPORT: A WIDE SPECTRUM

One of the most consistent findings in psychological research with youth is the importance of caring, trusting relationships with adults. Such a relationship with even one adult has been demonstrated to give children and youth the resilience to cope with some of the difficult experiences they might face growing up.[23] And, as decades of adolescent development research has demonstrated, adolescents need adult role models to help them envision their futures, a central aspect of the identity development process. Many adolescents, including some LGBT youth, find the caring relationships they need with parents or other adult family members. For many sexual minority youth, however, coming out can mean being rejected by their families, even in today's society, where LGBT issues are discussed more openly than in the past.[24]

Given the unpredictability of parental support for LGBT youth and the importance of nonparent adult mentors even for youth from supportive families,[25] teachers, counselors, principals, and other adults in the school environment play especially important roles. Yet as both statistical and interview data indicate, the attitudes and actions (and, in some cases, inaction) of some educators may be a significant detriment to LGBT youths' school experiences. One of the most damaging ways some school staff contribute to the creation of identity-detrimental environments for LGBT students is their failure to respond to hostile language and harassment. Forty percent of GLSEN's survey respondents indicated that the faculty and staff at their schools never intervene when they hear students use anti-LGBT language, and another 43 percent said their teachers intervene only "some of the time." Kate, the student I interviewed who had been harassed sexually, explains, "I got harassed and people—I didn't really go to the school about it because I didn't think anything would happen. Like, when it happened in front of teachers, they would, like, turn a blind eye." And Daniel, the student who experienced constant harassment at school from seventh grade on, adds:

> I went to the guidance counselors, some people that saw it [the harassment] happening went to the guidance counselors, who did nothing. Teachers did nothing. I had several teachers at that school even witness me being in physical fights and turn around and walk away. One guidance counselor told me not to walk around in school like a little puppy dog, that maybe that would deter some of the harassment, if I just—acted a little more masculine in the hallways.

In addition to highlighting the inaction of teachers and other school staff, Daniel's story illustrates the tendency among some school staff to "blame the victim" in cases of anti-LGBT harassment, as other researchers have noted. In *Hatred in the Hallways*, authors Michael Bochenek and A. Widney Brown cite situations in which LGBT students were removed from classrooms and even schools as a "solution" to their having been harassed (while the perpetrators faced minor consequences), as well as one in which an assistant principal reportedly said of a student who had been harassed, "If he didn't walk around telling people that he's gay, there wouldn't be any problems."[26]

Many LGBT students also report that even adults at their schools use homophobic language and openly express negative attitudes about LGBT people. In the latest GLSEN survey, nearly one-fifth (19%) of the youth said they hear faculty and staff use such language. Kim, a student I interviewed, says many of the teachers at her school failed to address anti-LGBT harassment, and that her chemistry teacher ignored—and even contributed to—her own victimization so much that she stopped attending his class:

> Like, if somebody walked by me they could say, like, "faggot" to me and he would—wouldn't even blink an eye to it. He didn't care if people called me things in class. I actually went to the principal a few times about him and a few other teachers, too, and the principal would talk to them and they still wouldn't stop, they wouldn't stop the abuse that people were putting me through. When he asked me what kind of car I had because I was always late to school, because it was my first period class, and I told him I had a Subaru station wagon he said, "Oh, that's typical." Because I guess it's like a big stereotype that lesbians drive Subarus.

Kim also says that the chemistry teacher's class was the only one she was failing when she ultimately decided to drop out of school:

> When I dropped out I had all As and one F. So I did well in the classes that I liked and the subjects that I liked. I had an F in chemistry when I dropped out, but I had an A in public speaking and an A in music, an A in art.

While it is unclear what other factors might have led to Kim's dropping out of school, her story illustrates how teachers' anti-LGBT attitudes can have serious academic consequences for students.

Along with educators who ignore and even contribute to the harassment of LGBT students, however, there are many teachers, administrators, and school personnel who make crucial, potentially life-saving differences in these youths' lives. In the latest GLSEN survey, 58 percent of students said they had at least one teacher or other adult in school with whom they felt comfortable talking about LGBT issues, and many of the students our research team interviewed cited teachers, administrators, and school staff members as valued mentors and sources of support. For Lindsey (the student quoted at the beginning of this chapter as saying, "I love school"), Janice, an openly lesbian school nurse who also advises the school's gay-straight alliance, is one adult that she believes she "can just talk to":

> The person I trust most in my school to talk to as, like, an adult would be Janice, and she's a nurse. I talk to her about anything, you know, because

I'm just—she's a GSA leader and she just listens and she's been there and, you know, I can just talk to her.

In addition to having teachers and school staff serve as trusted mentors and confidants, several students we interviewed appreciated the efforts of teachers who allow space in their curriculum for LGBT topics, demonstrate an interest in LGBT issues, and try to educate other students about them. As Lindsey, who wrote a paper about transgender identity for her English class, explains:

> Mr. Martin, my English teacher, he—he lets us write a lot of essays about things like sexual orientation and gender and things. And he just lets us, like, go wherever we want with them. I wrote one essay on gender. It was, like, twelve pages long. So that was pretty cool.

Similarly, Jason says he appreciates the fact that many of the teachers at school have LGBT "Safe Space" stickers on their doors—a quiet way of indicating that their classrooms are "safe zones" for sexual minority students.[27] On a more personal level, Jason says he also likes the way teachers sometimes subtly use the fact that he is openly gay to make a positive point about LGBT people. An avid bicyclist, Jason says he felt particularly honored recently when his English teacher used him as an example to help expand other students' notions about masculinity during a discussion of the play *Macbeth*:

> He's like, "Well, what do you think is a man? This guy over here [pointing at another student], who spends like, who spends the day, like, sitting around on a tractor plowing the fields, or this kid over here"—and he was pointing at me, and he's like—"who just for the heck of it will hop on his bike and bike 20 miles to school and 20 miles back and like if he doesn't have school, will bike from like before the sun comes up until after the school—after the sun goes down" or whatever. And he's like— they're comparing those people to me. Because—and people are realizing this more and more and that—like, the typicalness of, like, being gay, is like, you're all femme and you're really not—you can't be, like manly, you can't be doing all these things. And then, like, he's sort of like trying to open up their horizons and stuff, and I've noticed that teachers do that periodically in other classes just because it's a good contrast and—I don't know. I think it's cool because it sets me away from all the other kids in a way that they can't copy me.

GAY-STRAIGHT ALLIANCES: CRUCIAL SITES OF PEER SUPPORT

Perhaps the most common form of in-school support for sexual minority youth, gay-straight alliances (GSAs) now number more than three thousand in schools across the country. These groups are extracurricular organizations in which students can seek the support of peers and faculty advisors, discuss issues such as homophobia and heterosexism that might exist in the school and community, and plan programming about sexual orientation and gender identity issues. Twenty years ago, these organizations were virtually nonexistent, so the research on their effectiveness is still new. Still, a few studies have resulted in some promising findings.

In an evaluation of the Safe Schools Program for Gay and Lesbian Students, an initiative to support GSAs and other programming administered by the Massachusetts Department of Education, researcher Laura Szalacha found statistically significant differences on several measures between schools that had GSAs and those that did not. Based on questionnaires completed by 1,646 randomly selected students, Szalacha discovered that 35 percent of students in schools with GSAs said gay, lesbian, and bisexual students could be open about their sexual identity in school, compared to 12 percent of students in schools without GSAs. In addition, while 58 percent of students in schools with GSAs said they heard anti-gay slurs every day in school, 75 percent of the students in schools without GSAs said they heard such words daily.[28] Similarly, GLSEN's most recent survey found that students who attended schools with GSAs were less likely to feel unsafe at school than those without access to GSAs, and a recent analysis by Carol Goodenow, Laura Szalacha, and Kim Westheimer found that students attending schools with GSAs were less likely than other students to report having been threatened or injured by a weapon at school or to skip school out of fear for their safety.[29]

For a number of the students we interviewed whose schools had GSAs, these groups were important aspects of their high school experience that helped give them a sense of connection, purpose, support, and even pride at school:

> We had the GSA, and I liked that because it was, like, the only place that I got to meet other gay kids that went to school with me. (Kim)

> It [the GSA] gave me something to concentrate on the first year that I had it—that I started it. . . . I became kind of lost that year, and just—it was one of those things that gave me a purpose, kind of. (Travis)

Our GSA is really supportive, and a lot of the people in there, like, if you're just getting like, picked on by like, a few people or whatever, like if they're around they'll actually, like, go and stand up to the people with you. (Jason)

I think my GSA was probably the biggest step towards making high school bearable for me. (Phil)

You know, like, I was very proud of saying that I was in GSA. I was just a proud individual. (Matt)

As Beth Reis, co-chair of the Safe Schools Coalition of Washington State, explains, "GSAs offer kids a safe place to socialize without having to watch your back, without having to worry that something you say will be used against you, without having to pretend to be someone you're not—whether that's social time, just playing Scrabble, or more therapeutic time, having people that you can talk with about having been harassed or about having broken up with your girlfriend or boyfriend."

WHAT EDUCATORS CAN DO

There is strong evidence that many middle and high schools in the United States are still not safe, identity-affirming places for LGBT adolescents, yet the stories of supportive teachers, administrators, staff members, peers, and afterschool groups that my colleagues and I heard—as well as the glimmers of hope in some of the recent statistics—point to numerous steps educators can take to effect positive change in their schools. These steps include, but are certainly not limited to, the following:

Frank discussion of anti-LGBT language and harassment. Perhaps the easiest and most obvious thing educators can do to make schools better places not just for LGBT youth but for all students is to take active steps toward interrupting and discouraging anti-LGBT language and harassment. While much of the success of such efforts depends on the vigilance and consistency of individual teachers, principals and school leaders can also play an important role by setting a schoolwide tone of mutual respect and addressing the issue with both staff and students in proactive, rather than just reactive, ways.

Reis, who has facilitated many LGBT awareness programs in schools, recommends that at the beginning of each school year principals hold assemblies or class visits in which they frankly discuss the kinds of harassment and bullying that are "not OK" at school and explain why. In such presentations, she says, it is critical for school leaders to use terms such as gay and lesbian, as well as the slurs associated with them, in order to communicate strongly and clearly with both would-be harassers and potential targets: "I think the leadership of having a principal be the one who [talks about anti-LGBT harassment] is critical for every kind of child who's experiencing difference or being bullied," Reis says. "Even if they don't go to an adult when it happens, it means something to know that they could, and to know that the principal knows that this happens sometimes."

Visibility and inclusion. Another benefit to discussing anti-LGBT harassment in specific and frank terms is that such discussion shatters taboos and raises the visibility of sexual minority issues at school. On the other hand, only presenting LGBT issues in the context of problems such as harassment or anti-LGBT language can be damaging. As a starting point toward a more positive approach, educators can use inclusive language when discussing families and other relationships rather than assume that all students—and their parents, brothers, sisters, or friends—are heterosexual and traditionally gender identified.

Still, as every educator knows, the curriculum is at the center of any student's instructional experience. If a school's curriculum silences lesbian, gay, bisexual, and transgender people and issues, then the isolation in which LGBT students experience this aspect of their identities is exacerbated. In making the case for an LGBT-inclusive curriculum, Arthur Lipkin, author and former teacher, writes:

> In addition to these pragmatic considerations [including that virtually all students will know and work alongside LGBT people at some point in their lives], educators should be spurred by their professional duty to impart accurate and complete information in their classes and counseling sessions. Expurgation is dishonesty.[30]

Specific guidelines for an identity-positive (and age-appropriate) curriculum in the various school subjects are beyond the scope of this chapter, but as Lipkin points out, opportunities exist not just in health and sex education, but also in English/language arts, history and social studies, science, the arts, and a variety of other subject areas. And, while embedding LGBT themes into curricula in integral ways is essential for LGBT students to feel truly included, the examples Lindsey and Jason cite of inclusive projects and discussions illustrate how teachers can also bring these themes into the classroom in subtle but powerful ways.

Adult support and role models. As indicated previously, many sexual minority youth receive crucial support from teachers, counselors, and other adults at school. GLSEN's survey found that students who said their schools had a supportive faculty and staff were more likely to feel they "belonged" in school than those who did not. Also, the latest MYRBS found that students who believe there is a teacher or other school adult they could talk to "if they had a problem" are less likely to skip school, use drugs, or attempt suicide. While there are, of course, limits on the kinds of advice noncounseling school staff can and should give to students, gestures like the "Safe Space" stickers some of Jason's teachers had on their doors can send a subtle message that a teacher's room is a safe place to bring up an issue they don't feel they can discuss with any other adult—or simply to be themselves.

Along with "straight" teachers who demonstrate that they are supportive of LGBT youth, it is becoming clearer that LGBT adolescents benefit greatly from "out" teachers and other role models who can represent for them what it means to be a successful LGBT adult and to whom, as Lindsey says, they can "talk about anything." Since Erikson and others have noted that a key part of identity development is the ability to envision a future role for oneself in adult society, such role modeling can be especially meaningful for sexual minority youth, for whom positive portrayals are often all but invisible.

"I've heard young adults talk about how there was an openly gay teacher in their school, and they never let the teacher know at the time that they were also gay or lesbian or bi or trans," says Reis. "Yet having that teacher present was the thing that kept them from committing suicide."

Truly inclusive gay-straight alliances. Along with supportive and accepting adult/student relationships, there is clear evidence that positive and open peer relationships make a difference in the way LGBT adolescents experience school. For this reason, it is essential that every school have a gay-straight alliance, a place where LGBT adolescents can belong to a community and be accepted as they are (particularly if other aspects of the school culture do not fully support the inclusion of LGBT students).

GSAs can only fulfill their mission of providing a safe, identity-affirming place for all youth, however, if all feel they can participate. In an analysis of the issues facing queer youth of color at a California high school, Lance McCready notes how the racial and gender composition of some GSAs or other groups intended to support LGBT students may actually be alienating to sexual minority youth of color, leaving these students without the identity affirmation such organizations are intended to provide. McCready cites the example of David, a gay biracial student he interviewed, who did not participate in his school's GSA because he perceived it as "pretty much a select group of white girls," and an African American gay youth, Jamal, who similarly avoided the group because he believed it was "not particularly safe or confidential." It is therefore important for any school with a new or existing GSA to consider whether students of all races, ethnicities, genders, social groups, and abilities can feel welcome and supported there.[31]

A central principle underlying all these recommendations is that LGBT students, like all students, need to have a positive relationship with school—free from harassment and marked by mutual respect, inclusion, and community connection—in order to achieve to their full potential. Based on our research, my colleagues Stephen Chow, Constance P. Scanlon, and I have recommended that educators evaluate the extent to which their schools provide *relational assets* for LGBT students; that is, whether there exist opportunities for LGBT young people to form "authentic, affirming relationships with peers, adults, and the institution of school."[32] GSAs are clearly a crucial relational asset for LGBT youth, as are relationships with teachers in which they can bring this important aspect of their identity into the classroom and have it reflected in the curriculum; peer interactions in which they can feel free to be "out" (if they so choose) without fear of rejection or harassment; and a school community in which LGBT issues are discussed with respect and openness.

THE CHALLENGE AND THE RESPONSIBILITY

It would be naive for any educator to expect that efforts to make a school environment more identity-supportive for LGBT students would not meet with some form of opposition on religious or political grounds. Changes in curriculum to include LGBT people and issues, even if made in age-sensitive ways, have prompted especially strong protests in the past. Gay-straight alliances, though their number is rapidly growing across the country, continue to meet with challenges from administrators, school boards, and parents in some communities, and the majority of high schools in the United States still do not have a GSA. Moreover, despite the apparent benefits of LGBT students' having both openly LGBT role models and teachers they can count on as "straight allies," few administrators and school boards seem willing to risk the political difficulties they might encounter in incorporating such considerations into their hiring practices.

Many if not most schools have mission statements that articulate their commitment to provide a high-quality education for *all* students on an equal basis. Yet, if such mission statements are truly worth the glass cases that surround them in school lobbies, then meaningful efforts to support the needs of lesbian, gay, bisexual, and transgender students must be part of that commitment.

NOTES

1. All student and teacher names in this chapter are pseudonyms.
2. For detailed case studies of some of the students quoted in this chapter, as well as a complete description of the study for which they were interviewed, see Michael Sadowski, *Aligned at the Core: Relational Connections and Disconnections in the Lives of Lesbian, Gay, Bisexual, and Transgender Youth* (Cambridge, MA: Harvard Graduate School of Education, unpublished dissertation, 2005).
3. Erik H. Erikson, *Identity: Youth and Crisis.* (New York: W. W. Norton, 1968).
4. Erikson, *Identity*, 128.
5. When discussing the issues that affect youth who are lesbian, gay, bisexual, or transgender (LGBT), language is a problematic issue. Before the 1990s, most studies referred only to gay and lesbian youth, but researchers have become increasingly aware that bisexual people are a distinct group with specific concerns. More recent research also has recognized the special issues affecting transgender youth and adults, those who do not conform to traditional man/woman or boy/girl gender norms in a variety of ways. (Some transgender youth also identify as gay, lesbian, or bisexual, while others do not.) In addition, some individuals identify as "queer," a designation that implies a rejection of societal norms around sexuality and gender, or "questioning," if they are unsure of their sexual orientation or gender identity. Also, see Arthur Lipkin, "What's in a Label?" on pp. 142–146 for a discussion of some of the newer identifications used by sexual minority youth. When speaking of the studies and sources cited in general, I use the terms lesbian, gay, bisexual, and/or transgender, the abbreviation LGBT, or the inclusive (though admittedly problematic) term sexual minority youth. When citing specific studies, I use the terms the researchers used to describe the specific populations they sampled.
6. Lindsey reports that she experienced intense anti-LGBT harassment in middle school, but that her high school is much more accepting of LGBT students.
7. John Cloud, "The Battle over Gay Teens," Time, October 10, 2005, 42–51.
8. Lisa Machoian and I served as co-principal investigators of the study. The other researchers were Steve Anderson, Stephen Chow, Constance P. Scanlon, Andrea Sexton, and Travis Wright.
9. Massachusetts Department of Education, *2005 Massachusetts Youth Risk Behavior Survey Results* (Malden, MA: author, 2006); Vermont Department of Public Health, *2005 Vermont Youth Risk Behavior Survey: Statewide Report* (Burlington, VT: author, 2006).
10. *2005 Massachusetts Youth Risk Behavior Survey Results* (Malden, MA: author, 2006); Massachusetts Department of Education, *2003 Massachusetts Youth Risk Behavior Survey Results* (Malden, MA: author, 2004).

11. Forty states administer Youth Risk Behavior Surveys as part of the federal Centers for Disease Control and Prevention's Youth Risk Behavior Surveillance System, but only Massachusetts and Vermont ask students to identify their sexual orientation on the survey and are thus able to break out their data in this way. No state surveys include specific information on the risks affecting transgender youth.

12. Joseph G. Kosciw and Elizabeth M. Diaz, *2005 National School Climate Survey: The Experiences of Lesbian, Gay, Bisexual, and Transgender Youth in Our Nation's Schools* (New York: Gay, Lesbian and Straight Education Network, 2006).

13. California Safe Schools Coalition and 4-H Center for Youth Development, University of California, Davis, *Consequences of Harassment Based on Actual or Perceived Sexual Orientation and Gender Non-Conformity and Steps for Making Schools Safer* (Davis, CA: author, 2004); Harris Interactive and Gay, Lesbian and Straight Education Network, *From Teasing to Torment: School Climate in America, A Survey of Students and Teachers* (New York: GLSEN, 2005); Joseph G. Kosciw, *2003 National School Climate Survey: The School-Related Experiences of Our Nation's Lesbian, Gay, Bisexual, and Transgender Youth* (New York: Gay, Lesbian and Straight Education Network, 2004). Although the GLSEN school climate surveys are not based on random sampling of students (youth self-select to participate), their findings on the pervasiveness of anti-LGBT language and harassment have been consistent over multiple administrations of the survey and are supported by the reports listed herein and others.

14. The percentages in this paragraph are for students who indicated on the GLSEN survey that they'd experienced that type of harassment either "sometimes," "frequently," or "often." Students who indicated "rarely" for a given type of harassment on the survey are thus not represented in these figures.

15. GLSEN, *National School Climate Surveys*, 2001–2005.

16. The figures in this paragraph are for students who report any experience of harassment at school based on these identity factors.

17. Michael Sadowski, "Sexual Minority Students Benefit from School-Based Support—Where It Exists," *Harvard Education Letter* 17, no. 5 (September/October 2001): 1–5.

18. Michael Bochenek and A. Widney Brown, *Hatred in the Hallways: Violence and Discrimination against Lesbian, Gay, Bisexual, and Transgender Students in U.S. Schools* (New York: Human Rights Watch, 2001), 120.

19. Beth Reis, *They Don't Even Know Me! Understanding Anti-Gay Harassment and Violence in Schools* (Seattle: Safe Schools Coalition of Washington State, 1999).

20. Two earlier studies that included data showing the lack of representation of LGBT issues in school curriculum were: Rita M. Kissen, "Listening to Lesbian and Gay Teachers," *Teaching Education* 5, no. 2 (1993): 57–67; Kathleen P. Malinsky, "Learning to Be Invisible: Female Sexual Minority Students in America's Public High Schools," *Journal of Gay and Lesbian Social Services* 7, no. 4 (1997): 35–50.

21. Massachusetts Governor's Commission on Gay and Lesbian Youth, "Recommendations of the Governor's Commission on Gay and Lesbian Youth Based on Testimony Received at the Commission's Tenth Anniversary Forums" (Boston, MA: author, 2004).

22. Students using computers in New York City public schools, for example, are sometimes denied access to websites that contain words such as *lesbian, gay, bisexual,* or *transgender* and receive a message that a site contains blocked words if they attempt to access one.

23. Michael D. Resnick, et al., "Protecting Adolescents from Harm: Findings from the National Longitudinal Study on Adolescent Health," *Journal of the American Medical Association* 278, no. 10 (1997): 823–832; Michael D. Resnick, Linda J. Harris, and Robert W. Blum, "The Impact of Caring and Connectedness on Adolescent Health and Well-Being," *Journal of Pediatrics and Child Health* 29, Supplement 1 (1993): S3–S9; Michael Rutter, "Psychosocial Resilience and Protective Mechanisms," *American Journal of Orthopsychiatry* 57, no. 3 (1987): 316–331; Peter C. Scales and Nancy Leffert, *Developmental Assets: A Synthesis of the Scientific Research on Adolescent Development* (Minneapolis, MN: Search Institute, 1999); Renee Spencer, Judith V. Jordan, and Jenny Sazama, "Growth-Promoting Relationships between Youth and Adults: A Focus Group Study," *Families in Society* 85, no. 3 (2004): 354–362; Emmy E. Werner and Ruth S. Smith, *Vulnerable But Invincible: A Longitudinal Study of Resilient Children and Youth* (New York: Adams Bannister Cox, 1982).

24. Anthony R. D'Augelli, Scott L. Hershberger, and Neil W. Pilkington, "Lesbian, Gay, and Bisexual Youth and Their Families: Disclosure of Sexual Orientation and Its Consequences." *American Journal of Orthopsychiatry* 68, no. 3 (1998): 361–375; Norweeta G. Milburn et al., "Discrimination and Exiting Homelessness among Homeless Adolescents," *Cultural Diversity and Ethnic Minority Psychology* 12, no. 4 (2006): 658–672.

25. See citations in note 23.

26. Bochenek and Brown, *Hatred in the Hallways*, 83.

27. GLSEN sells packs of 25 LGBT "Safe Space" stickers for $3.00; available at http://www.glsen.org/cgi-bin/iowa/all/library/record/1641.html

28. Laura A. Szalacha, "Safer Sexual Diversity Climates: Lessons Learned from an Evaluation of the Massachusetts Safe Schools Program for Gay and Lesbian Students," *American Journal of Education* 110, no. 1 (2003): 58–88.

29. Carol Goodenow, Laura A. Szalacha, and Kim Westheimer, "School Support Groups, Other School Factors, and the Safety of Sexual Minority Adolescents," *Psychology in the Schools* 43, no. 5 (2006): 573–589.

30. Arthur Lipkin, *Understanding Homosexuality, Changing Schools: A Text for Teachers, Counselors, and Administrators* (Boulder, CO: Westview Press, 1999), 332.

31. Lance McCready, "When Fitting In Isn't an Option, or, Why Black Queer Males at a California High School Stay Away from Project 10," in Kevin K. Kumashiro (ed.), *Troubling Intersections of Race and Sexuality: Queer Students of Color and Anti-Oppressive Education* (Lanham, MD: Rowman & Littlefield, 2001), 37–53.

32. Michael Sadowski, Stephen Chow, and Constance P. Scanlon, "Meeting the Needs of LGBTQ Youth: A 'Relational Assets' Approach," *Journal of LGBT Youth* 6 (forthcoming, 2009). Our relational assets framework is based in part on the developmental assets framework outlined in Scales and Leffert's book (see note 23).

Profile

The Story of Matt, "Transgender Superhero"

MICHAEL SADOWSKI

Although many sexual minority adolescents experience harassment, a lack of peer acceptance, and tensions both at home and at school (see previous chapter), transgender youth—those who express their gender in ways contrary to expected male or female norms[*]—can face some of the biggest challenges. First, whereas most adults understand what a young person means when she or he "comes out" as gay, lesbian, or bisexual, many still lack a clear sense of what the word "transgender" even means or why it is important to many young people that they identify themselves as such. Second, there is reason to believe that many people feel even more threatened by the transgression of gender norms than by nontraditional sexuality: Transgender people are at heightened risk for violent hate crimes[1] (the rape and murder of Brandon Teena depicted in the film *Boys Don't Cry* being only one such example), and transgender students experience school-based harassment in even greater proportion than lesbian, gay, or bisexual youth.[2] Third, parents who raise a child as a son or daughter may have an especially difficult time accepting that young person as transgender, especially if this involves the child identifying as—and possibly even transitioning to—the opposite gender.[3]

Following are excerpts from my interview with Matt[4], a friendly, soft-spoken, female-to-male transgender youth, from a qualitative study I conducted with six other researchers on the family, school, and peer relationships of lesbian, gay, bisexual, and transgender (LGBT) young people.[5] At

---

[*]The U.S. Surgeon General defines transgender people as follows: "Individuals whose gender identity, expression, or behavior is not traditionally associated with their birth sex. Some transgender individuals experience gender identity as incongruent with their anatomical sex and may seek some degree of sex reassignment surgery, take hormones, or undergo other cosmetic procedures. Others may pursue gender expression (masculine or feminine) through external self-presentation and behavior."

the time of his interview, Matt had graduated from high school and was regularly attending YouthWest, a community-based LGBT youth support group in a rural area of the Northeast. Though still biologically female, Matt presents primarily as a young man through clothing, haircut, and the use of a traditionally male name. During our interview, he shares with me his plans to start taking male hormones within the next few months and to work toward a biological sex reassignment in the near future, although he still has many questions about how he will pay for the surgical procedures involved. He also discusses the dilemma he faces between his own self-fulfillment and the central relationships in his life by drawing analogies to Spider-Man. (A new Spider-Man film had been released just prior to the time of our interview.)

I was wondering if you could talk about the things you like about being transgender and the things you don't like about it.

I do like being so in tune, you know, with myself and who I am. And it just really makes me happy when I realize that I've finally found, you know, the one thing that identifies me the most. I don't like the relationships that it's kind of testing. I mean, my parents—my mom pretty much cries whenever I talk about it, and seeing her in that much pain just hurts me beyond anything . . .[6]

Can you give me an example of when you've spoken to your mother about being transgender and what exactly you talked about? What was the conversation? How did she react?

When I first identified as transgender, I told her that, like, I was going to see a therapist soon, I was going to look into that. And I told her that Youth-West was my main support for that and that Shane [one of the adult advisors] was helping me with it a lot. Her reaction was basically that she was kind of just shocked and then she was kind of flabbergasted. You know, she didn't—she hadn't even heard of this before really, and to think of her daughter as her son is just something she can't—it's unspeakable to her. And so I think at first she was just totally shocked, and then it just turned into anger and then sadness.

Can you remember any particular things that she said or did?

She thought it was just incredible that I wanted to be a guy. You know, she just didn't even think that it was possible. And she says a lot of things about hormones that are very degrading. She thinks—basically she said to me that

I'm going to die if I go on them, even though, you know, a doctor will be monitoring my health and everything. And whenever I tell her about the good points of hormones, she just goes into denial and says, "You know, they're going to kill you. They're going to hurt your liver and you'll never be the same." She says a lot of things like, "You're going to do this so young, and then, you know, be upset about it in three or four years and wish you'd never done it." And just things like that.

How does it make you feel when she says things like that?

It hurts a lot. Like I feel like she'll never accept me for who I am, and that's one of the things that hurts the most . . .

Do you remember when you started to accept [your transgender] identity yourself?

Pretty much around the time that I came out to my mother. You know, I never really was depressed about being a lesbian [how Matt identified before adopting a male gender identity] because it seemed mostly that everyone was accepting. But I did have a hard time in high school. I went to Smith County [high school] for about two-three years [before transferring]. And a lot of people were accepting there, but then there were people who weren't. . . .

What happened at Smith County that made it hard?

I lost a lot of friends when I told, you know, them about my sexuality, and they were very derogatory, very—they would laugh at me behind my back and say stupid shit. It just was so bad that I just didn't want to be there anymore. Like I didn't really feel comfortable being there. I mean I had like four or five friends who stood up for me and accepted me, but to me, that wasn't really enough. I actually used to get harassed, too, for looking like a guy. People used to come up to me and say, "Are you a guy or a girl?" You know, and that really pissed me off at the time because I don't think it was more, like, how I felt about my gender, it was more that I knew they were doing it just to be an asshole. So it really upset me when I was younger. Now it doesn't faze me anymore.

How did you deal with it when things like that would happen or things would get tough?

I mean, I have gotten mistaken for a guy, like, many times. Before I identified as trans, I would kind of just laugh it off, you know? But now it's just nice to have people call you "sir" and stuff because that's how you want to identify. But before, it was more, like, funny to me. Like, I didn't realize the significance of it. You know, I was kind of like, "Well I do have really androgynous features," and I started to realize more and more, the more I got mistaken for a guy, that I actually really felt like I was a guy and wanted to *be* a guy. . .

How do you feel most of the time?

Lately I've been okay, but the last month or two I have been really depressed because of the family issues. I get really upset, you know, because I've—I've told my mom flat out that I'm going to do hormones. You know, she told me that she would respect the decision if I waited a few years, when I was around twenty-three or twenty-four. And basically her exact words were, "If it doesn't go away, then at least we know that you've had more time to think about it." I try telling her that I have thought about it my whole life. You know, like I've always wished that I was a guy, and she just says, "No. No, you haven't. You haven't thought about this. You haven't thought about that." And she actually—she kind of conned me into telling her that I would wait [to begin taking hormones]. You know, she was crying and she was upset, and I was upset, I was crying . . .

In a way, I think of it like being Spider-Man, you know? Like he's so strong and brave, but he can't really identify as Spider-Man because he knows it will hurt everyone he loves. And I think I war between that. You know, like a part of me wants to be, you know, the person that my mom wants me to be, but then I realize that I'm a greater person when I'm not the person she wants me to be. So it's kind of like a war between myself. 'Cause I know if I don't go through with the hormones and the surgery, I know I would just be miserable. But my mom and my family would be happy. You know, it's just kind of like a war . . .

Have you seen the new Spider-Man movie?

Yes.

I haven't seen it. I've heard it's good . . .

Well, it was a very emotional movie for me. You know, I found myself crying through it because in the movie he gives up being Spider-Man to make himself happy. And when he does, he realizes that he's not happy at all. And that's how I felt when I told my mom I would wait three years. I mean, I was going along with that for at least a good two weeks. When I talked to Marlene [Matt's therapist] about it, I realized how ever since I'd made that decision, I had gotten more and more depressed. And it just totally—I related to it more than I've related with anything because I gave up being transgender in a way. You know, I put a halt—a very big halt—on my transition, and I wasn't happy at all. And I realized that if I did wait three years, that would be three years of being untrue to myself, and that's one thing I just can't do. . .

So that was the realization that kind of made you say, "No, I'm not going to wait?"

Yeah, it was. Yeah, I realized that I feel exactly how he feels. It's almost like being transgender is being a hero to me because, you know, there are so many people that just won't come to the realization and they don't advance on their transition because of the pain and suffering it causes. But I just realized it's something I had to do . . .

What are things that give you hope when you look ahead?

I think my career, you know, and the fact that I am transitioning. I just feel like I'll be more comfortable, you know, in a better environment. It's kind of like almost like I'm seeing a movie, you know, when I think about my future. You know, like I picture myself this young guy striving to find that right career in New York City, and it just makes me smile, you know, because I realize that I do have the potential to have a great career and a good life. And I think that gives me a lot of hope.

When you think of trans people as heroes, are you thinking about other people, maybe kids, who might be trans but either don't have the circumstances where they can do anything about it or—

I do. Yeah, you know, I think a lot about myself and other people, you know, when I'm thinking about that because I do know a lot of trans guys, like online and otherwise, and they are all struggling. . . . A lot of people would call it selfish, but I think we're brave, and I think it takes a lot of emotional stress out of us to do these kinds of things. And people don't realize these things. They don't realize the emotional circumstances. They think you're this selfish asshole, you know? And it's not that at all. You know, you're just doing it to be happy, and it takes a lot of guts to do that, to go against everyone you know.

NOTES

1. While the number of bias crimes against individuals based on their gender identity or expression is difficult to measure, the organization Gender Education and Advocacy (www.gender.org) estimates that there has been at least one antitransgender murder per month in the United States since 1989. Numerous national organizations, including the Gay, Lesbian and Straight Education Network now officially recognize an annual Transgender Day of Remembrance in honor of these victims. For more information, see www.dayofsilence.org/tdr.html.

2. Joseph G. Kosciw and Elizabeth M. Diaz, *2005 National School Climate Survey: The Experiences of Lesbian, Gay, Bisexual, and Transgender Youth in Our Nation's Schools* (New York: Gay, Lesbian and Straight Education Network, 2006).

3. Bernadette Wren, "'I Can Accept My Child Is Transsexual, But If I Ever See Him in a Dress I'll Hit Him': Dilemmas in Parenting a Transgendered Adolescent," *Clinical Child Psychology and Psychiatry* 7, No. 3 (2002): 377–397.

4. Matt is a pseudonym for the traditionally male name by which the youth I interviewed identified himself. All other names mentioned are also pseudonyms.

5. Lisa Machoian and I served as co-principal investigators of the study. The other researchers were Steve Anderson, Stephen Chow, Constance P. Scanlon, Andrea Sexton, and Travis Wright.

6. Ellipses indicate breaks in the sequence of the actual interview.

Commentary

What's in a Label?
Adolescents and *Queer* Identities

ARTHUR LIPKIN

> First, there was the term "homosexual," then "gay" and "lesbian," then
> the once taboo "dyke" and "queer." Now, all bets are off.
> —*Rona Marech*, San Francisco Chronicle[1]

> That's genderqueer. It's not just crossing the lines, it's erasing them.
> —*Craig Malisow*, Houston Press[2]

A number of years ago, a substantial percentage of youth whom others might
classify as lesbian, gay, bisexual, or transgender (LGBT) began calling themselves *queer*. In a 2001 California survey of high school gay-straight alliances (groups for the support of sexual minority students and the advancement of LGBT rights), queer-identifying youth made up about 12.5 percent
of those who did not identify as *straight*. Another 12.5 percent chose *bisexual* to describe themselves; those identifying as *gay* and *lesbian* were evenly
divided at 37 percent each.[3]

Today, several new sexuality and gender-defying identifiers like *pansexual, heteroflexible, tranny,* and *genderqueer* are expanding the popular lexi-
con beyond *queer*, particularly in urban centers and among academics and
young activists on the left of the political spectrum. In the context of the
vanishing clinical term *homosexual* and the still resilient *gay, lesbian,* and
bisexual, these new signifiers might baffle conventional and liberal minds
alike. Educators should understand the political and psychological roots of
this rapid evolution and variety of terms, since they are central to the ways
in which many young people view their emerging identities.

A BRIEF HISTORY OF *QUEER*

Academics first employed *queer* to contest what they saw as arbitrary and oppressive sexuality labels, thus undermining the rigid binary categories *straight* and *gay*. Beginning in the 1980s, many campus Gay Studies programs came to be called Queer Studies. The 1990s activist organization Queer Nation took the label into the streets, and then adolescents picked it up as a form of self- and community identification. For adolescents, the term *queer* was a public appropriation of a demeaning epithet. Other stigmatized groups have also tried to weaken the venom of name-calling by remaking hurtful words into prideful ones. The adoption of the "N-word" by some African Americans is one such example.

Besides representing an attempt to de-fang their tormentors, *queer* offers some youth a relatively comfortable and open-ended way to say that they are "not straight." Rather than boxing them into a narrow, fixed gay or lesbian social script, it allows for greater flexibility and promises a freer identity trajectory. Even as more youth begin to come out at earlier ages as lesbian, gay, bisexual, or transgender, others may wait indefinitely in what psychologist Esther Rothblum calls the "lingering" category.[4] For both groups, *queer* seems an appropriate fit.

For some adolescents attracted to both men and women, the word *queer* also is more appealing than *bisexual*, either because they aren't sure of the scope of their attractions or because they reject common misconceptions about the meaning of *bisexual*: "omnivorously promiscuous" to many heterosexuals and "confused or cowering" to many gays. Those judgments, of course, are undeserved. Being open to exploring one's full sexuality is not the equivalent of being oversexed, confused, or frightened.

Although some youth still hesitate to identify as lesbian, gay, bisexual, or transgender out of internalized homophobia or fear of family and peer rejection and harassment, others wait because they doubt the worth of sexuality categories altogether—even *queer*. One research subject, Matthew, seems just such a case:

> Just because he has a boyfriend, that in itself doesn't mean much about who he is. Matthew notes that many of his friends are uninterested in labels or categories referring to sexual identities. His generation, he maintains, is beyond terms like "gay" or even the reclaimed identity label "queer."[5]

Yet it is difficult to tell whether such rejection of labels is a consequence of heightened post-*gay*, post-*queer* awareness or a product of lingering shame, or at least reticence, about identifying oneself as part of a stigmatized group. Matthew insists that sports, academics, and career aspirations are more indicative of who he is than the gender of the person with whom he shares an intimate relationship. Yet, if he and his cohort are so blasé about labels, why is it also reported that it took a probing question from Matthew's mother about dating for him to "come out" (his words) to her? There appears to be a more complex psychological context here than the researchers concede.

Just a few years ago, the spaciousness of *queer* seemed sufficient to create a sense of community among sexual minority youth. As one San Francisco high school graduate observed:

> Queer unifies the community. We're so used to being sectioned off into our groups and subcultures. This is one word that embodies all of us. It's something we are struggling for in the younger generation. It's saying we're all in this together, this is who we are, our history, culture and everything we've been through.[6]

The word even came to incorporate youth who do not view themselves as LGBT but identify as "politically queer," sympathetic to their sexual minority peers and resistant to cultural norms of sexuality and gender.

When it first appeared, *queer* also encompassed a spectrum of gender identity and expression that *gay, lesbian,* and *bisexual* still do not necessarily imply. It represented the fundamental trangenderedness of all people who violate common male and female norms—in the bedroom, the wardrobe, the schoolhouse, the playing field, and so on. And with recent transgender emergence, it is not surprising that many of the newer signifiers young people are using to identify themselves spring from variations in gender identity, from the all-inclusive *genderqueer* (echoing *queer* itself) to *trannydyke* or *trannyfag* (reclaiming those old pejoratives) to *boi* (subversion through spelling).

Finally, the breadth of *queer* created space for those who bring a non-Western, non-white perspective to their same gender desires and sexualities. They may resist *gay, lesbian,* or *bisexual* being applied to feelings and pursuits that are understood differently in their native and community cultures. Adopting such labels could estrange them not only from their established sense of themselves but also from their cultural supports, families, and friends who consider such identities alien. Of course, multiple-minority people may find *queer* no less problematic than *gay*. Many Native Americans, for example, have historically favored the term *two-spirit,* and the terms *on the down low* and *same gender loving* are still common among African Americans. That said, one gay African-American rapper, Deadlee, a self-described "queer bastard child of DMX & Lil' Kim,"[7] calls his music "homohop," and organized a "HomoRevolution Tour" of other queer hip hop artists. Queer has also found appeal among other ethnic groups in the U.S. (e.g., "The Queer Arabs Blog: Rantings of Angry Sarcastic Bitchy Queer Arab Americans"[8]) as well as internationally (e.g., Iranian Queer Organization, the name for the former Persian Gay and Lesbian Organization, and the UK's Queer Youth Network).

The appropriation of *queer* and all its variants, however, has not meant that the word has lost its poison. Like the "N-word," context is everything: who says it, where, and how. From kindergarten on, homophobic invective continues to be a favorite weapon among bullies and bashers:

> Jackie Chesson's heart sank last month after discovering her school notebook had been defaced with the words "gay," "faggot" and "queer." She felt even worse after realizing the vandalism was linked to her participation in a student panel of Gay-Straight Alliance members two days before.[9]

So it should be no surprise that, although it retains its positive currency (e.g., California's *Queer Youth Advocacy Day*), some sexual minority youth might remain squeamish about *queer* or its double-edged successors.

"QUEER" IDENTITIES IN CONTEXT

The factors that influence anyone's sense of self and determine how one presents oneself to the world are an interdependent matrix. Gender, race, ethnicity, faith, and location are some of the factors that affect one's sexual identity and expression; conversely, sexuality has an impact on one's gendered, racial, ethnic, religious, family, and community "selves." Political identity can also figure in the mix. Writer and activist Kate Bornstein calls the term *genderqueer* "a gender version of beatnik, hippie—whatever you want to call it. It's punk. It's that kind of radical voice and expression against conformity."[10] Conversely, a young gay contributor to the *Yale Daily News* writes:

> To those heterosexuals who feel pressure from noisy activists to use the word "queer" but are understandably uncomfortable doing so: not to worry. I'm gay, and I'd like to keep it that way.[11]

In the end, of course, young people growing up an a complex (and still homophobic) world need and deserve to call themselves whatever they wish—even as those of us who want to support them rush to keep up with the nomenclature.

NOTES

1. Rona Marech, "Nuances of Gay Identities Reflected in New Language: 'Homosexual' is Passé in a 'Boi's' Life," *San Francisco Chronicle*, February 8, 2004.
2. Craig Malisow, "Genderqueer: Straight or Gay, These Kids Refuse to Play Dress-Up by the Rules," *Houston Press,* March 16, 2006.
3. Geoffrey Winder, "GSA Network Anti-Racism Initiative Report, Summer 2001" (San Francisco: Gay-Straight Alliance Network).
4. Tori DeAngelis, "A New Generation of Issues for LGBT Clients," *Monitor on Psychology* 33, no. 2 (2002): 44–53.
5. Bertram Cohler and Phillip Hammack, "The Psychological World of the Gay Teenager: Social Change, Narrative, and 'Normality.'" *Journal of Youth and Adolescence* 36, no. 1 (2007): 47–59.
6. Greg Zhovreboff, as quoted in Christopher Heredia, "Older Generation Sneers at 'Queer,'" *San Francisco Chronicle*, June 24, 2001.
7. PlanetOut News, "Gay Rapper Deadlee Takes on 50 Cent," available at planetout.com (accessed January 30, 2007).
8. Sarah Klein, "Inside the 'Double Closet,'" *Detroit Metro Times*, available at alternet.org/story/36012 (accessed May 13, 2006).
9. Alexandria Rocha, "A Matter of Respect—and Safety," *Palo Alto Online*, available at paloaltoonline.com (accessed February 1, 2006).
10. As quoted in Craig Malisow, "Bois and Grrls," *Houston Press*, March 16, 2006.
11. James Kirchick, "Young, Out, and Gay—Not Queer." *Yale Daily News*, February 14, 2006.

CHAPTER EIGHT

Who Wins and Who Loses?

Social Class and Student Identities

ELLEN BRANTLINGER

Waiting to get my hair cut a while ago, I saw a familiar-looking woman sitting across the reception area thumbing through *Vogue*. She looked about thirty-five or forty years old. I puzzled for some time before I realized that this woman who looked so much older than I remembered her was Marissa, whom I had interviewed when she was entering her sophomore year of high school.[1] As her name was called and she walked by me on fashionable, high-heeled clog sandals, the skimpiness of her miniskirt and halter top revealed a woman who was probably five feet, ten inches tall and could not have weighed more than one hundred pounds. I recalled that a decade earlier she had been a slim but healthy-looking teenager, with a gracefully rounded face and figure, and her hair had been a darker blond. She complained then that her mother would not let her bleach it; now it was streaked with light tones and framed her face in shaggy layers. It looked perfect even before her hair appointment, and her darkly tanned face was made up with great expertise. Marissa's parents were acquaintances of mine. A few years earlier I heard from them that Marissa had graduated from an MBA program and was engaged and living in another state. When I saw her at the beauty salon, I assumed that she was in town to visit her parents.

One of the things an ethnographer hates to admit—especially to herself—is that she does not particularly like certain participants in her study. I began my research with affluent adolescents after having interviewed forty youth who lived in subsidized housing. I was still numb from hearing about the poorer youths' degrading school careers and how they had been treated by teachers and by students from wealthier families. These low-income adolescents were bitter that their affluent peers monopolized the high-status activities and accelerated academic tracks in their socioeconomically mixed secondary schools. They worried about their current circumstances and bleak futures and envied the better school conditions and brighter prospects of "preps," "jocks," "good students," and "respectable kids." I had come to care about the low-income youth I interviewed. As I extended my study to include the high-income adolescents, I felt as though I were moving into enemy territory. These were the schoolmates my earlier participants had accused of humiliating them with degrading epithets and of otherwise bullying, excluding, and ostracizing them.[2]

MARISSA

Marissa epitomized my preconceptions of an elite student. She lived in the most expensive area of Hillsdale and had attended the only elementary school in town that didn't enroll students poor enough to be on free lunch. Having completed her freshman year of high school at the time of our interview, Marissa was on the honors track and had been a cheerleader since middle school. During that summer interview, Marissa proudly announced that she was among only four sophomores selected to be in the prestigious swing choir. She joked that she was "really tone deaf," indicating that she was aware that she likely had been chosen because of her attractive appearance and the fact that her parents could afford the expensive show costumes and trips to contests. When discussing social groups in school, Marissa usually referred to herself and her friends as "preppies" or "jocks." When asked what others would call her, she replied, "Um, maybe an airhead," which she defined as "someone pretty, [with] good hair, good figure, nice clothes . . . interested in looks, with good taste." Marissa's friends were, in her words, "popular kids, preppies." As she explained, "We all dress the same, go to the mall, hang out at somebody's house or pool, play tennis." She added that she and the girls she spent time with "talk together all the time, but never about anything important." Expressing real feelings or talking about serious topics apparently was not permitted.

Marissa's vaguely stated post–high school plans included "going to college and getting a great job," which she defined as one with a high salary and some prestige. Her ideal goal was "to be a famous model." She had not decided on a college or a major. She later confessed that her PSAT scores were "not great—nowhere near as high as my nerd of a brother." She lamented, "I'm not anywhere near as smart. He's a brain." However, Marissa got what she called "good grades, mainly As." Chris, her older brother, excelled in science and had been offered scholarships to several prestigious universities, one of which he would attend in the fall. Marissa admitted that she had to work hard to keep her high GPA, but she still resented that her mother disciplined her to a mandatory nightly study time at home and kept track of schoolwork. This was something she did not tell peers about because it was "not cool to study." It seems that it was best to be seen as someone who was naturally smart, which meant that you got good grades without trying or caring. Marissa conjectured that her friends probably also lied about not studying, as she gave the example that before a test her peers would say, "Oh my god! I didn't study. I know I'll fail," then feign surprise at doing well. She suspected that in talking to each other about homework, they all underreported the time they put into writing papers or completing assignments, as well as the amount of support they received from their parents.

Assessing her relationships with teachers, Marissa said, "Most like me. We get along. They know I'm a good kid." When asked if she ever got into trouble, Marissa said, "Not really. I get away with stuff because teachers trust me; they know I'm just messing around when I'm, like, a little late to class or something. Oh, sometimes they give me a dirty look when I goof off too much, like complain about the work or talk to my friends when I am supposed to be listening." Marissa implied that teachers were respectful to her (and perhaps intimidated by her) because they knew that her parents closely monitored her schooling, both what Marissa herself did in school and what teachers did. She volunteered that teachers knew of her before she got to high school because Chris had been an honor student and a championship tennis player. Marissa confidently said she had been in "the most popular freshman clique." After naming "grits" as the least popular students at her school and hypothesizing that "grits don't have cliques, I don't think," she clarified her statement:

> Grits are poor. I think they mostly live in the country. We—[quickly correcting herself] some of my friends call them hicks or rednecks. I guess

most live on the Hill—that's over on the west side of town. It's the slums. Grits smoke, do drugs, dress grungy. They have those hick accents. I think they usually get bad grades. They don't like school, so I think they drop out a lot. They don't really fit in. They are troublemakers. I don't see them much; they aren't in any of my classes.

Marissa admitted that she did not personally know any low-income students and had little contact with them: "I see them hanging around in the parking lot by the vocational wing before school. They smoke, try to look tough, and—excuse me for saying this—but the girls look slutty."

TRAVIS

In terms of home and school circumstances, Travis—someone Marissa would have called a grit—was her polar opposite. The third of four sons, Travis lived with his recently widowed mother in the same apartment in subsidized housing where he had been born seventeen years earlier.[3] His two older brothers, who he said "mostly don't have jobs," also lived at home "most of the time." During my interview with Travis, one of his brothers worked on a car in the parking lot and occasionally glanced over at us with what looked like either suspicion or derision. Travis informed me that his younger brother Jimmy, a 16-year-old, had been incarcerated in a juvenile treatment center after having been convicted on burglary and drug charges two months earlier. Several times during the interview, Travis condemned Jimmy for "getting in trouble with police" and "being stupid and getting caught," but mostly for "hurting Mom."

I had heard of the four Ramage brothers, each a year apart, well before my interview with Travis. The second oldest, Mike, was a fighter who ended up being classified emotionally handicapped due to problems with anger management and opposition to school authority. While doing special education field supervision, I had watched this bright and active youngster through the five or six years that he was placed in special education classes up until the time he dropped out of school. I knew that Child Protection Services had been involved with Mike a few years earlier when he and his mother had been severely beaten by his father, who spent some time in prison because of the incident. However, teachers mainly spoke of the four Ramage boys because they were remarkably alike in appearance—and were therefore constantly being confused with one another—and because of their amazingly good looks. Variations of Brad Pitt, these blond, brown-eyed, small youths had muscular builds and walked with a spring in their step, looking as if they had important business that they must attend to quickly, although they rarely made it to class on time, if at all.

The boys' physiques made it clear that they were athletic, and they were reputed to be bright, though mostly unmotivated to do schoolwork. Junior, the oldest, had been the best student, but even his achievement and attendance were erratic. The Ramage boys frustrated school personnel because, in spite of their talents and considerable encouragement from teachers and coaches, they never sustained an interest in their classes or school-organized sports. T-shirts with various car and motorcycle motifs communicated their real interests. They were described as leaders among their equally disengaged but somewhat more rebellious peers from the housing project. As one teacher observed, "These kids live close together, have gone to all the same schools, and are in the same classes, so they are like siblings, squabbling all the time." Friction mostly involved arguments, threats, and scuffles, but there were sometimes brawls for which they would be suspended or, if weapons were involved, expelled. Nevertheless, the Ramage boys were mostly cooperative and personable, so teachers liked them. They had a lively sense of humor but also could be unpredictably moody and unaccountably angry. From the time each of the brothers entered middle school, they conveyed that their major objective was to turn sixteen so that they could quit school. When asked about the particulars behind his own dropping out, Travis reminisced:

> The dean was giving me a bunch of trouble. She did that with all us boys. She'd hassle me about being late, missing school—I was having problems with everything. She'd call my mom and threaten her. When I quit going for a week after my dad died, she said she'd take me to court if I wasn't there every day. My mom said I did not have to go until we got things straightened out. So she suspended me. She said I couldn't come back until I had a letter from the doctor or welfare. I never liked school anyway. It was all right at Hillview [elementary] some of the time, I guess. I did not like Downing [middle school] or high school. When I was sixteen, I stopped going. I just got tired of going.

When I asked if he had any regrets about quitting school, his prompt reply was simply, "No."

The first part of the interview took place in the family living room, where Travis, his mother, and his brother Mike sat smoking and watching a soap opera. I had introduced myself as a teacher educator interested in what teenagers thought about school and told them I might be writing about their experiences for teachers and others. At that introduction, his mother smirked and said, "Travis has plenty to say about school!" When Travis said he sort of liked elementary school and felt he was "pretty good" in math and reading, his mother interjected, "Travis got lots of As when he was at Hillview. He liked that school." Travis said middle school was "all right some of the time" and that his favorite classes were math and shop. His mother proudly pointed to a wooden clock Travis had made that was sawed into the shape of the state and painted in the local university colors. The clock hung on the wall in the middle of a cluster of school pictures, which showed her sons' cute faces representing their first-grade to early teenage years. No prom or graduation pictures were among them. Travis added that his middle school gym teacher was "nice" and "got me to wrestle." His mother then bragged, "Travis won trophies in wrestling," as she pointed to two gleaming statues on top of the television. Travis' older brother piped up, "Yeah, you was good at wrestling, right Travis?" Then he turned to me and said, "Me and Junior taught him wrestling," at which point Mike guffawed sadistically and Travis shrugged.

Shortly thereafter Travis agreed to move out to a grassy area a short distance from the housing complex to complete the interview. When outside, Travis promptly denied his mother's claims about his good grades at Hillview:

> God, I flunked first grade even, but I never was in special ed—I wasn't that dumb. I never did really like school. Me and teachers did not get along. I guess I sort of did okay until in high school, then I did terrible. All they [teachers] cared about was me being on time. The dean, she did not like me. Some girls got in a fight over me and she blamed it on me—said, "You get around, don't you!"

When I asked how long he had participated in wrestling, Travis confessed that his wrestling career was cut short in eighth grade when he was not allowed to be in extracurricular activities because of school absenteeism, tardiness, and low grades in several courses.

Although Travis asserted that "me and teachers didn't get along" and reiterated that belief in response to several questions, when asked to describe a favorite teacher, Travis responded without hesitation:

> I loved Mr. E. [his fifth-grade teacher]; he was a real cool teacher. He helped me a bunch of times when I did not understand—he cared about

me. Other teachers did not care. They'd just get mad and say, "You'll flunk if you don't do your work." They didn't care what happened to me. We'd argue a lot. I wouldn't understand something and they'd say, "Well I just showed you how to do it!" [When quoting teachers, he raised his voice and mimicked a sharp, ugly tone.] And I liked Mr. F. [his middle school gym teacher and wrestling coach]. He was nice. All the kids liked him and he liked us. We had fun in his class. Most teachers was snobby; some was all right. If you didn't understand, they didn't treat you like a piece of trash. Some teachers helped you if you had a problem. Most didn't. They helped some kids, their pets, but they didn't care about most of us, didn't care about me, if I flunked or anything.

When asked if he thought that some kinds of students had an easier time in school than others, Travis's immediate response was, "Yeah, preppies, rich kids. They got away with things. Teachers were hard on me and my friends." Regarding his relations with other students when he went to high school, Travis said:

> I had some friends—we stuck together. The punks were smart alecks—we avoided them. They would start fights and things like that. The preps ran the school. They would smart off and call us grits and stuff like that. They didn't bother me. I just kept away from them. I didn't care.

Travis emphasized "not caring" at several points in our conversation, but his animated and emotional tone belied the validity of this assertion.

Travis dropped out of school in the middle of the second semester of his freshman year when he was of legal age, sixteen years old. He admitted that he had been suspended twice in the fall for "missing class and being late" and so had not successfully completed any high school courses prior to his officially dropping out. Travis said of his mother, "[She] didn't want me to quit, but said, 'If that's what you want to do, then do it.'" He went on to explain, "She'd rather see me quit than in trouble. Besides, she let my brothers drop out, so it wouldn't be fair to make me go. Anyway, she didn't finish herself, and my dad dropped out when he was real little."

When I asked about his plans for the future, Travis said he would like to "find a job that pays good, maybe work in a factory." He said that because his father died in a quarry accident he was not interested in quarry work, adding, "That's not steady work anyway—never was for my dad." Travis was vehement that he intended to keep out of trouble and out of jail, again mentioning how upset his mother was about his younger brother's incarceration. When asked about the availability of factory jobs, he shrugged, then volunteered in a bitter tone, "Junior [his oldest brother] had a job that paid real good, but they let him go. Most of that factory moved to Mexico, so only guys with seniority got to keep jobs." According to Travis, Junior had a good salary during the approximately two years he worked and had been able to move into a mobile home he rented until he was laid off. Neither Travis nor Mike, his second-oldest brother, had found full-time employment in the year since both had dropped out of school. All three brothers had done some temporary maintenance work at a local stock-car race track and at a demolition derby site in a nearby town. Junior sometimes was called in for pick-up work at an auto mechanic shop, but this did not happen often enough for him to fully support himself and live on his own. When asked about his ideal goals, Travis said he would like to work on motorcycles or race cars—a love he and his brothers shared. Most of all, he wanted to be a race car driver.

SOCIAL-CLASS RELATIONS IN SCHOOL

Marissa and Travis were part of an interview study I did with forty low-income youths[4] and thirty-four high-income youths in the 1990s.[5] A major finding of that study was the high degree to which the nature of adolescents' school careers correlated with their class status: Affluent students were making good grades and were on or above grade level and in advanced-track classes, whereas 35 percent of low-income participants were identified as learning disabled, emotionally handicapped, or mildly retarded and were receiving special education services. Also, 37 percent had been retained one or two years, and few of those on grade level claimed to be making decent grades.

The extent to which social-class issues permeated adolescents' stories about school and their views of themselves in the school environment was a surprise to me. Echoing the words of sociologist Philip Wexler, I "was not prepared to discover how deeply the differences of class run in the lives of high school students."[6] Social class certainly figured as prominently as gender or race in their identity construction. As illustrated by Marissa and Travis, adolescents are not passive imitators of class-distinctive ways of being; rather, they are agents that perform class-distinctive roles in innovative ways, and thus they actively contribute to the reproduction of class roles in their own social setting.[7]

When examining the schooling of youths from different social classes it would be easy to portray such students as Marissa as winners and those like Travis as losers. However, although I earlier alluded to Marissa's worrisome thinness and anxious demeanor in the beauty parlor to hint at her difficulties as a young adult, I omitted statements she made in her interview that indicated all had not been ideal in her adolescent world. First, she expressed resentment that her parents expected her to be in all the advanced classes and prestigious activities in school as well as to be popular with peers and teachers. She implied that they cared more about what others thought than how she felt. She mocked her parents' bragging about "Chris' genius" to their friends, was distressed that they thought he was more likely to succeed in an important career, and expressed worry about her own future. In spite of my reassurance that her sterling grades indicated she was smart, Marissa reiterated that those grades resulted from hard work, help from her parents and tutors, and parental intervention with teachers. She insisted that she "did not catch on easily or really understand" in all of her subjects and implied that she was an academic imposter. As she discussed being an "airhead," there were glimmers of awareness that this image allowed her to mask her feelings about many things in her life, and, because the airhead role included not being serious about anything, it also served to hide her insecurities about not being as bright and competent as others expected her to be.

Neighborhood youths who were interviewed identified Marissa as "having it all," yet she was bitter about her peer interactions. Sensing her peers' envy and readiness to unseat her, Marissa felt her clique membership was fragile. When asked about friendships, she first reeled off a few names and then recanted to say that these girls were not true friends because they were "two-faced" and she could not depend on them. As the interview progressed, Marissa emotionally poured out information about her problems in a way that suggested she had nobody to whom she could confide her feelings on a regular basis.[8]

After seeing Marissa in the beauty parlor this year, I learned that she had moved back home after resigning from her job because she felt she had been passed over for a promotion. She also had serious marital problems that remained unresolved.[9] Her mother categorized Marissa as "sort of having an emotional breakdown." When I asked Marissa's mother, Catherine, what Chris was up to, she retorted, "Good question!" She then anxiously confided that in the many years since having completed his undergraduate work he had started and dropped out of two distinguished master's degree programs. Although he had an "okay job," he was unsettled about a career and "had no steady relationship."

Apparently, Travis' fate after his immediate postschool years continued to be pulled by the difficult currents of poverty. Several years ago, I read in the local newspaper that Travis hanged himself from a tree in the park by his housing complex—probably close to the site where I had interviewed him seven years earlier. Travis was twenty-four. His obituary listed three off-spring with different last names, presumably their mothers' surnames.

Occasionally I have reason to go to the neighborhood where I first interviewed Travis. I see the effects of poverty on space and people—the nature of his diminished environment is blatant. It not only offends my middle-class sensibilities, but people in the neighborhood also understand its impact. As Larry, one of Travis' neighbors, elaborated:

> This part of town is run down—trash everywhere, nobody's got money to fix things up. There's no grass, no flowers, only a few scraggly trees. In the area of town that we live in, the children are more or less pushed off. . . . The school system says you're underprivileged and your parents are failures, so you'll be failures. I'm not going to say all the faculty does. There are some teachers that go out of their way to help the kids get the tools so they don't fall into the same sorts of traps their parents did. But the majority of teachers over there feel that your parents are no good, so you're going to be no good, so why should I care. . . . If you come from a certain part of town, certain things are expected of you.

Or perhaps, as Travis seems to have believed, little is expected of you and little is available to you. When I asked Travis in our interview what he wanted to do over the next few years, he simply answered, "I don't know—don't know. What is there to do?"

Although there is no redemption for Travis, perhaps Marissa will recover from her struggles and find happiness with future pursuits. Marissa's break-down, or fall from middle-class grace, may not be typical. Marissa's parents perceive it as something she will recover from and believe she will go on to reattach herself to her former ambitions. However, because they were oblivious to the generalized nature of her pain when she was an exemplary high school student, it is unlikely that they understand the depths of her alienation as a young adult or how difficult it will be for her to achieve the intimacy and self-coherence that she needs. One of the things I learned from my interviews with affluent adolescents is that, although they were often annoy-ingly arrogant in taking their advantages at school and their high status for granted, they were not always content with their lives. Indeed, many were anxious, tense, and unhappy regardless of their relatively high achievement and apparent social success. This is not to say that because affluent students suffer in school that they suffer to the same extent or in the same way as low-income youth; nor do I intend to imply that circumstances are the same for both groups.

The stress felt by both affluent and impoverished youth originates, to some extent, from the same source: the stratifying and alienating aspects of their schools and communities. The divisive, differentiating, and humili-ating school practices offered few rewards to low-income adolescents and resulted in their being angry. They described coping with school by deliber-ate nonparticipation, avoidance (skipping school or missing classes), and/or minimal compliance with routines. High-income youths played the winning game, but with mixed enthusiasm and at some personal cost. They worried that they did not always live up to their own and others' expectations of them. Some seemed so driven by the need to win that they could not gauge for themselves whether winning was important.

A decade after my interviews with high- and low-income adolescents, I have come to believe that though there are many losers in the complex and troubled dynamics of social-class relations in school, there may be no true winners. It therefore seems important that educators understand how class identities are reinforced in students' performances on the high school stage and how these relations might reveal the roots of some adolescents' suffering.

CLASS IN AMERICA AND THE ROLE OF EDUCATORS

There is not a conscientious educator in the United States who would not want poor children to succeed in school in the hopes that their achieve-ment might allow them to move out of poverty. The irony, however, is that America is a country deeply divided by class and, apparently, is becom-ing more so all the time. In my town, for example, each newly constructed suburb has larger, fancier houses than the last one, while at the same time more and more subsidized housing units are built for the poor. There is an underpaid working class as well as a chronically underemployed or unem-ployed surplus class.[10] So regardless of individual aspirations or efforts, at least a portion of American adults can be predicted not to move up from their impoverished status. Their children will be the "at-risk" students of the next generation.

In my town, conditions for the working class have worsened over the past few years. Several factories where organized labor had secured good salaries and fringe benefits closed down when their work was moved to developing countries that offer cheap labor and less stringent environmental regulations. Travis' mother, who had worked intermittently as a motel maid because of the seasonal demand for motels that is typical of a university town, had not been called back after her employer (a well-established national motel chain) found it more profitable to hire a team of cleaning and maintenance staff from Eastern Europe. (They were willing to work a 48-hour week for $2.00 an hour and expected no fringe benefits.) And although construction in the suburbs is booming, workers in that trade are imported by the truckload from south of the border.

Travis was acutely aware of the lack of job opportunities and poor working conditions; he and his brothers had been unable to find steady jobs even at minimum wage. His father had never earned enough to get the family out of the projects, and eventually he and a coworker died laboring in the quarries that harvest and carve limestone for the impressive federal buildings in our nation's capital. Travis was profoundly depressed about his own lack of work opportunities, and as far as he was concerned, nobody in school cared about the "trash from the projects." For Travis and his low-income peers, school personnel were members of the other (respectable, preppie, "to-do") class who looked down on them.

The message of an uncaring world bombarded Travis at school, and as he tried to find a place in his community, his bitterness about unfairness dominated his telling of his life story during our interview. Although Travis knew that school achievement and attainment were equated with securing employment, his appraisal that good jobs would require a college degree and that there was no way he could afford college were also correct. As far as Travis was concerned, high-income students monopolized the high-status school positions just as they would dominate life opportunities in their postschool lives. Legitimately skeptical of his own ability to break class barriers, Travis invested his interest and identity in other pursuits, which were depressingly fanciful in terms of being achievable for a young man like Travis—and he knew it. Travis was bright, healthy, attractive, articulate, and personable. He was so rational and astute that he realized that investing in school was not worth his while. He found other ways to boost his self-esteem temporarily and ease the pain connected with his class condition—ways that generally expressed anger at and resistance to school personnel and other "respectable" citizens who he felt were responsible for the conditions of his social class.

Given the dire conditions for the working and unemployed classes, as well as the vulnerable state of the middle class in our current economy, what should educators do? One thing we cannot assume is that we, as an educated class, necessarily have it right. We cannot simply preach that other classes need to get their acts together and be like us, because in some ways even we are not doing so well. As high-stakes accountability measures intensify our work, we have to ask the corporate world if more jobs with better salaries will be available to "at-risk" students who do better in school as a result of our sincere efforts. We must tell what we know about the inequities that affect a substantial number of our students to people outside of schools so that they will vote for leaders whose policies will benefit a broad range of Americans and, ultimately, the students we teach.

In her disparaging description of low-income people, Marissa did not mention structural inequities related to poverty but only personal characteristics that she felt distinguished her from her low-income schoolmates. One reason Marissa did not know about students' unequal chances was that she never crossed paths with low-income people, either in her segregated elementary schools or in tracked secondary schools—or, for that matter, anywhere else in her relatively small town. Another reason that Marissa did not know about social-class conditions and relationships was that subject matter related to the working class (e.g., the history of organized labor, the extent to which the working class is overrepresented in the risky responsibility of defending America during wars) was not part of her formal school curriculum. As Marissa gloated about the worthiness of her own class compared to others, had she been asked to analyze which social class has the most negative impact on the environment? Perhaps she had learned the various parts of government and could display her knowledge of American heroes on exams, but had she been asked to evaluate the conditions necessary to ensure a truly inclusive democracy and an equitable economic system?

In addressing what students need to know, it seems that both high- and low-income students need curriculum and texts that include the stories of ordinary working-class people as well as people who are poor. They need to learn about empathetic and brave activists who have struggled to improve the lives of the oppressed. On their trips to our nation's capital (if they are fortunate enough to be able to take such trips), they must be asked to consider why war monuments dominate the Mall and why there is an absence of memorials to those who have fought to improve democracy and equity within the boundaries of our country.

Educators must be imaginative in finding ways to bridge the great divide between the social classes. A principal recently told me that in order to prepare students for a high-stakes exam, school personnel decided to break the sophomore class into groups of ten to twelve students, which he called "families." Every adult at the school worked with a family for two or three days preparing them for the tests, then for the several days while the tests were administered. Families took breaks and ate lunch and snacks together. Students were assigned to groups by alphabetical order, so a variety of students suddenly crossed social-class and achievement-track boundaries for the first time in their ten years of schooling. The principal confided to me how inspiring it was to see these students take a real interest in each other and treat each other respectfully. He told me that, in a relief celebration following the exams in the teachers' lounge, the main topic of conversation was the disappearance of inter-class friction. In a short period of time, these adolescents were able to recognize their common humanity and see their schoolmates as peers engaged in the common task of passing these exams so that they would not have to repeat them the next semester. Indeed, the school's aggregate test scores were several points higher than expected. As might have been predicted, however, the principal also reported that after the tests everyone returned to their previously class-segregated spaces in the school.

Regardless of the longevity of their effects, efforts like these can help to reduce the effects of social class in schools; they can also be small steps toward eliminating the deep and pernicious class divisions that persist in our society. Certainly, educators need to become powerful advocates for all of our nation's children and be vocal about the ways social-class divisions make it difficult for them to educate all children to high standards. American education is often seen as a "great equalizer," but this mission is difficult if not impossible to accomplish as long as children continue to attend school and live their daily lives under such unequal circumstances.

NOTES

1. This name is a pseudonym, as are all names of people and places in this chapter. Certain other characteristics of schools and people also have been modified to ensure anonymity.
2. Don Merten provides an astute analysis of why middle-class youngsters act this way toward each other and their lower-income counterparts in school in "The Cultural Context of Aggression: The Transition to Junior High School," *Anthropology & Education Quarterly* 25, no. 1 (1994): 29–43.
3. Her husband had died at work in a quarry accident about a year before the interview.
4. I use the term *low-income* rather than *working-class* because 78 percent of the adolescents were from single-parent homes in which only 40 percent of parents were employed. Most of these parents had part-time jobs.
5. Ellen Brantlinger, *The Politics of Social Class in Secondary Schools: Views of Affluent and Impoverished Youth* (New York: Teachers College Press, 1993).
6. Philip Wexler, *Becoming Somebody: Toward a Social Psychology of School* (London: Falmer, 1992), 8.
7. Dorothy Holland, William Lachicotte, Jr., Debra Skinner, and Carole Cain, *Identity and Agency in Cultural Worlds* (Cambridge, MA: Harvard University Press, 1998).
8. Because of the extreme unhappiness (depression) shown in the interview, I asked Marissa if I could help her find support. She was vehement that she could "handle it" and that she had just "lost it" temporarily. Confidentiality requirements prevented my intervening without her permission.
9. Marissa's parents were acquaintances of mine, but I had not seen Marissa in years. Although I suspect Marissa recognized me in the beauty parlor, she seemed to purposely turn away as she walked past me. She still may have been embarrassed by her outpouring of troubles at fifteen.
10. Barbara Ehrenreich, *Nickel and Dimed: On (Not) Getting By in America* (New York: Henry Holt, 2001).

Interview

Class and Identity in a Socioeconomically Diverse High School

A DISCUSSION WITH ELAINE BESSETTE, JOAN LOWE, AND BILL QUINN

Greenwich High School is a well-manicured, spacious, handsome collection of buildings set back from a wooded road in Greenwich, Connecticut. Known throughout the New York area as a wealthy suburb where multi-million-dollar mansions are graced with tennis courts, swimming pools, and stables, Greenwich in many respects lives up to its well-heeled reputation. But Greenwich is also a town of socioeconomic diversity where other housing consists of smaller homes, condominiums, apartment buildings, and even public projects. Close to 90 percent of the eligible youth in Greenwich attend the public high school, making it a place where the daughters and sons of lawyers, financiers, and the independently wealthy attend school alongside those of service workers, struggling recent immigrants, and families on public assistance.

Prior to publication of the first edition of Adolescents at School, *editor Michael Sadowski visited Greenwich High School to talk with school staff about the ways social-class differences affect their students' perceptions of themselves and their peers. Following are excerpts from one discussion that included Elaine Bessette, then the school's headmistress, and Joan Lowe and Bill Quinn, both social workers at Greenwich High.*

In what ways do you believe students' awareness of their socioeconomic status, especially in comparison to their peers, affects them at this school?

Quinn: For many kids coming into this building, especially those who come from modest or middle-class backgrounds, getting a sense of the wealth of the community and the wealth of many of the kids can be overwhelming. You can see these things just by noticing the way some of the kids dress. I think it makes it difficult for some students. It can easily make them feel that they don't belong or fit in here.

Bessette: I also think the reverse is true. Some of the wealthier students who perhaps attended more homogeneous neighborhood elementary schools hit the middle school and then the high school, and they suddenly become aware of kids who don't have what they have. I sometimes wonder what that does to their sense of self, to their concept of who they are. A student might ask one of his peers, "Where is your mom sending you during April vacation?" And the kid he's talking to has a job and is going to be working in town over vacation, whereas the other kid is going off to Cancun. Those kinds of experiences might make the wealthier student realize, "Wait a second. Maybe there is another kind of life besides what I have had all along, what the people around me have always seemed to have, and what I see on TV. There are actually people who have free or reduced-price lunch. There are actually teenagers who don't have their own cars."

Lowe: I hate to say this, but I think there are also some kids who are oblivious. They are so self-absorbed that they don't really see beyond their own wealth. They think, "This is the way I am, so this is the way it is." Then there are other kids who reject their wealth. They are embarrassed by how wealthy they are, so they downplay it—the clothes they wear, and especially the cars they drive. They could drive an expensive car and they opt not to. So it really depends on who the kid is, what their values are, and how they want to relate to other kids.

To what extent do you think the awareness of socioeconomic issues plays a part in how students group together as friends, who hangs around with whom?

Bessette: Our soccer team this year was an interesting example of that. We had kids from all over the world, from every walk of life, and from every socioeconomic group who bonded together. The parents have told me several times, "What an interesting dynamic that was." But I don't know how long-lasting their bonding experience was as they moved away from soccer to other things.

Lowe: The most interesting thing about the soccer team to me was that the carryover socially was not as profound as one might think. They were buddies on the field. There was some carryover in the student center. But as far as sustaining the friendships in their social lives, that didn't really happen.

Bessette: Right. When the kids go out into the student center, they start to gravitate toward the kids they are comfortable with or those they see as the most similar to them. Some of that may arise from social-class differences. For example, a member of a team or club might say, "Let's all go over to Jane's house." Jane lives in a very nice section of town, and everyone drives over there. Then when it comes time for Anita to have everybody to her house, maybe she lives in a very modest home and she can't throw the party that Jane can. So there is definitely an aspect of class that comes into it.

Do you also see situations in which students would like to be part of a certain social circle but they don't have the money to belong? Are there kids, for example, who are jealous and wish they could go sailing on weekends like some of their peers? To what extent have you seen or heard about situations like that?

Lowe: It is not so much about money as it is about kids wanting to be in the popular group. They don't necessarily say, "I want to be like the kids who have money." But they want to do the things that the popular kids—who are also often the wealthier kids—do. Take the prom, for example. We have students who really cannot afford to do the prom the way some of the other kids do, but they do it. They pay a lot of money for their gown. They rent a big limousine. And you just know that they don't have the money to do it. I work with kids who live in the projects and are on free lunch. Yet they spend a bundle of money on the prom because that's what everyone else is doing. But I don't have many kids saying, "I wish I were one of the wealthy kids so that I could go sailing." They look at who is in the popular group and what they're doing more than they look at economics.

In what ways do you think issues of class identity affect students academically?

Quinn: Many students come into our school and compare themselves to others who may have more means or seem to have a better life. They might be extremely successful academically, but their sense of themselves is still affected by the socioeconomic disparity they see. They say to themselves, "I may fit in here academically, but there is still a disparity between what they [the wealthier students] can do, the opportunities they have, and what I can do." For some of these students, school can be a negative experience they remember for a long time. Unfortunately, I've talked to several former students for whom this has been the case.

Bessette: I also think there is an achievement difference between kids who have had very rich cultural experiences and those who haven't. Some students here have been brought up to read books from an early age, as well as to go to libraries and to plays, and others have really had television as their only entertainment. Some of the reasons for these differences are cultural, but I think it also has something to do with class.

Another thing that almost all the students here get caught up in, which is largely driven by the parents who are well-heeled, is the game of reputation and status that is associated with the "name-brand" colleges. I think many kids feel that they *have* to get into Yale, or they *have* to get into Harvard, and that seeps pretty deep down into the culture of the school. Even the kids who are somewhere in the middle socioeconomically get caught up in that.

It is both a positive and a negative thing about attending a high-performing school—there is an expectation for you. This year's class did very well in terms of getting into most of the colleges where they applied. But in last year's class there was some consternation. I heard laments like, "Dad went to Yale, Mom graduated from Harvard, and Johnny didn't get into either one of those two."

How else do you see perceptions about class affecting students' expectations for their own futures?

Quinn: I think class plays a tremendous role for many of the students here in that regard. For some of our Hispanic students, for example, those who are not from wealthy families already have a sense that they are not going to make it, that they cannot be more than a custodian. Even though we may tell them about the opportunities available to them—such as the scholarships available to Hispanic students who do well in school—it is very difficult for them to overcome their expectations and to feel that they can rise above them. That is why some students are not successful in this building. They really feel that they cannot make it. This is not just reflective of the family of origin from which they come, but from looking at society as a whole. These kids are not stupid; they are just aware of what is going on socioeconomically. They know that most of the Spanish-speaking people here live in certain parts of town and hold certain jobs. It's very difficult for them to overcome that.

Lowe: Expectations can also affect the wealthier kids in a different way. I've known a number of great, high-achieving kids here who had altruistic goals to go out and do good things in America. Some were going to be teachers, like we are. They really wanted to make some contribution to society. Then we would hear about these students years later, and we'd find out that a lot of them had, in a sense, "sold out." One student I can think of, who was planning to be a teacher, is an investment banker now. He belongs to a country club, he wears the right shoes, he drives the right car. He is not the altruistic kid that we knew when he was eighteen years old and he was going to go out and join the Peace Corps. He got into money. I could tell you more stories like that.

So even though kids want to shrug it off from their parents and they want to be altruistic, somewhere that piece of identity is deeply ingrained. They are what they were groomed to be as little children, going to the right nursery schools and then all the way up through the right colleges. It's not that there's something wrong with students living their lives this way, but it bothers me sometimes when I think about what they could have done.

How can educators support students' positive identity development, especially those students who might not be part of the dominant social groups at school?

Bessette: I think the teachers who really acknowledge a student, not just whether he got the right answer or not, but acknowledge him for who he is, make a big difference. Such teachers don't just bring students to my office and say, "Mary has the top average in my class." They might also say something like, "Mary has a new job after school." Or, "Sandra is on the dance team. Have you ever seen her dance?" Or, "Who is your favorite writer, Jeremy?" Then Jeremy will answer, "Vonnegut," and the next thing you know we are having a discussion about Vonnegut. We want every student to feel that someone knows him or her well on a personal level. I think that helps develop a sense of self.

Quinn: To me, identity is based on many things, but two things are most important. One aspect of a student's identity is, "How do I experience myself given all my capacities? Am I defined by what I can do academically? What I can do athletically?" That part of them that is the center of their own experience is a major part of identity. But another major contributing factor in identity is, "Who do the people outside of me say I am? Who does my family say I am? Who does the school say I am? And what does the larger culture say I am?" For students who are minority students—whether it be economic minority students, racial or cultural minority students, sexual minority students—outside society may be giving them messages that are not supportive of their true selves. And the question we need to ask as educators is how we can begin to counteract those messages.

CHAPTER NINE

The Impact of Disability on Adolescent Identity

MICHAEL L. WEHMEYER

Any discussion of adolescent identity and disability must begin with an acknowledgment that, fundamentally, there is no such thing as a unitary "disability identity." Indeed, it is difficult to generalize almost anything as applying to the group referred to as "people with disabilities," due in part to the sheer number of people in this category. According to a U.S. Census Bureau report, there are more than 51 million Americans with disabilities, roughly 4 million of whom are between the ages of fifteen and twenty-four, a large and diverse group of young people.[1] Some are born with a disability, and their identity emerges with that "characteristic" as part of how they think about themselves and how others think about them. Others experience injuries or are identified later in childhood or adolescence and must therefore accommodate this new aspect of themselves into their still forming identities. Some disabilities are "hidden" and known only by the young people who have them and those close to them, while others are openly discernible. Some disabilities affect cognitive development and performance, while others do not.

The Individuals with Disabilities Education Act (IDEA) defines a student with a disability as "a child with mental retardation, hearing impairments (including deafness), speech or language impairments, visual impairments (including blindness), serious emotional disturbance . . . orthopedic impairments, autism, traumatic brain injury, other health impairments, or specific learning disabilities."[2] The most recent report to Congress on the implementation of the IDEA indicates that about 2.9 million students ages twelve to seventeen receive special education services funded under the act.[3] The majority of students receiving special education services are those with cognitive disabilities, such as learning disabilities and mental retardation.

In light of the variety of disabilities that exist and the diversity of young people who have them, it is a daunting task to try to describe an identity associated with adolescent disability. Still, some experiences are nearly universal to people with disabilities and provide a way of describing the impact that disability can have on identity during adolescence. It is important for educators to understand these issues so that students with disabilities have instructional experiences that promote a healthy, positive sense of self.[4]

IDENTITY AND DISABILITY

If we define identity in the simplest and most straightforward manner, an identity is, in the words of psychologist David Moshman, "an explicit theory of oneself as a person."[5] This "theory of oneself" is derived from multiple sources, including important input from peers. Thus, one's understanding of self is derived not only from personal attributions of identity, but also from understanding others' perceptions. This metarepresentational process (thinking about how others are thinking about you) is particularly salient when one of the primary "descriptors" of oneself is "person with a disability." How disability is understood and viewed by peers and others in society is a key component of the construction of identity for young people with disabilities, and the fact that disability is associated with stigma also greatly impacts the construction of self for these youth.

It can be helpful to view the relationship between identity formation and disability through a historical lens. Since the early 1900s, disability has been associated with a variety of negative stereotypes. In the early part of the century, people with cognitive disabilities were perceived as menaces responsible for many of society's ills, including crime, pauperism, and prostitution, and people with physical disabilities were seen as subhuman ("vegetables") or as economic burdens to society. By mid-century, the stereotypes associated with disability became more charitable, but they were still stigmatizing. The return of large numbers of soldiers who had been injured and disabled during World War II led to a flurry of rehabilitation and training initiatives. Medical advances that conquered diseases linked with disability, including polio, began to move public opinion about disability away from stereotypes of menace and burden. These were replaced by perceptions of people with disabilities as objects of charity and pity. The ubiquitous poster-child images and the constant pleas to "help the retarded" or "aid the victims" of numerous diseases portrayed people with disabilities as not quite menaces or subhuman, but still not equal citizens. Many of these perceptions persist today.

It is self-evident that these kinds of stereotypical perceptions can have an impact on an adolescent's developing sense of self. For example, if one is thought by others to be a burden or in some way responsible for the problems experienced by others, one's self-worth and self-confidence, not to mention one's image of oneself as a valued person, will be adversely affected. If you are a teacher, consider the number of times you have heard adolescents teasing, harassing, or even bullying their peers using terms like *idiot*, *retard*, *moron*, or *spaz*. Clearly, these perceptions still simmer close to the surface.

The perceptions of disability associated with pity and charity are manifest in a number of ways. People with visual impairments are spoken to in loud voices with clearly (and slowly) articulated measure; adults with cerebral palsy are patted on the head by well-meaning strangers; adolescents with Down syndrome are assigned to classrooms with children with disabilities from the elementary and secondary grades.

Exacerbating the impact of all of these stereotypes and misperceptions are the expectations that arise from them. People with disabilities are sometimes seen as "holy innocents" and are therefore not expected to be sexual beings, marry, or have children. "Victims" and "charity cases" are seen as worthy of being helped but unable (or maybe just unwilling) to help themselves by working. "Eternal children" will, it is assumed, never live independently. Even for students with so-called hidden disabilities, such as epilepsy or learning disabilities, these stigmatizing perceptions lower expectations and limit their options and possibilities.

New images of disability are beginning to replace these older, stigmatizing perceptions, albeit slowly. These newer conceptions frame disability as a natural part of the human experience, not separate or distinct from it, and focus on the interaction between a person's capacities and his or her social context or environment. Rather than placing an emphasis on "fixing" or "curing" the person, new perspectives on disability involve efforts to modify the environment to provide more effective supports, which will in turn enable the person with a disability to succeed despite limitations. By viewing the relationship between students with disabilities and their context in this way, teachers, administrators, and others who work in schools can envision ways to change aspects of learning environments in order to support the positive identity development and academic success of adolescents with disabilities.

FACTORS THAT AFFECT IDENTITY FORMATION FOR YOUTH WITH DISABILITIES

A beginning point for making positive changes in schools is understanding the factors related to disability that uniquely contribute to identity formation, some of which are "internal" to the adolescent and others of which arise from the experience of living with a disability. Unfortunately, most of the factors that have been studied by researchers have shown a negative impact on identity development, including cognitive impairments, social isolation, segregation, ineffective social skills, and other problems that often affect students with disabilities.

Self-definition, self-concept, and self-image

How students think about or define themselves is critical to the development of a positive self-identity. Students who have a disability often hold self-concepts and self-perceptions that are negative because of the way disability is perceived in our society. However, the experience of disability is not *always* associated with negative self-perception. In reviewing the research on self-concept and students with learning disabilities, developmental psychologist Susan Harter concluded that there are both similarities and differences between the self-evaluation patterns of normally achieving students and special education students.[6] Other research has found that the self-concept of students with mental retardation is strongly determined by the quality of their interpersonal relationships and their personal sense of well-being.[7] A student with mental retardation who has an adequate social network and a positive sense of well-being, then, may hold a very positive self-image and have positive self-esteem, independent of the fact that she or he has mental retardation. Based on these findings, it seems clear that school environments can strongly affect these students' self-esteem and self-image.

Self-efficacy and perceptions of control

Another factor contributing to students' "theories of self" is the degree to which they perceive themselves as able to act successfully *in* and *upon* their environment. This perceived *self-efficacy* is defined by psychologist Albert Bandura as "beliefs in one's capabilities to organize and execute the courses of action required to produce given attainments."[8] Psychologist Julian Rotter defined a related concept, *locus of control*, as the degree to which a person is able to perceive the contingent or causal relationships between his or her actions and outcomes that might result from them.[9]

Research examining the self-efficacy, locus of control, and outcome expectations of students with disabilities has shown that many students with cognitive disabilities hold perceptions that are not conducive to promoting autonomy and enhanced self-determination. That is, they perceive themselves as either not capable of acting on their environment, not in charge of outcomes caused by their actions, or not believing that anticipated outcomes will occur. As a result, students with disabilities may be more capable of acting successfully on their environment than it appears to teachers or others (and perhaps even themselves). Students may have more skills and knowledge than they demonstrate, yet they may not display these skills because they do not believe that it will make any difference. A student with a disability who on a number of occasions has approached a group of popular students and tried to initiate a conversation but has been rebuffed will eventually quit trying to initiate conversations because he or she believes it doesn't make a difference. This has little to do with the student's social skills, and much to do with his or her belief about efficacy and control. Other students come to believe that they cannot succeed when they try to do something, so they stop trying new or challenging things because they don't believe they can achieve them, even if that belief is not based on experience. These students will, in turn, form self-identities that are based on these negative beliefs and perceptions.

There is sufficient evidence, however, that these perceptions can be changed through intervention. For example, teachers can ensure that students with disabilities experience success in classroom tasks by using "errorless" learning strategies, "scaffolding" on students' prior knowledge, and verbalizing the links between students' contributions and the successful achievement of learning outcomes. Such learning experiences, repeated over time, will support more positive efficacy and locus of control perceptions.

Self-determination

Beliefs about control over one's life form an important component in the development of self-determination. Fundamentally, self-determination refers to the degree to which someone acts as a causal agent in his or her life; that is, they act to make things happen in their lives instead of having someone else act for them.[10] Enhanced self-determination is, theoretically, an important contributor to the process of individuation (the movement from being largely dependent on others to being largely dependent on oneself) and adolescents' movement toward autonomy. In fact, setting goals, making decisions, solving problems, and advocating for oneself are all elements of self-determined behavior and essentially describe the role of the adult in our society.

Students with disabilities are not often provided with experiences that enable them to learn to make decisions, solve problems, or set goals. Particularly with regard to students with cognitive disabilities, many parents, educators, and other adults assume that students with disabilities cannot perform these kinds of tasks. However, there are numerous examples of students with cognitive and other disabilities acquiring skills related to self-determination.[11] Moreover, research has shown that students with learning disabilities or mental retardation who are more self-determined upon graduation from high school are more likely to achieve positive adult outcomes such as competitive employment, higher wages, and greater independence.[12] As such, it is important that teachers consider ways to focus instruction on promoting self-determination both to improve outcomes and to promote more positive identity development. Some suggestions follow:

Teach students the skills and knowledge they will need to become self-determined. The educational programs of all students, not excluding students with disabilities, should promote the skills students need to:

- set personal goals
- solve problems that act as barriers to achieving these goals
- make appropriate choices based on personal preferences and interests
- participate in decisions that influence the quality of their lives
- advocate for themselves
- create action plans to achieve goals
- self-regulate and self-manage day-to-day actions

Promote active student involvement in educational planning and decision-making. Planning for special education services is an important aspect of educational programming for students with disabilities, and students can and should be active participants in such planning sessions. Students can learn goal-setting skills that enable them to develop personal objectives for learning in advance of the meeting and then have those objectives considered in the planning of their educational programs. Similarly, students can be taught basic skills for participating in meetings (such as compromise and negotiation, listening skills, and assertiveness) and be encouraged to use those skills to contribute meaningfully to the discussion. Finally, students can be taught simple skills that enable them to assume a leadership role at the meeting, such as introducing meeting participants, reviewing previous goals and progress, or identifying areas of future instructional need.

Teach students to direct their own learning. Many instructional models emphasize teacher-directed learning strategies, in which the teacher is primarily responsible for providing content information, directing student response, and guiding learning. It is important, however, also to teach students self-management strategies that enable them to direct their own learning. This can be done by teaching students skills such as self-instruction, self-monitoring, self-evaluation, and self-reinforcement that put the student in charge of instructional activities typically performed by teachers. Creative teachers can easily develop self-monitoring tools that enable students with a wide array of abilities to track progress on educational goals. These might include developing a checklist to fill out at the end of the day or class period, using graphing or charting features of word processing software, or dropping a marble in a jar upon completion of a task (and teaching the student that when the marbles reach a certain level, a larger goal has been met).

Communicate high expectations and emphasize student strengths and uniqueness. One simple yet powerful thing educators can do to promote student self-determination is to have high expectations for students and to communicate those expectations often. Students with disabilities are often all too aware of what they cannot do, and are not as aware of their unique strengths and abilities.

Create a learning community that promotes active problem-solving and choice opportunities. Students who learn to solve problems do so in classrooms that value diversity of opinion and expression and that create "safe" places for students. All students, but particularly students with disabilities, can benefit from the opportunity to provide answers to problems that might be incorrect, knowing that they will be provided the support they need to learn from their mistakes. Such learning communities often emphasize collaboration and student involvement in classroom rule-setting.

Create partnerships with parents and students to ensure meaningful involvement. While much can be done through the school to promote self-determination, unless there are parallel activities occurring in the student's home, efforts at school will not be sufficient. Parents are a student's first and longest-lasting teachers, and it is important that, from elementary through secondary education, teachers work to ensure the meaningful involvement in educational planning and decisionmaking of both parents or family members and the students themselves.

THE INTERSECTION OF DISABILITY WITH OTHER FACTORS

The experience of disability does not exist in a vacuum, and in many ways the issues pertaining to disability that teachers need to consider occur at the intersection of disability and other identity-related characteristics. Gender and race/ethnicity are particularly important, in that girls and young women with disabilities and students of color with disabilities often encounter stereotypes and biases that have a more negative impact on them than on other students with disabilities.

Gender, disability, and identity. Considering issues of gender alongside disability and identity makes an already complex situation more so. It is clear that stereotypes and biases related to gender combine with stereotypes and biases related to disability to create a "double jeopardy" for girls and women with disabilities.[13]

Though employment is primarily an aspect of life that affects adults, the special issues that face women with disabilities in the job market have strong implications for the education of adolescent girls with disabilities. The authors of a Harris Poll on the employment of people with disabilities conducted in the mid-1980s concluded that perhaps the best definition of disability in the country was "unemployed." Indicators vary across time, but today it is not unusual to have unemployment rates reach 80 percent among people with disabilities. As negative as these conditions are, however, the situation is even worse for women with disabilities. In a comprehensive overview of vocational and employment outcomes for women with disabilities, educational researchers Bonnie Doren and Michael Benz found that:

- Women with disabilities are less likely to be employed than women without disabilities and men with and without disabilities.
- Women with disabilities earn substantially less than men with disabilities, and the wage gap between women and men with disabilities increases as the time since exiting high school increases.
- Women with disabilities are more likely than men with disabilities to be employed in low-status occupations, and they are less likely to be engaged in full-time or uninterrupted employment.

Although research documenting the relationship between educational experiences and these adult outcomes for women with disabilities is scarce,[14] it seems evident that the root of these problems lies in a combination of two factors: (1) the social and educational experiences available to girls with disabilities in school, and (2) societal expectations for girls with disabilities in general. Educators need to be alert to the ways that girls with disabilities are treated differently, and how the curriculum content to which they have access reflects gender stereotyping and/or differs from that offered to males. In addition, educators need to provide girls with opportunities to see themselves as capable of achieving in a wide range of careers.

Race, ethnicity, and disability. As with gender, it is likely that issues of race and ethnicity affect identity formation for students with disabilities in a variety of ways. In fact, these issues underscore the need to consider the whole child and not try to parcel her or him into discrete segments.

Although there is little data available on the combined impact of race and disability on adolescent identity formation, it is a well-established fact that students from minority groups are overrepresented in the population of students receiving special education support (and male minority students are even more heavily overrepresented). In *Racial Inequity in Special Education*, Daniel J. Losen and Gary Orfield note that, while African American students account for 16 percent of the total U.S. student population, they represent 32 percent of students in programs for students with mild mental retardation, 29 percent of those in programs for moderate mental retardation, and 24 percent of students enrolled in programs for serious emotional disturbance.[15] Similarly, Hispanic students are overrepresented in special education services. Again, there are multiple reasons for such overrepresentation, including cultural and linguistic bias in testing procedures, stereotypes related to gender and race that affect referral to special education (or, often, simply out of the regular education classroom), and issues pertaining to the economic availability of educationally enriching experiences.

Presumably, this overrepresentation influences identity formation in multiple ways. As with gender and disability issues, expectations for the academic performance of students of color with disabilities are affected by stereotypes and biases about disability, stereotypes and biases related to race (and sometimes language), and interactions and combinations thereof. One area of particular concern for both students of color and students with disabilities—and so particularly, perhaps, for students of color with disabilities—is the school dropout rate. Recent federal statistics place the national high school graduation rate at about 85 percent. The rate for African American students, however, is 81 percent, and for Hispanic students it is just 59 percent.[16] The dropout rate for students with disabilities ranges from 25 to 30 percent, but varies by disability category. Slightly more than one-third of students with learning disabilities drop out, while almost half of students with emotional and behavioral disabilities drop out before graduating. Similarly, nearly half of all minority students receiving special education services in urban settings drop out of school. This illustrates one of the drawbacks of being labeled as having a disability. Presumably, students who receive special education services get the individualized instructional assistance they need, but only about one-fourth of students with disabilities graduate from high school with a regular diploma.

FOSTERING SCHOOL SUCCESS

Issues affecting "disability identity" are closely tied to the contexts in which adolescents live, learn, and play. Much of the discussion about this issue (including this chapter) focuses on factors that have a negative impact on the identity formation and development of youth with disabilities. It is important, however, that educators not dwell exclusively on these negative factors but focus as well on the "whole" student. Having a disability is, after all, only one aspect of the life experience of a student with a disability. Too often, educators behave as if this one factor were the only factor to consider. Students with disabilities are more *like* all other adolescents than they are *different from them*, if one can see past the disability. Students with disabilities have the best opportunity to develop a positive, healthy identity when they are included in the educational and social contexts that other adolescents experience and are provided the supports they need to succeed in these environments.

Unfortunately, a large percentage of students with disabilities receive their educational services in settings outside the regular education classroom. According to Department of Education data, fewer than half of students with learning disabilities, fewer than 30 percent of students with emotional or behavioral disorders, and fewer than 15 percent of students with mental retardation receive their education primarily in the regular classroom.

When adequate supports are available in the general education classroom (which remains an ongoing problem in many schools), it is evident that inclusive practices promote enhanced social inclusion and more positive self-concepts and self-esteem than segregated settings.[17] In a study I conducted with Kathy Kelchner, we found that that the self-perceptions of students with cognitive disabilities, as well as their perceptions of the classroom environment, differed from their nondisabled peers based on the setting in which they received their education. Students in separate classrooms perceived their classroom environment to be more controlling, thus offering fewer opportunities for exerting control themselves.

In addition to including rather than segregating students with disabilities, there are a variety of other strategies teachers can employ to promote their positive identity development. Cynthia Warger and Jane Burnette have identified several of these strategies as follows:[18]

Respect diverse backgrounds. Students come into learning environments with a variety of experiences. The educational process needs to take into account cultural, linguistic, racial, ethnic, and other differences in addition to disability-related variables.

Make the curriculum relevant and conducive to the success of all students. Students with disabilities can succeed in the classroom. This is not a theory but a fact. Educators who value diversity and who want to enable students with disabilities to develop a positive self-identity can do so by ensuring that all students are engaged in a curriculum that meets their needs and that promotes academic and social success.

Build on students' strengths. Perhaps the most important thing educators can do is to focus on what a student does well. Students with disabilities are very aware of their differences and their failures. Special education has, historically, been a deficit-focused process. Yet all students have strengths, and by focusing on those strengths, teachers can enable students to learn what they do well and to capitalize on that knowledge.

Provide district support to build the capacity of personnel. One frequently mentioned limitation to supporting students with disabilities is the lack of training that many educators have had to work with this population. With adequate support and ongoing training, however, all educators can provide the needed support and appropriate instruction to students with disabilities.

Adolescents with disabilities are, first and foremost, adolescents. There has been too little focus on enabling this group to develop a healthy, positive identity—one that enables them to use the skills and knowledge they have and to learn new skills and knowledge so that they can become contributing members of their communities and experience a more positive quality of life. Educators play a critical role in this process, since they can provide the instructional experiences and supports that make the difference.

NOTES

1. U.S. Census Bureau, *Survey of Income and Program Participation* (Washington, DC: U.S. Department of Commerce, Census Bureau, 2002).
2. Individuals with Disabilities Education Act (IDEA) Amendments of 1997, PL 105–17, 20 U.S.C. §§ 1400, Sec. 602 (3)(i).
3. U.S. Department of Education, *Twenty-Seventh Annual Report to Congress on the Implementation of the Individuals with Disabilities Education Act, 2005* (Washington, DC: 2007).
4. This chapter is written from the perspective of an educator in the field of developmental disabilities. Had a person with a disability written the chapter, the focus might have been different, although it is likely that the same themes would appear. The discipline of disability studies provides excellent resources for perspectives from scholars with disabilities, and readers should review Simi Linton, *Claiming Disability: Knowledge and Identity* (New York University Press, 1998) for an excellent overview of these issues.
5. David Moshman, *Adolescent Psychological Development: Rationality, Morality, and Identity* (Mahwah, NJ: Lawrence Erlbaum Associates, 1999), 78.
6. Susan Harter, Nancy R. Whitesell, and Loretta J. Junkin, "Similarities and Differences in Domain-Specific and Global Self-Evaluations of Learning-Disabled, Behaviorally Disordered, and Normally Achieving Adolescents," *American Educational Research Journal* 35, no. 4 (1998): 653–680.
7. Andrea G. Zetlin and J. L. Turner, "Salient Domains in the Self-Conception of Adults with Mental Retardation," *Mental Retardation* 26, no. 4 (1988): 219–222.
8. Albert B. Bandura, *Self-Efficacy: The Exercise of Control* (New York: W. H. Freeman, 1997), 3.
9. Julian B. Rotter, "Generalized Expectancies for Internal versus External Control of Reinforcement," *Psychological Monographs* 80, no. 1 (1966): 1–28.
10. Michael L. Wehmeyer, "Self-Determination and Mental Retardation: Assembling the Puzzle Pieces," in Harvey N. Switzky (ed.), *Personality and Motivational Differences in Persons with Mental Retardation* (Mahwah, NJ: Lawrence Erlbaum Associates, 2001), 147–198.
11. Sharon Field, James E. Martin, Robert J. Miller, Michael J. Ward, and Michael L. Wehmeyer, *A Practical Guide for Teaching Self-Determination* (Reston, VA: Council for Exceptional Children, 1998); Michael L. Wehmeyer, Martin Agran, and Carolyn Hughes, *Teaching Self-Determination to Youth with Disabilities: Basic Skills for Successful Transition* (Baltimore: Brookes, 1998).
12. Michael L. Wehmeyer and Michelle Schwartz, "Self-Determination and Positive Adult Outcomes: A Follow-Up Study of Youth with Mental Retardation or Learning Disabilities," *Exceptional Children* 63, no. 2 (1997): 245–255.

13. Harilyn Rousso and Michael L. Wehmeyer, *Double Jeopardy: Addressing Gender Equity in Special Education* (Albany: State University of New York Press, 2001).

14. Wehmeyer and Schwartz, "Self-Determination."

15. Daniel J. Losen and Gary Orfield, *Racial Inequity in Special Education* (Cambridge, MA: Harvard Education Press, 2002).

16. U.S. Census Bureau, *Statistical Abstract of the United States: 2006* (Washington, DC: author).

17. Gail McGregor and R. Timm Vogelsberg, *Inclusive Schooling Practices: Synthesis of the Literature That Informs Best Practices about Inclusive Schooling* (Baltimore: Brookes, 1998).

18. Cynthia Warger and Jane Burnette, "Five Strategies to Reduce Overrepresentation of Culturally and Linguistically Diverse Students in Special Education," ERIC Clearinghouse on Disabilities and Gifted Education Digest #E596 (Arlington, VA: Council for Exceptional Children, 2000). While Warner and Burnette focus specifically on the needs of culturally and linguistically diverse students, their ideas certainly warrant consideration for the education of all students with disabilities.

Profile

Making Their Own Way:
The Perspectives of Three Young People
with Disabilities

MICHAEL L. WEHMEYER

A discussion of disability and adolescent identity like the one in the previous chapter almost necessarily focuses on the challenges these youth face. Yet the stories of these three young people with different disabilities illustrate how they have learned to develop a positive sense of self, even in the face of considerable obstacles, and become ambitious, effective, self-determining individuals.

CECELIA

Cecelia Ann Pauley is a young woman with Down syndrome who speaks frequently at meetings and conferences. In the following essay, written while the author was in college, Cecelia discusses the importance of making her own decisions as a high school and college student.

In the eighth grade my parents asked me if I wanted to go to Churchill High School with my classmates. I said I did. The county did not want to let me go to Churchill, so we had to fight to get them to change their decision. I'm glad they did. At the end of the tenth grade, my guidance counselor asked me what courses I wanted to take the next year. I picked my classes. I liked that. I also made my own choices about what I would do after school. I was in a lot of different things, and in my junior and senior years in high school I had to choose between several different activities. For example, I was in Girl Scouts. I also was in the tennis clinic at Potomac Community Resources.

In my senior year I made a lot of decisions myself. I wanted to go with the chorus on an overnight bus trip to Orlando, Florida, to sing in a national competition. I had to save my money. I decided not to go to some movies to save enough money to pay for the trip. On this trip I decided I wanted to visit Disney World and Universal Studios with four of my friends.

During my junior year I visited several colleges. All of my friends visited colleges that year too. I visited Trinity College in Burlington, Vermont. I liked it. I decided I wanted to go there. Trinity has a neat program called Enhance for kids like me. I decided to go to Trinity. I made a smart decision.

What subjects am I taking? I had to take two life-skills courses and the freshman seminar. The other two courses I could pick. I am taking a computer course and an English course. I will take music and acting later. The two life-skills courses are "Jobs: Finding Them and Keeping Them" and "Adult Problem-Solving." My favorite class is my computer class. I can log on to the computer and send e-mail to my family and all my friends. They all send e-mail to me too. I love Trinity. I have a lot of friends. I like my teachers. Everyone likes me. I am learning a lot. I have a telephone in my room and I call home whenever I want. I usually call home on weekends. I decide when I want to call home.

I keep a calendar and I write in it when I am going to clean my room, do my laundry, study with my friends, watch TV, go to meetings, work, do aerobics, walk, help teachers, go shopping, go to a restaurant, and go to the fitness center. My favorite restaurants are a Chinese restaurant, a Pizza Hut, and a Ben and Jerry's ice cream store. Every day I make my own decisions. I love it.

Trinity has an alternative spring break week. Instead of going to Fort Lauderdale, Florida, on spring break, the students spend the week working with the poor. This year we can go to Washington, D.C., or West Virginia. Last night we had a meeting to decide where we wanted to go. I listened to what we were going to do in both places. I decided I would go to West Virginia. In West Virginia we are going to help people repair their houses. I want to learn how to repair houses and build them.

After I graduate from Trinity I will have to decide whether I want to live in Vermont, return to Maryland, or live somewhere else. I also will have to decide what job I want and whether I want to get married. I don't know what my decisions will be, but because I make decisions now I know I will be able to make good decisions later on. All I want is a chance to make decisions about my future. Give me a chance and I will learn.[1]

JILL

Jill Allen is a young woman with cerebral palsy. She expresses her thoughts about herself and her disability through poetry, including "A Conversation with Cerebral Palsy."

A Conversation with Cerebral Palsy

Well, cerebral palsy—
Do you mind if I call you CP for short?—
You've been with me for fourteen years:
My constant companion.

I accept that you are with me,
Yet I resist you.
I ignore you most of the time, CP.
I hope you don't mind.

Why am I,
Of all people,
Stuck with you?

It's not fair!
Oh, well.
That's the way it's gotta be.

I must thank you, though, CP.
If it wasn't for you,
I wouldn't be me.

Because of you,
I am more determined than ever
To make something of myself:
To succeed.

Jill reflects on her poem with the following insights:

My poem underscores two crucial points with regard to teens with disabilities taking charge of their lives. First, in order for them to be independent, they must not let their disabilities take too much control of their actions. If this happens, the teens may start to view themselves as "disabled teens," not as "teens with disabilities." Second, the teen's disability shouldn't be treated as an obstacle that has to be overcome. Instead, it should be viewed merely as something to be dealt with. If seen as something insurmountable, then the disability is always cast in a negative light. This hurts the outlook of the person with the condition. The disability needs to be viewed realistically.[2]

JOSHUA

Joshua Bailey is a young man with a learning disability. On June 4, 1997, while still a high school student, he introduced President Bill Clinton at the signing ceremony for the 1997 amendments to the Individuals with Disabilities Education Act (IDEA). His remarks included the following:

My fellow students here today are deeply honored to represent America's disabled students at this historic ceremony. We thank you for giving us the opportunity to get a good education and to have a bright future. I know that in years to come, we will make you very proud of us. We want you to know that we can learn, and learn just as well as anybody. All we need is the appropriate help and the chance.

I am someone who insists on having that chance. I have a learning disability called dyslexia. . . . When I entered high school, I had a discussion with one of my advisors, who said that I should take courses that I could handle easily. I looked him right in the eye and said, "No, thanks. I'll take the tough courses and do my best." And I have. Next September, when I return to school, I will take seven classes. They are Advanced Placement American History, accelerated English III, accelerated Algebra II, accelerated Chemistry, Latin III, Drafting III, and psychology/sociology. Like I said—we can learn. My advisor wasn't trying to put me down. Maybe he was being a little overprotective. Sometimes people just don't understand what we need.

As one teacher said about me, "He's the first dyslexia student I've ever taught." I think I was the first one she ever knew about. But I have found that teachers and others are willing to learn. They have good hearts and they want to help—they just need to know how. . . .[3]

NOTES

1. From "The View from the Student's Side of the Table," by Cecelia Ann Pauley, in D. J. Sands and M. L. Wehmeyer (eds.), *Making It Happen: Student Involvement in Education Planning, Decision Making and Instruction* (Baltimore: Brookes), 123–128. Copyright ©1998 by Paul H. Brookes Publishing Co., Inc. Excerpts reprinted with permission.

2. From "A Conversation with Cerebral Palsy," by Jill Allen, in L. E. Powers, G. H. Singer, and J. Sowers (eds.), *On the Road to Autonomy: Promoting Self-Competence in Children and Youth with Disabilities* (Baltimore: Brookes), 93–95. Copyright ©1998 by Jill Allen. Reprinted with permission.

3. Joshua Bailey, remarks, U.S. Department of Education, Office of Special Education (1997).

Commentary

Multiple Intelligences in Adolescence

HOWARD GARDNER

In addition to the other factors addressed throughout this book, an adolescent's "intelligences" can play an important role in her or his emerging sense of identity and, thus, relationship to school. In the following commentary, researcher, professor, and author Howard Gardner explains his frequently cited theory of multiple intelligences (both what it is and is not) and discusses the relevance of these "computational capacities" during the adolescent stage of human development. He also addresses how common testing and educational practices tend to privilege certain intelligences over others and how educators can design instruction in ways that tap into more of their students' strengths.

WHAT ARE MULTIPLE INTELLIGENCES?

I first devised the theory of multiple intelligences (MI theory) in the early 1980s[1] based on findings from a variety of disciplines, ranging from anthropology to neuroscience. MI theory's principal assertion is that human beings are best thought of as having a series of relatively autonomous intelligences (the 8 multiple intelligences), including *linguistic, logical-mathematical, spatial, musical, bodily-kinesthetic, interpersonal, intrapersonal,* and *naturalistic* (see Figure 1). Individuals can be strong in some intelligences, while weak in others. The theory is evidently devised as a counter to the single intelligence (or "g") theory, which asserts that all individuals can be arrayed along a single "bell curve" of intelligence. At most, standard intelligence tests focus on linguistic and logical capacities, with some also looking at certain spatial abilities. But the other intelligences—vital for many vocations and avocations, and for getting along in the world—are ignored by standard intelligence theory and standard intelligence tests.

FIGURE I   *Summary of Multiple Intelligences*

Linguistic intelligence involves sensitivity to spoken and written language, the ability to learn languages, and the capacity to use language to accomplish certain goals.

Logical-mathematical intelligence involves the capacity to analyze problems logically, carry out mathematical operations, and investigate issues scientifically.

Spatial intelligence features the potential to recognize and manipulate the patterns of wide space (those used, for instance, by navigators and pilots) as well as the patterns of more confined areas (such as those of importance to sculptors, surgeons, chess players, graphic artists, or architects).

Musical intelligence entails skill in the performance, composition, and appreciation of musical patterns.

Bodily-kinesthetic intelligence entails the potential of using one's whole body or parts of the body (like the hand or the mouth) to solve problems or fashion products. (Obviously, dancers, actors, and athletes foreground bodily-kinesthetic intelligence. However, this form of intelligence is also important for craftspersons, surgeons, bench-top scientists, mechanics, and many other technically oriented professions.)

Interpersonal intelligence denotes a person's capacity to understand the intentions, motivations, and desires of other people and, consequently, to work effectively with others.

Intrapersonal intelligence involves the capacity to understand oneself, to have an effective working model of oneself—including one's own desires, fears, and capacities—and to use such information effectively in regulating one's own life.

Naturalistic intelligence involves the capacities to recognize instances [in the natural world] as members of a group (more formally, a species); to distinguish among members of a species; and to chart out the relations, formally or informally, among several species.

Synthesized from Howard Gardner, *Intelligence Reframed: Multiple Intelligences for the 21st Century* (New York: Basic Books, 1999).

Intelligences are often confused or conflated with learning styles. A learning style is an approach that an individual putatively brings to all kinds of tasks: for example, one has a planful, or laid back, or impulsive style. An intelligence is a computational capacity. A person with strong musical intelligence can easily compute (i.e., learn, perform, and remember) musical passages. A person with weak musical intelligence can improve his or her performances on such tasks as well, but that improvement requires more effort, more resources, higher motivation than is indeed in the case of someone who has high musical intelligence. Undoubtedly, there is a heritable component in all of the intelligences; but just as clearly, intelligences can be enhanced through hard work, just as they will atrophy through disuse or misuse.

MULTIPLE INTELLIGENCES IN CHILDHOOD AND ADOLESCENCE

Empirical evidence from Project Spectrum[2], a decade-long collaborative effort to examine the intellectual profiles of young children, suggests that individual differences in intelligence profiles can be discovered early in life. They are also quite malleable in the first years of life. By the time of adolescence, and certainly by late adolescence, an individual's profile of dominant and weaker intelligences is pretty well set and rather difficult to change. That is one reason why it makes sense to attempt to bolster weak intelligences early in life, while playing from strength (i.e., making maximum use of one's stronger intelligences) by adolescence and beyond.

Adolescents are also far more introspective than younger children about their own strengths and weaknesses; this reflective capacity draws on intrapersonal intelligence (see Figure 1). It is likely that one's intrapersonal intelligence undergoes qualitative shifts during adolescence, as young people become preoccupied with issues of identity, experiment with various identities, and ultimately establish a more consistent persona. Identity has always been an amalgam of whether one's persona makes sense to oneself and whether it makes sense to the community. In America, peers play an especially important role in the establishment of identity; and in recent years, much experimentation with identity occurs in virtual social networks, like Myspace and Facebook.

THE IMPLICATIONS OF MULTIPLE INTELLIGENCES THEORY FOR TEACHING

Students who are fortunate enough to have a combination of linguistic and logical strengths will typically do well in school and so academics will be relatively unproblematic for them. It can be said that schools have been devised to cater to that combination of intelligences. Challenges arise when students lack the academic combination of language and logic. In the past, these students were often labeled as dull and efforts were made to exclude them from higher education. One of the dividends of MI theory has been to call attention to other strengths that can be useful in life, whether or not they happen to help with school work.

Another dividend has been far greater flexibility in how subjects are taught. Almost any concept can be conveyed in a number of ways, thereby reaching a range of intelligences. When a teacher presents a topic like evolution in biology, or democracy in history, in a number of ways, two important things happen. First of all, the teacher reaches more students, because some learn better from logical analyses, some from narratives, some from works of art, some from hands-on activities, etc. Second of all, the teacher conveys what it is like really to understand a topic. Any person who understands a topic well can represent it in a number of ways. And if one's understanding is limited to only one explanation, drawing on only one intelligence, it is likely that one's own understanding is tenuous and in need of bolstering. MI theory applied to education thus has the potential to educate the broad range of learners and to do so in ways that are helpful to each and every learner.

NOTES

1. Howard Gardner, *Frames of Mind: The Theory of Multiple Intelligences* (New York: Basic Books, 1983); Howard Gardner, *Multiple Intelligences: New Horizons* (New York: Basic Books, 2006).
2. Howard Gardner, David Henry Feldman, and Mara Krechevsky (eds.), *Project Zero Frameworks—Building on Children's Strengths: The Experience of Project Spectrum,* Vol. 1; *Project Zero Frameworks—Early Learning Activities,* Vol. 2; *Project Zero Frameworks—Preschool Assessment Handbook,* Vol. 3 (New York: Teachers College Press, 1998).

CHAPTER TEN

A Question of "Faith"

Adolescent Spirituality in Public Schools

ERIC TOSHALIS

> [E]ven as my colleagues and I taught academic disciplines born of the
> great curiosities and passions of humankind, our classes somehow focused
> on closed answers, definitions, and formulas rather than on the questions,
> the sense of wonder, and the yearning for understanding that gave rise
> to the disciplines in the first place. I suspected that we were not teaching
> what matters.
>
> —*Katherine Simon*[1]

First, let me be clear: it is absolutely crucial that public school teachers
in an ostensibly democratic nation *never* attempt to proselytize or in any
way direct a student's religious convictions. Nothing I present in this chapter should be construed to contradict this essential point. Especially in an
era when religious affiliations and beliefs seem to drive some of humanity's
most violent conflicts, the requirement that public schools remain free of
religious indoctrination is paramount.

In an effort to keep teachers from violating students' First Amendment
rights, however, our injunctions against religion or spirituality in public
schools too often eliminate from classrooms many of the "ultimate concerns" youth are perhaps most eager to engage. Ignoring, evading, or dis-
missing adolescent spirituality to avoid the teaching of religion is akin to
throwing the meaning-making baby out with the religious bathwater. We
can and should do a better job at addressing, without violating, spiritual
matters in our work with youth in schools. This chapter seeks to argue this

perspective by demonstrating how we might understand adolescent "faith" and support its development in public school classrooms in legal, ethical, and academically invigorating ways.

WHAT IS "FAITH?"

To ask this question is to enter into one of the most ancient and vital lines of inquiry the human species has ever considered. Entire societies have been built around how it is answered, just as intractable wars have been justified based on the concepts people have embraced or rejected. In terms of how we might define faith in a manner appropriate for twenty-first-century public education, the scope and depth of the concept must be precise enough to be useful, but also open enough to invite diverse perspectives. This is tricky work! In a book about adolescent development I co-wrote with Michael Nakkula, we define faith as "the dynamic and symbolic frame of orientation or the ultimate concern to which a person is committed and from which she or he derives purpose in life."[2] This definition is designed to include the fundamentalist Christian whose religion is based on a literal understanding of Biblical texts, the Mahayana Buddhist whose frame of orientation is compassion and the renunciation of worldly desires, the secularist hedge fund manager whose ultimate concern is the growth of profit, the New Age spiritualist who is attached to Druid and Navajo symbols of mystical connection with a living earth, and the Muslim who is committed to jihad as an inward spiritual struggle against temptation. While any single definition of faith is unlikely to be adopted by many who believe in the work of grace, or God in history, or the Holy Spirit's influence in the human heart (not to mention those who do not believe in divinity at all), the definition above highlights the importance of recognizing faith when teaching adolescents. It underscores the foundational aspects of self and world understanding that emerge from religious and spiritual belief, matters that are also central to academic inquiry and school engagement.

When we work with youth in schools, it may be helpful to remind ourselves that deep concerns often lie underneath their stereotypical surface obsessions with music, clothing, movies, hairstyles, myspace.com, YouTube, and video games. Indeed, the developing adolescent is frequently immersed in existential questions: Who am I? Why am I here? What is my purpose? How do I make moral decisions? Whom should I love and how should I love them? What is sacred and what is taboo? In what or whom should I place my trust? These questions reveal powerful structures of meaning-making that drive many youths' decisionmaking processes. Relationships, habits, lifestyles, and commitments all connect to existential notions that are first grasped with cognitive complexity during adolescence. Sometimes as fleeting as they are passionate, these ultimate concerns can direct an adolescent toward experiences that promise fulfillment and meaning. Conversely, they often direct energies away from arenas that seem disconnected, meaningless, or devoid of wonder.

Regardless of whether these symbolic frames of orientation are understood as choices or as familial or cultural expectations, they can and do affect classroom learning in profound ways. To make sense of the reasons why educators might consider spirituality when designing instruction for and building relationships with students, I will articulate why it is important for teachers to consider faith concerns in their work. In the following section, subdivided into five related themes, I argue that faith is an important developmental and pedagogical consideration due to the adolescent's need for (1) belonging and community, (2) separation and individuation, (3) self-transcendence and purpose, (4) narratives of meaning, and (5) understanding her or his place in the postmodern world.

Belonging and Community

Being connected to a community and feeling as though one belongs are core components of psychological well-being for adolescents. Numerous studies have indicated that students who feel deeply connected to others, especially significant adults, are much less likely to take part in dangerous activities and are much more likely to invest in academic achievement than those who feel disconnected.[3] The natural defenses adolescents construct to protect their often fragile identities are lowered when it is clear that they belong. Knowing that they are cared for, that they are connected to others in meaningful ways, and that their presence is desired by those around them allows adolescents to relax into themselves and their surroundings. With less energy expended on the maintenance of defenses, more is available for connecting both to others and to what they understand as their ultimate concerns. When the shy student begins to speak, when facts give way to feelings and beliefs, when autobiographical disclosures outnumber putdowns—when these things begin to occur in the classroom—deep connections are being formed and learning takes on spiritual as much as academic dimensions.

The experience of belonging offers the adolescent much more than opportunities for socializing because it involves being known, being included, and being trusted. Both religious and secular scholars seem to overlap in their estimation of belonging's importance. As the theologian John McDargh puts it, humans have an "irreducible motivation to experience ourselves as selves-in-relationship."[4] Similarly, the psychologist James M. Day argues that belief itself amounts to an articulated "[effort] to belong somewhere to someone."[5] Conceived in this way, the need to belong actually requires a sort of faith that others can and should be trusted and even loved, that those around us are worthy of connection, and that a given community is safe enough for us to enter and take risks.

For adolescents, this faith can be very tenuous. Newly endowed with cognitive and relational capacities that allow the simultaneous consideration of another's point of view alongside their own, many teens begin to look at the world through the eyes of others. This creates opportunities for deeper, more reciprocal, and more empathetic relationships, but it also initiates experiences of fear and anxiety associated with their new self-conscious appreciation of being scrutinized by others. This peer scrutiny, what educator Sharon Daloz Parks has called the "tyranny of the they,"[6] can be diminished effectively in classrooms where youth are offered ample opportunity to engage one another's perspectives, feelings, and experiences within a culture of inclusion. To belong to a community where big questions are asked and answered bravely can be one of the most spiritually satisfying and academically invigorating experiences an adolescent may have.

While religious communities may understand belonging as communion or taking part in a covenant, teachers in public schools need only recognize the spiritual significance of feeling invited, included, and embraced in a group dedicated to one another's learning. With immersion in a self-affirming collective, youth can experiment with being authentically themselves without being alone, especially when the rules in such gatherings are constructed in terms that are partly theirs. After all, if we seek to develop in youth a commitment to the common good, we must recognize that they will only do so when we provide classroom environments that invite, embrace, challenge, and empower them to contribute. Experiences like these provide a foundation for identity and relationship development because they allow the adolescent to say "I know who I am because I know where I belong."

Separation and Individuation

The adolescent's need to belong contrasts with her/his need to separate. Since forming a cohesive and authentic identity is a primary task of adolescence, youth are forever exploring opportunities for both integration and autonomy as they attempt to connect who they think they are as individuals with the communities that shape them. The adolescent desire to be an *I*—an independent and unique self who possesses the capacity to direct her/his own destiny—is forever in tension with the need to be part of the *we*—any of an array of collectives in which the self is included and embraced. As the theologian Paul Tillich explains it, "the courage to be" is split in two: the courage "to be a part of" something and the courage "to be apart from" everything else.[7] This process is inextricable from youths' existential and spiritual growth and may reveal itself in a multitude of ways in the classroom.

Differentiating oneself from one's parent(s) is perhaps the first step toward the construction of an independent identity, and subsequent steps may include separation from one's extended family, friends, culture, heritage, and schooling. Though they may serve as primary role models, teachers are often also used by adolescents as exemplars of precisely who they want *not* to be. Such contrariness may be expressed in playful terms or in more defiant ones, depending on the relationship and context. If the teacher loves the subject matter of U.S. history, the student may proclaim his hatred for it. If the teacher shares her love of the Boston Red Sox, the student may express adoration for the New York Yankees. If we can remember the spiritual dimensions that often undergird these actions, we can avoid the temptation either to take personally our students' expressions or to attempt to force their compliance. Especially in communities that primarily reward obedience (such as schools), it may be prudent to remind ourselves that separation and individuation are necessary and valuable steps toward realization of the self.

Separation and individuation are about the need to find and express autonomy, to be independent of the whims and directives of the group, and to experience agency in one's innovations and decisions. They are the flipside to the need to belong, and therefore involve comparable spiritual elements. Like belonging and community, they allow the individual to say, "I know who I am," but this time with the clause "because I am unique, autonomous, and independent." They are about choice, self-responsibility, accountability, free will, self-efficacy, artistic expression, and voice. If adolescents are provided with sufficient opportunity to test the quality of their separation and the extent of their individuation, they will likely find ways to come back to the collective when the need for relationship and belonging arises.

But if such opportunities are not provided, separation can turn into isolation. The stress of divesting oneself from parental (or teacher) directives may actually introduce separation anxiety in the adolescent striving to construct an autonomous self. Just because they may vocally and energetically throw themselves into activities, habits, attitudes, and appearances seemingly opposed to their parents' or teachers' wishes does not mean they seek to sever relationships with these adults. These actions may be examples of invitations to dialogue rather than refutations of tradition or authority. Youth want to make identities and meanings that are theirs, but they rarely want to do so all by themselves. At the core of this process is the hope that they will be valued for who they are and want to be, and that their ultimate concern(s) will be deemed worthy of inquiry, support, and even adoration. Again, teachers are well positioned to anchor youths' separation and individuation through academic work; that is, to help them discover their unique part within a greater whole.

Self-Transcendence and Purpose

During adolescence, new levels of cognitive ability emerge. Though explained differently by various researchers, the basic view that adolescence marks the emergence of adult ways of reasoning and the construction of a durable identity is largely accepted.[8] Beginning with the work of Erik Erikson,[9] adolescence has been understood in psychological and social terms as a developmental era in which the individual attempts to resolve internal conceptions of the self with those reflected back to her by others and by her culture. This "identity crisis" often generates profound realizations about the adolescent's sense of self and how it is shaped by (and does some shaping of) others. If provided with the proper supports, a child's egocentrism expands during adolescence into a more complex worldview that is able to apprehend the needs and perspectives of others and incorporate them into a cohesive sense of oneself in the world.

With this expansion of mind comes the opportunity for deeper and more meaningful connection with others, but it also may come with anxiety stemming from the recognition of multiple audiences for whom one must perform (i.e., parents, friends, romantic partners, teachers, extended family, coaches, ministers/priests/rabbis/imams, etc.). In an attempt to silence the din of voices, whether real or imagined, that seek to direct or judge their development, adolescents sometimes withdraw into a simplified version of the world where they only consider their own needs and desires. In such cases, youth may appear narcissistic. They may express grandiose assessments of their capabilities, engage in fantasies that involve immense power and brilliance, act with a sense of entitlement, and even exploit interpersonal relationships for personal satisfaction.[10] But these occasionally self-absorbed modes of thinking and ways of interacting might best be viewed not as pathologies but as coping strategies employed by the adolescent to help manage an often complex and difficult transition. If we understand this behavior as a defense against uncertainty about the self, we can better see how an adolescent's temporary narcissism may actually be a transitional state toward a more robust self that can sustain its autonomy even during integration with others.[11] Seen in this way, narcissism is really an expression of hope.

To give that hope a chance to grow, adolescents need practice situating their growing identities, decisionmaking processes, and worldviews in the context of interdependent relationships, and they need to have faith that such work is worthwhile. Despite "rebellious" or "defiant" behaviors that sometimes suggest otherwise, youth yearn to connect to sources of meaning that provide escape routes out of narcissism and into reciprocal relationships with people and the world at large. Self-transcendence is therefore a reaching out to something or someone external to one's individualized experience. This takes courage. To transcend the self is to overcome the barriers of thought derived from the belief that one's experience is wholly unique and impervious to the insights or assistance of others. It is to recognize that one is not, never has been, and never will be an island.

Teachers are in a perfect position to support this self-transcendence, to show adolescents that there is meaning and purpose in the work they do, the pursuits they undertake, and the relationships they form in school. Regardless of whether the student's faith takes the form of a religious belief in God's plan, an expression of a more secular purpose in one's life (peace, love, justice, success, wealth, etc.), or an experimentation with situational factors that most compel the student to think outside their own experiences (i.e., their answers to "Why should I care?"), classrooms are ideal spaces where the need to self-transcend can be conveyed. Teachers attentive to this fact realize that since adolescents' withdrawal from or rejection of others is largely fear-driven, the engagement in relationships and the movement toward something bigger than oneself may require repeated invitations and earnest guarantees of safety. To transcend the self, youth need to know why it is worth the risked vulnerability, what ends might be achieved, and whose goals might be met. In short, they need a purpose.

In their survey of over a dozen studies relevant to the development of a sense of purpose in adolescents, William Damon and his co-researchers at Stanford University found such an orientation to be related to a host of other factors, including achievement, hopefulness, persistence, and "a sense of a compelling future."[12] Damon and his colleagues define purpose as "a stable and generalized intention to accomplish something that is at once meaningful to the self and of consequence to the world beyond the self."[13] They key word is *beyond*. To have a purpose, one must transcend the self, find meaning, and create consequences out there in the world with and for others, beyond the self. Consequently, if educators are able to read adolescent narcissism as a temporary rest stop on the way to more purposeful and meaningful connection, they will be better prepared to engage the many spiritual possibilities that lie underneath adolescents' temporary fixations on the self.

Narratives of Meaning

One way to understand the spiritual underpinnings of an adolescent's development is to frame it as a story. To make sense of their growth experiences, adolescents construct stories about what happened to them, how they became who they are, and where they are going. In this way, they are no different from adults. We all craft narratives to organize our lives into coherent storylines that explain our identities and decisions. These narratives provide characters, conflicts, and plots where there may previously have been only the raw data of experience and the basic needs of the psyche. When youth construct these narratives, they use the themes, motifs, tropes, symbols, archetypes, and vocabulary available to them, many of which are either drawn from religious traditions or are rife with spiritual meaning. In the lives of adolescents, heroic struggles, dangerous adventures, horrendous betrayals, and valiant self-sacrifices seem to abound at any given Friday evening's school dance, football game, or party, and school days themselves are often full of story-making sorts of events. ("Ohmigawd, did you hear what happened?!")

Adolescents' risk-taking, which invariably causes much anxiety and concern among the adults in their lives, is understood by some developmental psychologists in narrative terms.[14] Risk-taking experiences, these psychologists say, function to create intensity, drama, and group cohesion among youth who may be searching for life narratives that provide meaning and connection. Absent opportunities to share the stories that give structure to their sometimes disparate and confusing experiences, many teens engage in risky behaviors involving drugs and alcohol, sex, violence, and daredevil feats. Such experiences offer youth concentrated moments and critical decisionmaking experiences from which stories of crisis and commitment can be generated. If we want to know how youths' life narratives are being created and if we seek to participate in the development of their identities, we need to find ways to access those stories and value their significance.

Getting youth to share their narratives of meaning is not hard. Ask an adolescent to describe an experience, explain a dilemma, or discern a moral choice, and you will likely get a story. This is because stories are how adolescents transform fantasies and experiences into convictions that orient their lives. And, because narratives shape adolescents' life-orientations, they can be understood as expressions of faith. Even when narrative themes are drawn from ostensibly secular as opposed to religious sources, the stories adolescents tell of themselves (either internally or conversationally) convey a faith that there is indeed meaning in one's life, that there are morals to one's stories.

To recognize how important these stories are to the spiritual development of youth, teachers must appreciate their power and then provide opportunities for the construction, expression, and revision of narratives that have meaning for their students. Allowing students to write their own fictional accounts or beginning each language arts class by journaling are common methods teachers employ to channel youths' propensity for narrative into academic work. I would argue, however, that these are only starting points, and simplistic ones at that. A more nuanced and spiritually attentive approach would be to engage students in dialogues and assignments about the narratives they are telling themselves, then tease out and explore the dominant archetypes and tropes they may be infusing into their life stories (of which some will likely be religious), and write and rewrite their experiences using poetry, spoken word, short stories, plays, journalism, and essays. In fact, this sort of activity does not need to be restricted to language arts classes, since each of the other subject areas may be understood as having its own overarching grand narratives for explaining our world. What are the numbers, equations, and quantitative relationships that tell one's story? How does our biology form a narrative for who we are? What tales can be told about our history and culture that inform our identities and decisions? If James Day is right that "stories remind us that our life task is to make of our time here a story that will stick, a viable self-narrative in a world of competing tales,"[15] then any education that seeks to be relevant and powerful in adolescents' lives must draw out and provide safe audiences for these narratives of meaning.

Understanding One's Place in the Postmodern World

Most adolescents today receive information, imagery, and a multitude of conflicting perspectives daily from a variety of sources, including television, the Internet, magazines, billboards, movies, radios, mp3 players, cell phones, and the seemingly endless supply of catalogs that arrive at their homes. They then enter schools where posters, displays, announcements, flyers, textbooks, calendars, workbooks, schedules, reminders, tables, worksheets, novels, tests, and detention slips demand their attention. Drenched in such information, teens then have to endure some adults' comments about their apparent "short attention spans" or their supposed "inability to concentrate," as if it is the students' fault for finding it difficult to discern what is worth their focus. To meet the spiritual needs of adolescents in public schools, part of the educator's job is to help youth make sense of this informational deluge, to find meaning in what can seem like the meaninglessness of our postmodern era.

To construct a cohesive self and find purpose in one's relationships and decisions while enduring the bombardment of texts, photos, graphics, symbols, sounds, and ideas can be exhausting both physically and existentially. The psychologist Kenneth J. Gergen calls this phenomenon "the saturated self" to emphasize how over-full we can become when confronted with so many audio and visual stimuli, many of which make claims on our identities or seek to influence our decisionmaking.[16] For adolescents who are just emerging into a complex understanding of the world, this saturation can be troubling. They may ask: Where is truth if every person seems to possess their own version of it? What is worthy of my devotion if every next person seems to value a completely different set of priorities? What should I pay attention to when my teachers say one thing, my parent(s) says another, and the various media say anything they can to get me to buy what they're selling? Who am I and what am I to do in this crazy world?

Though many teens adopt the teachings of their religious traditions to find order in the chaos of contemporary existence, others frame it in all-or-nothing terms: Either there is one Truth, or there is none. In such cases, nihilism, or the belief that life has no meaning or purpose, can be read as an existential expression of despair. When coupled with evidence of depression or self-destructive behaviors, this expression should be addressed with immediacy and great care. However, nihilism is not necessarily just gloomy hopelessness. For the adolescent confronting the postmodern world, nihilism may sometimes function productively. As an overstated façade designed to cover deeper searches for truths and purposes on which a life can be built, nihilism establishes a moratorium on decisions about which truths to believe. Underneath this façade is often a yearning for dialogue on contentious issues, thorny ethical dilemmas, and philosophical disputes. If placed in learning communities where exploration of life's larger questions is welcome, nihilistic youth may be relied upon to serve as invaluable "devil's advocates" who forever keep discussions and investigations interesting. Indeed, if teachers can read some adolescents' nihilistic outlooks as temporary and clever coping strategies rather than arrogant negation and withdrawal, they might find tremendous critical resources there waiting to be channeled into solid academic work.

CREATING THE "FAITH-FRIENDLY" CLASSROOM

Many authors have provided compelling examples of how teachers in public school classrooms are legally, ethically, and with academic rigor promoting the spiritual development of adolescents.[17] These sources are worth consulting because they afford a much broader treatment of classroom techniques and the rationales for them than space permits here. What I highlight below are a few practices most closely connected to the ways I have outlined spirituality and faith in the previous sections.

Promote Imagination and Creativity

As adolescents discover their own uniqueness, they naturally look for ways to capture it, imagine it differently, and express it to others. Writing poems, drawing pictures, playing music, inventing games, choreographing dances, playing sports, cooking meals, planting gardens, building dioramas, making pottery, coordinating an outfit, getting to the math problem's solution differently from one's teacher—all these things thrill adolescents precisely because they involve the imagination and creation of something into being. Perhaps nowhere is the adolescent's sense of possibility more pronounced than in those moments where they use their creativity in the service of their ultimate concerns, when they bring a small part of the world closer to their vision of what it could be.

Especially in our era in which policymakers seem bent on reducing teaching and learning to preparation for reductive and spirit-numbing standardized tests, teachers must find ways to protect imagination and creativity in their classroom activities. Practically speaking, this means resisting the so-called "accountability" movement's capacity to rid classrooms of meaningful dialogue, even as we do our best to help students pass the tests they need to succeed. Channeling students' sense of wonder and guiding their passions toward relevant academic work can and should provoke youths' imaginations and invigorate their creativity without sacrificing the skill development needed to pass high-stakes tests. The youth I know don't come to school with a desire to learn how to pass a test—they come to engage issues and one another on matters that stir their intellect, rouse their sense of purpose, and connect them with concerns they understand as ultimate. While many may not bring their pencils or even their homework to school (!), they are always bringing their faith and their need to imagine and create.

If there is any doubt that imagination and creativity belong at the center of education, consider how many of us adults went into education in part because we knew it would provide an endless outlet for our own inventiveness. We get to imagine units, lessons, bulletin boards, diagrams, lectures, questions, discussions, tests, graphs, and timelines. Sometimes, however, if we are not careful, our own creativity may eclipse the imaginations of our students. This can happen if we stick too rigidly to our "plan," if we rely too heavily on lecture or rote learning, or if our goal is simply to "get through the chapter." Educator Rachael Kessler asks, "How many of us close down immediately when our plan appears to be thwarted, by reminding our students what we're 'supposed to be doing now?' By valuing openness and being willing to be surprised, we can override this reaction and discover a more creative response."[18] This does not mean we should abandon structure, nor does it mean we should refrain from challenging students. Often, some of the most inspiring imaginative activity comes in response to problems or tensions with clearly defined goals and timelines. Problem-posing and project-based learning have long, successful track records in this regard. Yet providing these challenges is not enough. Nothing shuts down our imaginations more quickly than an awareness of others' scorn for our creation, and so it falls on us adults to defend a challenging but safe environment for adolescent imagination and creativity.

Offer Experiences of the Extraordinary

With the enormity of developmental tasks and the often overwhelming character of the questions faced in young adulthood, the threat of meaninglessness and the seductiveness of nihilism persistently loom on the adolescent horizon. Desiring to transcend themselves and to reach beyond the limits of the self, teens look for ways to shake their frame of orientation to see what is worth holding onto and what may need letting go. Such yearning often manifests itself in the search for ecstatic experiences, and this leads some adolescents to turn to alcohol, drugs, sex, violence, or "extreme" risky behaviors to provide them with the intensity that confirms they are alive. Providing safer alternatives for extraordinary experiences may help youth test their commitments, form lasting bonds with others, and give shape and color to their ultimate concerns without exposure to danger.

Educators can provide extraordinary experiences by pushing adolescents to go beyond their perceived limits. By encouraging students to take risks and immerse themselves in activities with unknown results, we open youth to an awareness of their own possibility. Variously understood as "expeditionary learning,"[19] "flow experiences,"[20] or even "grace," these extraordinary moments may occur in art, music, athletics, academics, human relations, or any other seemingly normal domain suddenly electrified with meaning. Losing oneself (and therefore finding oneself) in play, beholding a piece of music or a work of art that confirms oneself or one's faith, confronting an essential truth underlying an intellectual argument, finding a person in history or literature to whom one feels a strong affinity—these are the moments in which teens (and adults alike) feel larger than life. Something profoundly clicks in those extraordinary moments, so much so that many of us find ourselves referring to them as sort of chapter titles in the story of our lives. ("It was when _____ happened that I knew ____ about the universe/myself.") Finding ways to inspire such experiences in adolescents is essential to the development of a robust and invigorating faith, and watching them happen is perhaps one of the best rewards in teaching.

Engage Moral/Ethical Issues

One of the chief drawbacks of the current obsession with high-stakes tests is the way it leaves our students stranded at the surface of subject matter we all know contains unfathomable depth. In the schools I visit, I have seen and heard too often what teacher and researcher Katherine Simon describes in the epigraph at the beginning of this chapter: classrooms in which the issues that matter most are discussed the least, classrooms where the minutiae outweigh the momentous. If we understand our vocation as educators to include being mediators of meaning and suppliers of symbols, we must be prepared for adolescents' big questions. Therefore, to meet the spiritual needs of youth, it is critical that we devote time, space, and energy in our classrooms to issues of morality and questions of ethics.

Research has provided empirical evidence of the profound and positive effect that "character education" programs, "service learning," and ethics-infused curricula can have on adolescents who are beginning to engage the world in moral terms. While many argue that schools should teach only "the basics" (i.e., literacy and math skills) and that the family and the church/temple/mosque should be the sole venues for discussions of morality, such an argument runs contrary to the purpose of public education as it has been expressed since its inception. To relegate moral inquiries only to those discussions among family and congregation members is to strip education of perhaps its most basic calling—to produce citizens capable of tackling the most difficult questions of the day. Likewise, if we restrict the settings in which moral questions will be entertained, we send the message to youth that moral issues are only relevant to specific activities. Despite our occasional efforts to hide it with the dismissive "do as I say, not as I do," the truth is that youth know already that moral and ethical decisionmaking is infused in all of our choices.

The need to explore ethical questions may help to explain why adolescents are so adept at steering classroom lessons into "tangents" that pertain to moral issues. Try as they might to stick to the lesson, teachers routinely confront their students' spiritual hunger for meaning, purpose, and agency in their classroom activities. Looking up from their lesson plans, teachers encounter rows of students who desperately seek investigations into moral quandaries, especially those in which the consequences are theoretical rather than real. Youth may not be ready to make actual decisions regarding stem cell research, poverty, torture, war, racism, weapons of mass destruction, global warming, and disease prevention—the very issues that will determine how we progress through the twenty-first century—but they relish opportunities to practice thinking through such problems nonetheless. Issues like these are the ones youth are often most eager to explore with audiences led by trusted adults who provide resources and direct energies to support a complex understanding of what we ought to do.

Classrooms that are devoid of moral inquiries risk becoming purposeless spaces where facts are dispensed at the expense of meaning, and information is relayed without wisdom. To avoid this, Simon contends that students in public schools "should regularly be asked two basic moral and existential questions about the topics they study: 'What are the implications of what I am learning for my own behavior and beliefs?' and 'How does this material help me understand my place in the world?'"[21] Asking such questions violates no First Amendment protections against the establishment of religion, nor does it limit its free exercise. In fact, written into many states' curricular frameworks are directives that require teachers across subject areas to address the core ethical concerns of their disciplines. To ask "What would God say?" or even "Is there a God?" is clearly an ethical transgression, but to frame classroom inquiries around questions such as "How do people make moral decisions about _____, and what do you think?" is to provide academically motivating as well as spiritually stirring educational content.

A truly integrated understanding of the academic and developmental needs of adolescents must include faith. Avoiding this fact because of narrow interpretations of church/state separation amounts to what researcher Angela Valenzuela calls a "subtractive" process[22] whereby students are expected to check central aspects of themselves at the door when they enter school. This is neither possible nor preferable. Powerful undercurrents of belonging, community, self-transcendence, and narrative convey meaning in and through youth both individually and collectively, whether we choose to honor them or not. Rather than being avoided or dismissed, adolescent spirituality should be recognized for what it is—a wellspring of curiosity, imagination, justice, interconnectedness, and compassion. Though ethical and cultural considerations make it essential that teachers never proselytize within the context of compulsory public education, questions of ultimate concern ought to form the core of why we teach, what we teach, and how we teach. In truth, those questions are already there, just waiting for the attention they deserve. The point is not to answer them for our adolescent students, but to open space in which they can explore them themselves.

NOTES

1. Katherine G. Simon, *Moral Questions in the Classroom: How to Get Kids to Think Deeply about Real Life and Their Schoolwork* (New Haven: Yale University Press, 2001), 2.

2. Michael J. Nakkula and Eric Toshalis, *Understanding Youth: Adolescent Development for Educators* (Cambridge, MA: Harvard Education Press, 2006), 211.

3. Roy F. Baumeister and Mark R. Leary, "The Need to Belong: Desire for Interpersonal Attachments as a Fundamental Human Motivation," *Psychological Bulletin* 117, no. 3 (1995): 497–529; Carrie Furrer and Ellen Skinner, "Sense of Relatedness as a Factor in Children's Academic Engagement and Performance," *Journal of Educational Psychology* 95, no. 1 (2003): 148–162; Gil G. Noam, "The Psychology of Belonging: Reformulating Adolescent Development," in Aaron H. Esman, Lois T. Flaherty, and Harvey A. Horowitz (eds.), *Annals of the American Society of Adolescent Psychiatry* (Hillsdale, NJ: The Analytic Press, 1999), 49–68; Robert W. Roeser, Carol Midgley, and Timothy C. Urdan, "Perceptions of the School Psychological Environment and Early Adolescents' Psychological and Behavioral Functioning in School: The Mediating Role of Goals and Belonging," *Journal of Educational Psychology* 88, no. 3 (1996): 408–422.

4. John McDargh, "Faith Development Theory and the Postmodern Problem of Foundations," *The International Journal for the Psychology of Religion* 11, no. 3 (2001): 194.

5. James M. Day, "Speaking of Belief: Language, Performance, and Narrative in the Psychology of Religion," *International Journal for the Psychology of Religion* 3, no. 4 (1993): 213.

6. Sharon Daloz Parks, *The Critical Years: The Young Adult Search for a Faith to Live By* (San Francisco: Harper and Row, 1986).

7. Paul Tillich, *The Courage to Be* (New Haven: Yale University Press, 1952).

8. For an insightful critique of this orientation and its cultural-historical agendas, however, see Nancy Lesko, *Act Your Age: A Cultural Construction of Adolescence* (New York: Routledge Falmer, 2001).

9. Erik H. Erikson, *Identity: Youth and Crisis* (New York: W. W. Norton, 1968).

10. Matthew C. Aalsma and Daniel K. Lapsley, "Religiosity and Adolescent Narcissism: Implications for Values Counseling," *Counseling and Values* 44, no. 1 (1999): 4.

11. Aalsma and Lapsley, "Religiosity and Adolescent Narcissism," 5.

12. William Damon, Jenni Menon, and Kendall Cotton Bronk, "The Development of Purpose During Adolescence," *Applied Developmental Science* 7, no. 3 (2003): 121.

13. Damon, Menon, and Bronk, "The Development of Purpose," 121.

14. See, for example, Cynthia Lightfoot, *The Culture of Adolescent Risk-Taking* (New York: Guilford Press, 1997); Lynn Ponton, *The Romance of Risk* (New York: Basic Books, 1997).

15. Day, "Speaking of Belief," 218.

16. Kenneth J. Gergen, *The Saturated Self: Dilemmas of Identity in Contemporary Life* (New York: Basic Books, 1991).

17. See, for example: James W. Fowler, "Reconstituting Paideia in Public Education," in Parker J. Palmer, Barbara G. Wheeler, and James W. Fowler (eds.), *Caring for the Commonweal: Education for Religious and Public Life* (Macon, GA: Mercer University Press, 1991), 63-89; Joan Montgomery Halford, "Longing for the Sacred in Schools: A Conversation with Nel Noddings," *Educational Leadership* 56, no. 4 (1999): 28–32; Ronald V. Iannone and Patricia A. Obenauf, "Toward Spirituality in Curriculum and Teaching," *Education* 119, no. 4 (1999): 737–744; Rachael Kessler, *The Soul of Education* (Alexandria, VA: Association for Supervision and Curriculum Development, 2000); Rachael Kessler, "Nourishing Students in Secular Schools," *Educational Leadership* 56, no. 4 (1999): 49-52; Michael J. Nakkula and Eric Toshalis, *Understanding Youth: Adolescent Development for Educators* (Cambridge, MA: Harvard Education Press, 2006); Parker Palmer, "Evoking the Spirit in Public Education," *Educational Leadership* 56, no. 4 (1999): 6–11; Sharon Daloz Parks, *The Critical Years: The Young Adult Search for a Faith to Live By* (San Francisco: Harper and Row, 1986); Sharon Daloz Parks, "Faithful Becoming in a Complex World: New Powers, Perils, and Possibilities," in *Growing Up Postmodern: Imitating Christ in the Age of 'Whatever'* (Princeton, NJ: Institute for Youth Ministry, Princeton Theological Seminary, 1999), 37–52; Katherine G. Simon, *Moral Questions in the Classroom: How to Get Kids to Think Deeply about Real Life and Their Schoolwork* (New Haven: Yale University Press, 2001); Charles Suhor, "Spirituality: Letting it Grow in the Classroom," *Educational Leadership* 56, no. 4 (1999): 12–16.

18. Rachael Kessler, *The Soul of Education* (Alexandria, VA: Association for Supervision and Curriculum Development, 2000), 100.
19. Denis Udall and Amy Mednick, *Journeys through our Classrooms* (Dubuque, IA: Kendall/ Hunt Publishing Company, 1996).
20. Mihaly Csikszentmihalyi and Reed Larson, *Being Adolescent: Conflict and Growth in the Teenage Years* (New York: Basic Books, 1984).
21. Simon, *Moral Questions*, 211.
22. Angela Valenzuela, *Subtractive Schooling: U.S.-Mexican Youth and the Politics of Caring* (Albany: State University of New York Press, 1999).

CHAPTER ELEVEN

Beyond Categories

The Complex Identities of Adolescents

JOHN RAIBLE AND SONIA NIETO

What does it mean to be an adolescent in the United States today? In this chapter we attempt to provide insights into this question, based on our varied experiences with young people of different backgrounds. We are both teachers and researchers with a special interest in how race and ethnicity, social class, language, gender, sexual orientation, and other differences manifest themselves in students' identities, and in how these identities are influenced by schooling. Both of us have taught for many years at levels ranging from elementary school through university. Our research—Sonia's previous work with students of diverse cultural backgrounds and John's ongoing research in "communities of adoption"—has rendered questions of identity enormously significant for both of us.[1] Our own backgrounds and developing identities are, of course, major reasons for this interest. Both John (biracial African American, adoptee and adoptive father, gay male teacher and professor, and grandfather) and Sonia (Puerto Rican, Spanish-speaking female, teacher and teacher educator, mother, and grandmother) recognize how our own identities have shifted over the years. Hence, we share a keen curiosity about young people and the identities they create and re-create, and how their identities change based on their experiences and the contexts in which they live and study at any given time.

Human beings are constantly evolving and redefining themselves over the course of a lifetime. Adolescence is a particularly significant phase of life, during which young people try to figure out who they are. The great task of adolescence is learning to express one's multiple identities in personally meaningful and socially acceptable ways. As educators, we need to understand the implications of adolescent identity formation for schooling. How are race and gender, for instance, affirmed or dismissed in school settings? What does it mean to be a lesbian in a school setting hostile to that identity? How can an adoptee explore his identity in a school environment where biological family ties are accorded higher status than ties of adoption? And how are students' quests for meaningful identities linked to learning?

The changes one undergoes in one's identifications are due not just to individual preferences and experiences; that is, they are not simply psychological transformations that take place in one's own head. Identities also change in response to the sociopolitical contexts in which people live. Our identities have been shaped and continue to be influenced by the people with whom we interact and the material and social conditions of our lives. In this chapter, we focus on two young people who several years ago allowed us into their worlds through a series of interviews. These students come from different cities and towns, and they hail from various kinds of families and different social classes. They identify in multiple ways, based on such factors as family structure, race, sexual orientation, and national origin. In spite of these differences, they share a need to belong and to feel free to explore who they are. Finally, to explore how a sense of self can reach a comfortable—although always changing—status as one leaves adolescence, we conclude with the thoughts of a young man in the early years of adulthood.

CREATING IDENTITIES: CASES OF TWO YOUNG PEOPLE IN TRANSITION

Whether we are seasoned adults or young children, our identities are always in flux. The human impulse to categorize, however, has resulted in labeling people in ways that restrict the expression of complex identities. This tendency has been especially evident in the past several decades, given the resurgent interest in race and ethnicity in education. However, although significant in and of themselves, race, ethnicity, gender, and other traditional markers of identity do not tell the whole story.

Culture is a great deal messier than these static terms might imply. Researcher Steven Arvizu's description of culture as a verb rather than a noun begins to capture the dynamic nature of identity, particularly as defined by youth in an increasingly globalized world.[2] For instance, in their research focusing on adolescents, Shirley Brice Heath and Milbrey McLaughlin found that ethnic labels provided only partial descriptions of the young people they studied. Their research suggests that, rather than serving as a primary identifier, ethnicity gives adolescents an "additional layer of identity" they can adopt as a matter of pride.[3] In her later work, Heath found that young people, particularly those who live in urban areas, are involved in the creation of new cultural categories based on shared experiences, not just shared identities. According to Heath, these young people "think of themselves as a *who* and not a *what*" (emphasis in original).[4]

Daniel Yon is another researcher who has found that conventional, static conceptions of culture are unsatisfactory for describing the multiple and hybrid realities of identities today. Yon conducted a study of high school students of various racial and ethnic backgrounds in Toronto, Ontario. In this research, he coined the term *elusive culture* to suggest the new and creative ways students made sometimes surprising and unpredictable identifications; for instance, a Serbian student identified as "Spanish" and a white male identified most closely with his Guyanese classmates. Yon concluded:

> Youth demonstrate tremendous flexibility in their capacity to make identifications, to experiment, take risks, discard and create ideas, and in these processes they resist an understanding of culture as something to simply embody, apply, or force others to have.[5]

Raquel Romberg describes a similar phenomenon among Puerto Ricans on the U.S. mainland. *Cultural chameleons* is Romberg's term for those who "manage their lives through the combination, merging, or shifting of different cultural strategies."[6] In this way, Puerto Ricans and other young people with hybrid identities provide a far healthier model of cultural adaptation than is commonplace.

Given the pressures to assimilate to both peer culture and, in some cases, a new national culture and society, it should come as no surprise that students develop unpredictable identifications. In her ethnographic study of immigrant youth at Madison High (her pseudonym for a racially and ethnically diverse school in California), Laurie Olsen found that adapting to a new culture often meant that young people needed "to abandon the fullness of their human identities as part of the process of becoming and being American."[7] In addition, Olsen found that many newcomers were surprised that coming to the United States did not automatically make them American. For some students, especially those whose backgrounds and physical characteristics differed most from the European American mainstream culture, factors such as skin color, religion, and language prevented a facile assimilation. Students at Madison High were often forced to construct narrow boundaries for themselves, limiting possibilities of multicultural interaction. This situation was especially painful for students of biracial and multiracial backgrounds, who were often forced to "choose sides," and for many immigrants who did not fit neatly into any of the already constructed categories. (See "Adolescents from Immigrant Families: Relationships and Adaptation in School" by Carola Suárez-Orozco, Desirée Baolian Qin, and Ramona Fruja Amthor, pp. 51–69, in this volume.)

Clearly, we live in a time of transition, one in which static labels can no longer contain the rich complexity of contemporary identities. We turn now to a closer look into the lived realities of two young people who shared with us their reflections on their own unique identifications. (In what follows, the names of the young people, as well as the towns or cities where they live and the schools they attend, are pseudonyms.)

NICK GREENBERG: THE IDENTITIES OF A TRANSRACIAL ADOPTEE

Nick Greenberg is a 14-year-old middle school student. He is tall and tan, with wavy black hair and a ready smile. In physical appearance, Nick might be taken for any number of ethnicities, races, or nationalities. That is, he epitomizes a racially ambiguous individual. Nick was adopted when he was a few months old, but he maintains contact with his birth mother and his older brother, who lives with her. During his interview, Nick spoke honestly about his feelings regarding his multiracial heritage and other people's expectations for how he "should" act:

> I look more like my birth mother than my birth father because he was African American and my birth mother is white. . . . My adoptive father is Jewish, and my adoptive mother is Christian. I usually check off "African American" and "Native American" because I know I'm at least part Native American. Sometimes when I say I'm Jewish, this one kid says, "No, you're not Jewish. You have to act more Jewish." To me, I have no idea what it means to "act more Jewish." Maybe it means to wear a yarmulke or go to synagogue.
>
> I've been told that I talk white, but that was in a joking way. Certain black kids will say I shouldn't listen to a certain kind of music since I'm black. It kind of gets annoying to be told what music I'm supposed to listen to. They continue to press on and say I'm supposed to "act black."

When I ask them how that's supposed to be, they can't really answer that because there's no way you're supposed to act if you're black, Chinese, white—you're just supposed to act the way you feel.

Nick identifies tastes in music and clothes, along with language styles, as important markers of identity that are frequently used to define him. Being raised by his white adoptive parents in a predominantly white environment, it is understandable why Nick "sounds white" to some. Yet partly because he listens to some rap artists, and partly because he regularly visits his birth family in a predominantly African American neighborhood of another city, Nick is able to "code-switch" and adopt an urban (some might say "black") manner of speech. Nevertheless, it has not always been easy for him to do so.

Talking about his interactions with African American students in his middle school, Nick related a few incidents that occurred in the halls during which he was forced to navigate tricky racial boundaries as a multiracial, racially ambiguous student. The names others hurl his way hint at their confusion about how to place Nick in the social circles at school:

> Most of the black people act kind of racist towards me because I don't act like them. They usually say "nigger," which I find pretty offensive. Like, "Out of my way, you nigger"—stuff like that. "Nigger" is probably the worst thing I've ever been called. Some people have called me "gay." "Gay" and "nigger" are the things they call me the most. One black person was picking on me because I didn't "act black." And two other people, they kept on telling him to stop, and they said, "He doesn't have to act black, he can act however he wants to. He can act Chinese for all I care." The first guy wasn't too happy, but he left. I thought it was pretty good.
>
> I think it's starting to sink in that people don't have to act like their race. They can act any way they want. Kids don't really have to tell anybody how they're supposed to act according to their race, or gender for that matter.

While on the surface Nick resists attempts by other students to get him to "act like his race," he nevertheless usually includes himself when he talks about black people; that is, he identifies as African American. At other times, Nick speaks about African Americans as others. This "now I'm one thing, now I'm something else, but I'm all of me simultaneously" approach reflects a hybridized, "both/and" approach to racial identification, especially characteristic of how identifications are made by individuals who are multiracial. Such an approach is a refreshing change from the outdated "either/or" model from an earlier era, which forced people to identify with only one or the other parent's racial designation.

When asked explicitly to describe where he feels he fits, Nick answered:

> I don't really choose friends by color; I choose them by who they are on the inside. I watch what they do. If they do a lot of laughing and smiling and are not acting like jerks, then I consider them nice people, and I'll see if I can make friends with them. I have a variety of friends from different races, not just a single race. I have white people, black people, Asian people, German, Russian, Canadian, et cetera, as friends.
>
> I don't feel I fit in with totally black people. I feel like if it's more mixed, I have a better chance of fitting in. I would actually have to say I fit in best in the water. I know it sounds kind of weird, but that's something that I'm really good at. I can just swim around and forget about everything that's happened to me.

Nick's comment about "forgetting about everything" when he's swimming serves as a poignant reminder of the strife he experiences as a result of rigid racial categories. For him, how people act is more important than how they identify. Nick explains that he "has a better chance of fitting in" in mixed settings. Although schools sometimes respond to diversity by offering cultural clubs (such as black student unions or Hispanic student associations), which are modeled after groups popularized on college campuses in the 1960s and 1970s, culture-specific clubs may not meet the identity needs of students like Nick. One hopeful sign is that there are more and more organizations for mixed-race students on college campuses around the country. Perhaps soon they will become established at secondary schools as well. Nick's situation further suggests that schools can do more to promote interracial activities for those who actively seek involvement in pluralistic, rather than ethnocentric, extracurricular experiences.

Elsewhere in the interview, Nick talked about visiting his birth mother and brother in the large northeastern city where they reside. Because he maintains contact with his birth family, Nick's adoption is considered an open adoption. Growing up in an open adoption has provided Nick with access to people who can answer many of the identity questions with which adoptees often grapple: Why was I adopted? Where did I come from? What does my biological family look like? Nick talked about how he handles being adopted and other people's curiosity about his unique family:

When people find out I'm adopted, they usually say, "You're adopted?" They are kind of shocked, because they thought that I was just—that they were my "real" parents and I just had a little bit darker skin.

I go to this group where everybody there is adopted. It meets maybe once or twice a month, maybe a little more. We do social activities, but we always talk about adoption and what our lives are like and how we feel about it. It kind of feels useful to be able to get it out and tell other adoptees what it's like, like children your age. We like the stuff we do, but we also like being able to talk to each other really well.

Nick's reference to people who wonder about his "real" parents indicates a common mistake made by well-intentioned individuals when discussing adoption. Some adoptees insist that the parents who raised them are their real parents, while others reject the term altogether. It is more appropriate to be specific and to talk about "birth" (or "biological") and "adoptive" parents, since all of them, whether they are known or not by the adoptee, are real people with real identities. Moreover, all have a real influence in the life of the adopted adolescent.

As an adoptee, Nick is fortunate to be able to integrate two powerful influences that shape his identity: namely, his birth family and his adoptive family. While open adoptions are becoming more commonplace, most adoptees are faced with knowing little, if anything, about their biological family origins. Discriminatory laws remain on the books and continue to deny teenagers knowledge about their birth parents, medical histories, possible siblings, and so on, until they reach the age of eighteen. At this age of majority, state laws usually allow adoptees to request access to their records, but even then information may be withheld, if it is available at all.

Nick's case is remarkably different. Because Nick's is a transracial adoption, when people see him with his adoptive parents it quickly becomes obvious that he is adopted. Furthermore, since he knows his birth mother and brother, should he ever decide he wants to meet his birth father, he can always ask them for his name and whereabouts. The open nature of Nick's adoption circumvents the problem of access to identity information; it is not restricted by outdated laws that privilege the rights of parents over those of adopted young people.

Whether adoptions are done in the innovative open manner or follow the traditional closed approach, the presence of adoptees in school raises questions for teachers who may inadvertently send biased messages to students and families. Schools help to maintain the higher status of families connected biologically by reproducing mainstream definitions of family. For instance, a school form that asks simply for "mother's name" and "father's name" dishonors the reality of the multiple parents in a complex family configuration like Nick's. Similarly, students and parents should be able to check or write in more than one category if authorities insist on asking students to identify themselves by racial group.

In addition, assignments to chart family trees in social studies or biology classes typically privilege biological ancestors and descendants, making it difficult for adoptees to participate fully. For adoptees who do have relevant information, fitting it all into the traditional linear family tree model poses a challenge. Quite simply, their huge family tree diagrams would look more like forests. For adoptees who don't have access to their birth families' histories, having to fill in the tree chart as if they were not adopted can feel dishonest at best and like a betrayal of family ties at worst. Moreover, adopted young people are often keenly aware of the contingent nature of their identities, as reflected in various family ties, family names, legal documents such as birth certificates (which in their case have already been falsified or "amended"), and other identity markers most people take for granted. Simply to appear more inclusive, if not to become more affirming of the array of student identities, schools can change to accommodate the reality of complex families that have been formed through adoption or otherwise.

REBECCA FLORENTINA: COMING OUT SAFELY IN HIGH SCHOOL

Rebecca Florentina is seventeen years old and attends public school in the small New England city of West Blueridge, which has a visible and active lesbian, gay, bisexual, and transgender (LGBT) community. Shortly before the time of her interview, Rebecca "came out"; that is, she began acknowledging her homosexuality openly. Rebecca wears her hair boyishly short and dyed green, and a string of multicolored pride rings hangs around her neck. During the interview she wore a T-shirt that read, "I'm not a dyke, but my girlfriend is." Rebecca belongs to the school's gay-straight alliance (GSA), one of a growing number of school-sanctioned clubs that provide a sense of safety and support to LGBT students and their allies. She describes the level of tolerance of homosexuality in her community and school:

> When I came out, my friends were awesome. I didn't lose a single one. So it was pretty cool. I think, in West Blueridge, if you don't approve of the lifestyle, you don't say it, because you're going to be offending

a heck of a lot of people. There are so many lesbians around. I think if people do mind, they keep their mouths shut. I just think that because we're in West Blueridge we get treated so much better than people in other schools. I mean, people have gotten killed. You know the school is accepting because the school has a gay-straight alliance. I'm in the school's GSA. We've gone around and asked teachers to put Safe Zone stickers on their door. The majority of them actually have them on their doors. Most of the teachers don't mind. There's a couple that are kind of iffy.

There are probably three of us who are "out" at school. I walk around wearing this shirt: "I'm not a dyke, but my girlfriend is." I'm lesbian, butch lesbian, whatever you want to call it. I just want people to know that I'm not a little femmie. That's basically how I define myself.

Rebecca identifies herself not simply as a lesbian student. It is important to her that people recognize her as a particular kind of lesbian, an out, butch lesbian (or, in her words, "not a little femmie").

As an openly gay student, Rebecca has taken advantage of the GSA offered at her school. There she has found allies who share her interest in increasing the visibility of LGBT issues and in promoting a more tolerant atmosphere. But other comments Rebecca makes suggest that not all spaces in the school make her feel equally safe to express aspects of her identity:

I'm in music, and everybody there knows about me and my girlfriend, because we're both in music. They're all cool with it. And if they're not, they don't say anything. But I'll be reluctant—like I wear my sweatshirt [over the T-shirt] all the time, but I'll be reluctant to wear this in the halls, or in the bathroom or something. I don't wear this T-shirt when I'm alone in school. I don't think teachers could do anything. You're not going to stop the kids from doing something they want to do. If I'm in the hall and some other kid is in the hall, and there's no teachers around, he can hit me if he wants. Or she.

Clothing arises as an important marker of identity in Rebecca's story. She talks about her desire to increase lesbian visibility within the school by wearing her "dyke" T-shirt. At the same time, she worries about other people's reactions and threats to her physical safety. In some schools, dress codes prohibit students from wearing T-shirts that might be considered offensive, or that contain a message that might distract students from learning. Rebecca's T-shirt, no doubt, would present a challenge for teachers and administrators in charge of enforcing dress codes in such schools. It is worth bearing in mind the important role that freedom of expression plays in adolescent identity, particularly for students like Rebecca. Being able to decide where and when to display her T-shirt serves a significant function in Rebecca's exploration of her newfound identity as an out lesbian.

Rebecca's fears for her safety came up at numerous times in the interview, as well as her belief that teachers play an important role in the extent to which she feels free to express who she is:

> This girl said, "Oh, you faggot" in one of my classes, but I don't know if the teacher heard or not. Students just say "faggot" all the time. It makes me angry. I mean, there's nothing you can do, really. It made me feel so much safer when I had a teacher say, in his class the first day, "There will be no swearing, there will be no slurs like 'faggot' or whatever in my class." I have had only two teachers in four years of high school that have ever said something like that. I think if you had to hold your tongue in class without saying that stuff, it would help a little bit.
>
> When you get out in the halls, it's a totally different atmosphere. People act basically the opposite of how they act in class. The climate is like, if you're generally like everybody else, you're fine. But if you're totally opposite of what everybody else looks like and acts like, you'll get shoved into a locker or something, or told to shut up. All we can do is hope to educate teachers, because there's kids in middle school getting beat up in the hallways because of homophobia, and the teachers don't do anything about it.

Even when teachers make it a point to set standards for respectful interaction in their individual classrooms, there is often a discrepancy, as Rebecca points out, between students' behavior in class and their actions in common areas, such as the school hallways, cafeteria, library, or restrooms. This discrepancy may reflect the need for some students to gain a sense of control over the ways their identities are being constructed by their schooling experience. For example, one common way adolescent identities get expressed is through resistance to adult norms. If teachers simply impose what may seem like superficial "political correctness" about the use of slurs and put-downs, then students may well reject these values when teachers are out of sight and out of earshot.

Similarly, Rebecca's remarks about the messages students receive from school curricula are particularly insightful:

> The health class in the high school looks at same-sex whatever, or queer whatever, in a derogatory way. The curriculum says, "Here's these lesbian people, and we should accept them," something like that. It's not like,

"Here's the great things about being gay." It's like, "Here's all the things that happen, and things that people think of them." And I don't even think it's that accepting. It's just like, "There are people who are gay." And that's the whole curriculum. And, "Here's a dental dam," and that's it. And the whole class would laugh, and they'd move on. So I think if you want to educate people better, get the health teachers to put better curriculum for teaching about same-sex, transgender, anything. Because it's looked at in a negative way instead of in a positive way.

Rebecca articulates the limits of supposedly inclusive health lessons, which do make mention of lesbians, but then don't provide students with accurate, possibly controversial information about real lesbian lives and gay-related health issues. Merely mentioning a dental dam in the context of a lesson on safer sex, for instance, only gives students something to snicker about, rather than increasing their understanding of lifesaving health concerns. Clearly, teachers need assistance not only with gathering appropriate resources but also with fashioning their own personal approaches to presenting issues that may make themselves or their students—not to mention parents or administrators—uncomfortable. By glossing over and oversimplifying LGBT issues in the way Rebecca describes, teachers reinforce simplistic labeling that can restrict the lives of LGBT students.

Rebecca sums up her assessment of how much teachers at her school support her lesbian identity as follows:

We have an English teacher who has a lesbian daughter. That's the only reason he brings stuff up like that. Now he's talking about gay issues, like every other day in class. He doesn't talk about his daughter, but he's letting the kids read books that are very liberal and very queer-friendly. I think the teachers who are like that are the teachers who have a lesbian daughter, or are gay themselves, or who have the kids in class saying, "I'm a lesbian. You're offending me in class, like me and my other friends." That's the only reason they do it.

Lesbians are just like everybody else. I mean, everybody sees it as somebody who's different and not normal. But it's just your sexuality. I don't identify myself as like, "Hi, I'm Rebecca and I'm a lesbian." It's like, "This is me, and this is my sexuality." That's as far as I'm going to go with it. I mean, I'll wear a T-shirt or something—I'm proud of who I am. But by wearing this T-shirt, all I'm saying is that here's a happy kid, I'm fine, whatever.

Teachers should value open-mindedness, I think, and being inclusive of everybody. It's hard to be politically correct in everything, every second in every word you say. But I don't know. There are some teachers you just don't want to approach sometimes, because they are very closed.

We cannot overstate the significant role played by the teacher in establishing the climate in the classroom. Even when teachers attempt to share power and run their classes in a democratic fashion, students may still see the classroom as belonging to the adult authority figure. Rebecca placed as much responsibility on her teachers as she took herself. For example, she expresses appreciation for the teachers who make an effort to use inclusive language, who set class expectations for tolerance, and who bring gay content into their lessons. At the same time, she doesn't wait for the world to change before she herself takes action. In the way she negotiates the expression of her unfolding lesbian identity, Rebecca is an inspiring example of the power of one individual to make a difference, simply by insisting on being true to herself. (See "Still in the Shadows? Lesbian, Gay, Bisexual, and Transgender Students in U.S. Schools" by Michael Sadowski on pp. 117–135 of this volume.)

IMPLICATIONS OF COMPLEX IDENTITIES FOR EDUCATIONAL PRACTICE

While identity construction might appear to be a profoundly personal matter, it is also a social and political matter, precisely because it is deeply implicated in the struggle to develop a sense of self within a social sphere. Thus, these are not just individual issues; rather, they have implications for educational practice, as well as for the social and cultural climate created in schools. These implications relate to teachers' professional development as well as school policy and practices. For educators who choose to provide a safe space for the free exploration of adolescent identities in schools, a number of important lessons can be drawn from the students' experiences presented in this chapter.

The themes of choice and flexibility are crucial for youth. Because their identities are in flux and more complicated than static labels can hope to convey, neither of the young people featured here would appreciate being labeled permanently with any one descriptor. For example, Rebecca is not simply a lesbian; she wants to be known as a butch lesbian, and not a "femmie." Furthermore, at the same time she makes visible her lesbian identity and advocates for its equality with other identities, she insists that she is more than her sexuality. She also identifies as Italian and as a musician, for example. Similarly, Nick is African American, European American, Native American, Jewish, and Christian simultaneously. He is also part of and loved by the members of both his birth family and his adoptive family, all of whom are real family to him. Schools need to catch up to the fast-changing identifications being created and re-created as today's students make their way through complicated social contexts.

Opportunities for peer association are valuable to students, in class and out. In their own ways, Nick and Rebecca articulate the benefits they gain from speaking with other young people who share similar situations. For example, Nick discussed the importance of his adoptees' group, and Rebecca mentioned the meaning she finds as an active member of the GSA. Although none existed at her school, Rebecca mentioned that she would join an Italian American cultural club, were one available; similarly, Nick might benefit from participating in a multicultural interest group, particularly one organized specifically for multiracial students.

While both students expressed the opinion that "teachers can't really do anything" about harassment in school, it is nonetheless incumbent upon educators to create school environments that are free from bullying. Teachers can do more to share power with students in order to develop school climates that genuinely respect diversity. Specifically, teachers can work with students in ways that go further than forcing them to pay lip service to politically correct verbiage only when adults are around.

How do teachers invite students to co-create respectful school climates? Rebecca's case suggests that modeling behavior that takes LGBT concerns seriously is one place to start. Elsewhere in her interview, Rebecca talked about a teacher who commented casually at the end of class that he had seen an article in the newspaper about a gay issue. Rebecca described feeling accepted and affirmed when he unexpectedly brought up a topic of concern to her as a lesbian. Having such conversations publicly, within earshot of other students, sends a clear message that LGBT topics are not taboo. Moreover, students learn that gay issues can be discussed seriously by gays and straights alike.

Teachers need more time to focus on issues of identity and diversity, both through their preservice education and through inservice professional development. Although schools and colleges of education are devoting more attention to concerns of diversity and identity, there is still much work to be done. Teachers who are planning curricula around themes of family heritage, genetics, or genealogy, for example, might benefit from professional time set aside to think through the implications of their lesson plans for marginalized groups, such as adopted, bicultural, or LGBT youth. Using curricula to reflect the realities of nontraditional families, such as those headed by two lesbian moms as well as families formed through adoption, invites all students to feel freer to express their unique identities in a climate of openness, safety, and mutual respect. Finally, providing teachers with time to reflect on and reconsider their own ideas about race and ethnicity, sexual orientation, and changing definitions of family can help schools become more affirming of the complex identities of today's students.

JOAQUÍN ROSARIO: BEGINNING ADULTHOOD WITH A STRONG SENSE OF SELF

We conclude our exploration of adolescent identity with the words of a man in the next stage of his life, young adulthood. Joaquín Rosario is twenty-two years old, and he currently attends one of the most prestigious liberal arts colleges in the nation. He grew up in poverty in a large urban area where he attended public schools, excelling so much that he received a full scholarship to the college. Joaquín confessed that in high school he had the "freedom" to excel academically because, besides being a strong student, he was an accomplished athlete. This identity gave him tremendous credibility in the eyes of his peers. But claiming his identity as both an urban Puerto Rican and a good student was not always easy. How could he be both in a context that only valued one or the other?

Joaquín noticed at the college's orientation that he was one of only two Latinos in the entering class. In spite of this context, it took going to a college steeped in privilege for Joaquín to be given the opportunity to study his heritage. It was after this experience that he began the process of claiming both identities of Puerto Rican and scholar, and along the way he picked up even more ways to define himself. Thus, Joaquín has emerged with a strong sense of self, comfortable with the complexity of his identity. And although he is "only" Puerto Rican, Joaquín recognizes that even what may seem to be a fairly straightforward identity is more complicated than it may appear. He says he can neither "limit his identity" nor define it solely in terms of his ancestral homeland. While he feels connected to the island of Puerto Rico through family stories and through cultural traits such as language, music, food, and clothing, to name a few, Joaquín remarks that his identity is always more complex than "just one thing." Here are his thoughts about who he is and how he arrived at this point:

Physically, I can only trace my roots as far back as my great-grandparents. One of my great-grandmothers is still alive. She's ninety-eight years old and can still remember how she had to fetch water from the well, and how her house was made of wooden planks and sheets of aluminum with a dirt floor. Historically, however, I am aware that as a Puerto Rican I come from a long history of merging and mixing of bloods and cultures. The indigenous inhabitants of the island now called Puerto Rico; the European traders, conquistadors, and slave owners; the African slaves (who were a diverse group to begin with) that were brought to the island both to work and be traded, are all ingredients of who I am.

But I cannot limit my identity to the history of the island where all four of my grandparents were born. Being born and raised in the urban center of a Northeast city, many more things have been factors in molding my life and my identity. I am an urban, bilingual, heterosexual, Roman Catholic, Puerto Rican male that enjoys listening to salsa as much as hip-hop, who can savor the taste of *tostones* as much as a side of collard greens. I can wear baggy jeans, a "hoodie," and "Timbs," put on a three-piece suit with high polished shoes, or a *guayabera* and Dockers, and fit in anywhere I go.

My multiple cultures allow me to move seamlessly across borders. I can speak proper English with an almost undetectable accent, I can talk as much trash about "yo momma" as anyone else in my neighborhood, or I can drop some knowledge while spitting/speaking my Spanish/Spanglish slang. My identity cannot be classified or contained into one or two categories. I am always much more than just one thing.

It is clear that border-crossing for Joaquín is not simply a metaphor, but an expression of his lived reality. Joaquín can and does move literally across boundaries marking different neighborhoods and even nations, as well as different social contexts and linguistic communities. This mobility leads to the hybridity, adaptability, and freedom of choice he enjoys.

LEARNING FROM YOUNG PEOPLE WITH COMPLEX IDENTITIES

Unfortunately, not all young people have the privileges that Joaquín enjoys. As elementary and high schools move to affirm students in their identity explorations, students will have fewer reasons to struggle through adolescence in silence and confusion before claiming their selfhood. It is imperative that all educators understand how race, gender, and other differences matter in school. Many teachers, particularly those at the secondary level, would rather focus on the content they teach than on the emotional and social concerns of their students. But it is becoming more obvious that these cannot be separated.

In her research at Madison High, Laurie Olsen found that the great majority of teachers did not believe that they needed additional preparation to serve the new diversity at the school. Most reported that being "color blind" was enough. Yet Olsen's research revealed tremendous discordance and rage among the students in the school, as well as a silence concerning racism and other forms of exclusion.[8] This underscores the need for teachers to come to grips with what impact identity has on students' learning and their sense of belonging at school.

For students who do not fit into tidy identity boxes, raising teachers' awareness of changing identifications among adolescents can enhance this sense of belonging. In our interviews with students who negotiate complex identities on a daily basis, they expressed a need for teachers to take notice of intolerance based on identities rendered invisible by the school. Both Nick and Rebecca spoke poignantly of the impact of harassment in the hallways, and even in classrooms, about which teachers apparently knew and did nothing.

The task of supporting the complex identities of students like Nick and Rebecca is as complex as these students are themselves. Yet as researcher Frederick Erickson has written, "When we think of culture and social identity in more fluid terms . . . we can find a foundation for educational practice that is transformative."[9] How can teachers and other educators engage in the kind of transformative practices that Erickson suggests? One way might be to envision multicultural school communities as "cultures of commitment" (to borrow a term from anthropologist Gerd Baumann).[10] These are associations of diverse individuals that cut across national, religious, ethnic, and other identifications but are united by a common purpose, a shared project and vision.

If educators, for example, united their school communities around a vision of high expectations and democratic participation for all students, schools might more effectively foster inclusive, respectful, accepting, and empowering school climates. In such environments, perhaps more students would find the freedom to explore their unfolding identities and form new identifications based not on outmoded, confining labels, but on their real needs.

NOTES

1. Sonia Nieto and Patty Bode, *Affirming Diversity: The Sociopolitical Context of Multi-cultural Education*, 5th ed. (Boston: Pearson/Allyn & Bacon, 2008); Sonia Nieto, "Lessons from Students on Creating a Chance to Dream," *Harvard Educational Review* 64, no. 4 (Winter 1994): 392–426; John Raible, "Re/Constructing Race: An Ethnography of Transracial Adoption," paper presented at the conference of Ethnography and Qualitative Research in Education, Pittsburgh, June 2002.
2. Steven F. Arvizu, "Building Bridges for the Future: Anthropological Contributions to Diversity and Classroom Practice," in Robert A. DeVillar, Christian J. Faltis, and James Cummins (eds.), *Cultural Diversity in Schools: From Rhetoric to Reality* (Albany: State University of New York Press, 1994), 75.
3. Shirley Brice Heath and Milbrey McLaughlin (eds.), *Identity and Inner-City Youth: Beyond Ethnicity and Gender* (New York: Teachers College Press, 1993), 222.
4. Shirley Brice Heath, "Race, Ethnicity, and the Defiance of Categories," in Willis D. Hawley and Anthony W. Jackson (eds.), *Toward a Common Destiny: Improving Race and Ethnic Relations in America* (San Francisco: Jossey-Bass, 1995), 45.
5. Daniel A. Yon, "Urban Portraits of Identity: On the Problem of Knowing Culture and Identity in Intercultural Studies," *Journal of Intercultural Studies* 21, no. 2 (2000): 143.
6. Raquel Romberg, "Saints in the Barrio: Shifting, Hybrid, and Bicultural Practices in a Puerto Rican Community," *MultiCultural Review* 5, no. 2 (1996): 16–25.
7. Laurie Olsen, *Made in America: Immigrant Students in Our Public Schools* (New York: New Press, 1997), 239.
8. Olsen, *Made in America*.
9. Frederick Erickson, "Culture, Politics, and Educational Practice," *Educational Foundations* 4, no. 2 (1990): 22.
10. Gerd Baumann, *The Multicultural Riddle: Rethinking National, Ethnic, and Religious Identities* (New York: Routledge, 1999), 153.

From Understanding to Action

Ten Principles of Practice

MICHAEL SADOWSKI

Throughout *Adolescents at School*, the contributors have drawn on the voices and experiences of young people to illustrate many facets of identity in vivid terms. Broadening and deepening readers' understanding of this complex set of issues has been a primary objective of this book. But in the enterprise of American education, where real adolescents enter real schools every day, a mere academic understanding is not enough. Thus, the second purpose of the book has been to provide educators with ideas for action: ways they can work with students to help put them on a course toward higher achievement and better lives. With this purpose in mind, many of the authors herein have provided practical recommendations that outline how educators and school communities can work toward a variety of goals. Pedro Noguera's recommendation to assign student groups to avoid self-segregation and Ellen Brantlinger's call for lessons that expand students' understanding about the contributions of poor and working-class Americans are two such examples.

Yet the practical implications of the concepts in this book extend beyond specific curriculum content or classroom organization strategies, as valuable and important as both of these may be. The previous edition of *Adolescents at School* ended with six central principles that emerged from the book's nine chapters, guiding notions that teachers, administrators, and school staff could apply in a variety of ways to their daily work with students. This expanded second edition points toward ten such "principles of practice" for supporting positive student identity development, learning, and success:

1. *Listen to students.* Perhaps the most recurrent theme among these chapters has to do with the importance of listening: hearing what students themselves have to say about who they are, how they see themselves in the school environment, and what they believe is expected of them as learners. The students who participated in the Fort Wayne workshops (highlighted in Thomas Fowler-Finn's piece) probably taught educators more about how to close the black/white achievement gap than did any of their analyses of test scores, dropout statistics, or other quantitative data. Similarly, the three students profiled in Michael Wehmeyer's "Making Their Own Way" reveal much about how students with disabilities might view themselves, their disabilities, and their learning. While we certainly cannot make assumptions about all students of color or all students with disabilities based on profiles like these, they remind us that students are at the core of our work and may hold more of the answers to their own success than we realize. Creating opportunities to listen to our students is therefore a crucial element in any effort to raise achievement.

2. *Make no excuses, but ask a lot of questions.* Under accountability-based reform, urban schools serving large percentages of poor children, who are often disproportionately students of color, are held to many of the same achievement standards as schools in higher-income areas. This is often called the "make no excuses" approach to improving education for low-income students. Poverty, racism, and other institutional factors are, in a sense, discounted, based on the assumption that such excuses only perpetuate inequities by encouraging separate standards for children living under more difficult circumstances.

While it is certainly true that lower standards serve no students well—least of all those for whom education may be one of the few tickets out of difficult socioeconomic conditions—it is essential to keep asking tough questions about why large numbers of these young people do not succeed academically. If, as Pedro Noguera and some of the researchers of the "acting white" theory suggest, for example, students of color perceive that they have fewer opportunities than their white classmates, it is incumbent on educators to do what they can to amend the factors that perpetuate these beliefs, even while they hold a uniformly high bar for achievement.

For very different reasons, Michael Kimmel calls on us to ask the right questions rather than accept mere excuses about school violence, such as the facile explanation that it is simply the result of media violence and therefore requires no examination of our culture or our schools. And Michelle Galley encourages us not simply to accept the "fact" that girls do better on tests of verbal ability and boys do better on math exams. Galley suggests that we consider *why* such conditions exist, *how* the work of educators exacerbates these conditions, and *what teachers can do* to support boys and girls as learners simultaneously.

3. Be willing to take risks. Beverly Daniel Tatum observes in her commentary that opening the conversation about race can seem like risky business in many school cultures. Yet, only by starting this dialogue can educators begin to understand—and break down—some of the barriers to school success that disproportionately affect students of color. Similarly, as I note in my own chapter, engaging in an honest assessment of the ways a school's environment affects lesbian, gay, bisexual, and transgender (LGBT) students is a difficult and often painful task. Taking action to improve the school climate for LGBT students can be even tougher, given the opposition that can arise in response to such measures. Ethnicity, ability, gender, social class— none of these is an easy topic to grapple with in a school community, but taking the risk to deal with these issues frankly and productively is necessary if we truly aim to serve all students well.

4. Rethink the curriculum. Ellen Brantlinger, Stacey Lee, Eric Toshalis, and other authors in this book suggest that teaching in a way that is responsive to the identities of all students requires rethinking what topics are represented in the curriculum. Although revising curriculum to represent diverse identities might be dismissed by some as "politically correct," it is important to remember that no curriculum is identity neutral. Curriculum as it has traditionally been developed in U.S. schools reflects choices about which aspects of American identities are to be represented and which are not. While much of these choices are based on centuries of our history and embedded cultural conditions that will not change overnight, we should at the very least be asking whether our curriculum truly reflects the identities of all the students in our schools as much as is practical. As Arthur Lipkin has aptly said about curriculum, "expurgation is dishonesty," yet such exclusion is often the rule in the slowly changing culture of schools.

5. Challenge yourself and your assumptions. Considering aspects of identity also means taking a look at ourselves: who we are, the experiences we've had, and the belief systems we've acquired along the way. For example, are we influenced in any way by the model minority or perpetual foreigner stereotypes about which Stacey Lee writes? Do we, as Angela Valenzuela suggests, subconsciously label immigrant students as less capable, not "honors material?" Do we assume that all families are based on the traditional model, or that all students who belong to a certain group experience their identities in a similar way? Do we dismiss the identities and experiences of transgender students as something we "just don't understand?" As products of our culture, we are all susceptible to stereotypes, assumptions, expectations, and prejudices that affect the way we see adolescents. Facing and challenging these assumptions—and perhaps questioning our own identities in the process—is an important step toward approaching our work in ways that reflect a better understanding of our students.

6. Offer diverse opportunities for students to succeed. Serving the wide diversity of students in our schools means, as a first step, making our schools more diverse. This does not mean returning to the model of the "shopping mall" middle or high school or abandoning a focus on core curriculum. But if we are, as Michael Nakkula suggests, to provide multiple opportunities for young people to invest psychic energy and explore diverse possibilities for themselves, then a "one-size-fits-all" approach to schooling will not suffice. We need to be willing to consider a wide range of curricular and extracurricular options—everything from mentoring programs to heterogeneous grouping to afterschool clubs for multiracial students—if we wish to encourage students' investment in school and their achievement.

The teaching implications of Gardner's theory of multiple intelligences are also important in this regard. As Gardner notes, schooling has traditionally privileged only two of the eight intelligences adolescents embody—linguistic and logical-mathematical. Rethinking the way we teach so that we tap into and develop *all* the valuable intelligences our students possess is key to fostering a belief in all students—not just those who write or do mathematics well—that they are learners and thinkers with the potential to make valuable contributions to society.

7. Form and facilitate relationships. As is evident throughout the chapters of this book, the importance of relationships in the school lives of adolescents cannot be overstated. Suárez-Orozco, Qin, and Amthor illustrate how positive relational connections with educators and peers can make a crucial difference in the school engagement and performance of immigrant students, for whom American middle and high schools can be overwhelmingly disorienting places. Yet, even for students born in the United States, relationships in the school context clearly are central to how they view themselves, whether they feel connected to others, and whether they feel they belong— all of which have much to do with both identity and learning.

Whether they are gay or heterosexual, black or white, male or female— whether they have a disability or not—students learn better and develop in more positive ways when they feel they have connections to others who are also involved in the teaching and learning enterprise. This does not mean, of course, that teachers should attempt to become friends with adolescents in the same way that their peers do. It does mean, however, that educators can foster students' success best when they open themselves up to genuine adult/ student relationships in which, as Nakkula says, "it is clear to the student that she matters to the adult as much as the adult matters to her." More specifically, student groups such as the gay-straight alliances I recommend or the organizations for multiracial students suggested by Raible and Nieto can be crucial lines of connection for students who otherwise might feel isolated or marginalized in their school settings.

8. *Keep it relevant.* As Toshalis states, and other authors throughout this volume suggest, adolescents yearn for discourses in school in which they can engage with the issues, questions, dilemmas, and concerns that are most salient to them. This is not to suggest, of course, that all school curriculum content that isn't related to burning teen issues be abandoned; it is, however, to suggest that teachers who truly want to support students' identity development and learning (and their identity development *toward* learning) search for ways to highlight the relevance of their course content to the real world. If adolescents can find positive answers at school to questions such as "Why should I learn this?" or "Who cares?" then the chances that learning will matter to them—and perhaps become deeply incorporated into their sense of who they are—will be that much greater.

9. *Leave* no *child behind.* One of the most offensive things I have observed in fourteen years of working in and with public schools is that some students seem to believe—perhaps because they are led to believe—that the school does not really belong to them, but to other, more "mainstream" students. As Angela Valenzuela points out, this can be a particular problem for

immigrant students, who often get placed in inferior learning environments and closed out of the most enriching experiences a school offers before they are even able to demonstrate what they can do. Students with disabilities, according to Wehmeyer, often face similar forms of segregation at school. In the research feature on "acting white theory," University of North Carolina researcher William Darity, Jr., notes how students of color sometimes stay away from AP classes because they view them as "belonging to the white students," and Lee demonstrates how many Asian American students don't even perceive themselves to *be* Americans.

The charge of U.S. public schools is to educate all students—and all means *all*. It means offering the best education possible to every student; making equitable efforts to ensure that all students' identities are represented in the curriculum; and (to borrow the Bush Administration's signature education reform slogan) truly leaving *no* child behind simply because she or he is not part of the majority.

10. Encourage students to break the rules. No, I am not suggesting that teachers advocate plagiarism, gambling on school grounds, or food fights in the cafeteria. Rather, I am suggesting that educators can help students' positive development as learners and as people by encouraging them to question societal "rules" that often place oppressive limitations on what adolescents believe they can do and be:

- "Girls should be quiet and not show off their knowledge, especially in math."
- "Boys should be tough, stoic, and self-sufficient, and, when they do have strong emotions, should express them only through anger."
- "African American and Latino students should stay away from AP courses, the gay-straight alliance, and any other areas of the school dominated by whites."
- "Immigrant students should be compliant and grateful for any opportunities the school affords, even if these are inferior to those available to native-born students."

As the authors in this volume suggest, these are just a few of the culturally embedded negative belief systems that can work their way into the thinking of adolescents and limit their success in school and beyond. Teachers, therefore, need to be alert to these ways of thinking among their students, work sensitively toward making students aware of them, and help them reframe their thinking toward what Nakkula calls "creating possibility."

Amid the fast-paced, day-to-day world of schools, it is all too easy to lose sight of the fact that real adolescents are what middle and high school education is all about. Getting to know more about this primary constituency, in all its fascinating complexity, is not a frivolous detour from a hard-driving focus on academic performance; rather, it is a crucial aspect of the work of educators, one that perhaps has a greater bearing on school performance than any other. Our hope is that this book has supported reflection, understanding, and action toward the goal of enriching adolescents' learning and their lives. This is, after all, the reason we teach.

Acknowledgments

The idea for the first edition of *Adolescents at School* grew out of my early experiences as a high school teacher. I sensed that issues of racism, sexism, classism, and other cultural forces strongly influenced my students' identity formation as well as their school engagement and performance, yet I lacked the breadth of knowledge to understand fully what I was observing. I invited a diverse group of authors—teachers, administrators, researchers, and others—to address these questions and was fortunate that nearly every person I invited to contribute to the original book chose to do so. I have been extremely gratified by the extent to which the book seems to have struck a chord with preservice teachers, teacher educators, and professionals working in secondary schools. (Clearly, I have not been the only teacher for whom these questions have been important.) Without the expert insight and practical knowledge of the original group of authors, the first edition of *Adolescents at School* would never have had the success it has enjoyed, and this second edition could never have been remotely imaginable.

Readers' responses to the first edition of *Adolescents at School* have helped to inform my choice of additional material for the second edition. Once again, I identified the teachers, professors, and researchers I thought could best articulate what I thought was important to add to this second edition, and again I was extremely fortunate that just about everyone I asked to contribute said yes. I am immensely grateful to the new authors who have helped me to make this an even better book—and have done so with more depth and clarity than I had ever hoped for.

Students in my courses in the Master of Arts of Teaching (MAT) Program at Bard College have been an especially helpful audience as I have considered new directions for the book. Through their work both in the graduate school classroom and in their middle and high school practicum placements, they have brought out new questions about the issues raised in the various chapters, suggested topics for additional chapters, and fleshed out in practical terms (and in their own individual ways) what it really means to teach with an awareness of adolescent identity and its cultural influences. Many of these students' ideas are written between the lines throughout this second volume.

Perhaps the truest test of the original edition's merit began in the fall of 2007, when principal Daisy Fontanez and assistant principals Kristin Arndt and Shadia Alvarez invited me to codesign and coteach a tenth-grade advisory curriculum with teacher Meg Hart at New Day Academy, one of Bard's partner public schools in the South Bronx. We designed a unit addressing many of the same issues that are central to *Adolescents at School,* and at the end of the unit students chose chapters of the book around which to base their final projects. The students' names and projects are too numerous to list here, but the insights of these "real experts" on the adolescent experience have also deeply informed many of the changes to this second edition.

As I have suggested elsewhere in this book, efforts to improve adolescent students' learning continue to focus more on testing and accountability than on identity and culture. I would like to think that *Adolescents at School* is helping to change that, and I am extremely grateful to several people who have supported me greatly by sharing this vision: Douglas Clayton, director of the Harvard Education Press (HEP), who believed in this book and its mission enough to publish it a second time and whose ongoing support for my work has been invaluable; Doug's colleagues at HEP, particularly Caroline Chauncey, Laura Clos, Tracy Patruno, Jeffrey Perkins, Dody Riggs, and Sheila Walsh, who have helped propel both the book and me forward not only through their hard work and expertise but their unwavering enthusiasm about the project; Ric Campbell, director of the Bard MAT Program, who has made an exceptional commitment to making issues of identity and culture central to teacher education; the William T. Grant Foundation, which generously supported publication of the first edition; and, on a more personal note, my husband Robb Fessler, an educator who has been a constant source of both support and inspiration through his deep commitment to the learning and lives of all his adolescent students.

Finally, I wish to thank from the depth of my heart all the young people whose stories are heard in these pages. It is to them that I dedicate this book. I truly believe that their willingness to open up their worlds and their stories to the people who interviewed them—and thus to the teachers, administrators, school staff members, and students who read *Adolescents at School*—will help make schools better places for the adolescents who come after them.

About the Contributors

Ramona Fruja Amthor is a doctoral candidate in the departments of education and sociology at Michigan State University, focusing on social foundations of education, immigrant youth, and ethnicity studies. Her scholarly interests include the intersections among immigration, ethnicity, and citizenship; multicultural and global education; and the teaching of social studies in increasingly diverse environments. She has previously worked with youth in multiple multicultural contexts, including the U.S.-based Upward Bound program and the American University in Bulgaria. Her teaching work has focused on such courses as "Human Diversity," "Power and Opportunity in Social Institutions," "Curriculum in Its Social Context," and "Global Diversity and Interdependence."

Darcia Harris Bowman has written about school security and health issues for *Education Week*, a newspaper that reports on school policy issues for a national readership that includes school administrators, state and federal policymakers, and teachers. During her five years at the paper, Bowman also reported on charter schools and vouchers, covered state education policy, and contributed to coverage of the aftermath of September 11th. Since 2004, Bowman has been a freelance writer and editor in the Washington, D.C., area.

Ellen Brantlinger is emeritus professor of curriculum and instruction at Indiana University. She is the author of *Who Benefits from Special Education? Remediating (Fixing) Other People's Children* (Erlbaum, 2006), *Dividing Classes: How the Middle Class Negotiates and Rationalizes School Advantage* (Routledge/Farmer, 2003), *Fighting for Darla: A Case Study of a Pregnant Adolescent with Autism* (Teachers College Press, 1994, with Susan Klein and Samuel Guskin), *Sterilization of People with Mental Disabilities: Issues, Perspectives, and Cases* (Greenwood, 2004), and *The Politics of Social Class in Secondary School: Views of Affluent and Impoverished Youth* (Teachers College Press, 1993). She also is the author of numerous journal articles, most notably "Using Ideology: Cases of Non-Recognition of the Politics of Research and Practice in Special Education," *Review of Educational Research* 67, no. 4 (Winter 1997): 425–460.

Theresa Squires Collins, a high school teacher since 1992, is a faculty member at the Francis W. Parker School in Chicago. Her primary interests are teaching writing and American literature, particularly African American writers of the Harlem Renaissance and American women writers. Her research interests include classroom gender dynamics, minority student achievement, and teacher-student relationships and their impact on learning. She was formerly a teacher and staff developer at Evanston (Ill.) Township High School and has taught a course to preservice teachers at Northwestern University entitled "Teaching and Learning in Social and Cultural Contexts."

Thomas Fowler-Finn is the superintendent of the Cambridge (Mass.) Public Schools. He began his educational career as a teacher in his hometown of Pittsfield, Massachusetts, and at age twenty-five became a teaching principal in Vermont. He also has served as a supervising principal, assistant superintendent for curriculum and instruction, and superintendent of schools over the past twenty-three years in New York, Indiana, and Massachusetts. In addition, he has served as a Soros Foundation consultant to the government of Albania, launched the first national education summit for mayors and superintendents, served as president of the national organization Large City School Superintendents, presented at national conferences, written numerous articles, and received state and national recognition for leadership in education. He was the founder of the Network for Equity in Student Achievement, a national organization of urban school districts working to close the achievement gap between minority and majority students.

Michelle Galley is a senior writer at the Academy for Educational Development, a Washington, D.C.–based nonprofit organization. She writes about the organization's efforts to improve education, health, and economic opportunities in the United States and in developing countries throughout the world. Previously, she was a staff writer for *Education Week*, where, in addition to gender issues in education, she wrote about such topics as philanthropic giving to schools, service learning, school partnerships with community organizations and businesses, and education in the states of Idaho, Oklahoma, and Texas.

Howard Gardner is the Hobbs Professor of Cognition and Education at the Harvard Graduate School of Education and senior director of Harvard Project Zero. Among numerous honors, Gardner received a MacArthur Fellowship in 1981. He has received honorary degrees from twenty-two colleges and universities. In 2005 he was selected by *Foreign Policy* and *Prospect* magazines as one of the 100 most influential public intellectuals in the world. The author of over twenty books translated into twenty-seven languages, and several hundred articles, Gardner is best known in educational circles for his theory of multiple intelligences, a critique of the notion that there exists but a single human intelligence that can be assessed by standard psychometric instruments. He has also written extensively on creativity, leadership, and professional ethics. His latest book, *Five Minds for the Future*, was published in April 2007 by the Harvard Business School Press.

Michael S. Kimmel is a professor of sociology at Stony Brook University. His books include *Changing Men* (Sage, 1987), *Men Confront Pornography* (Meridian, 1990), *Men's Lives* (7th ed., Allyn & Bacon, 2007), *Against the Tide: Profeminist Men in the United States, 1776–1990* (Beacon Press, 1992), *The Politics of Manhood* (Temple University Press, 1995), *Manhood in America: A Cultural History* (Free Press, 1996; Oxford, 2006), and *The Gendered Society* (Oxford University Press, 2006). His newest book is *Guyland: The Perilous World Where Boys Become Men* (HarperCollins, 2008), a study of young men aged 16–26. He also edits *Men and Masculinities*, an interdisciplinary scholarly journal. He is the spokesperson for the National Organization for Men Against Sexism and lectures extensively on college campuses in the United States and abroad.

Stacey J. Lee is a professor of educational policy studies at the University of Wisconsin-Madison. She is the author of *Unraveling the Model Minority Stereotype: Listening to Asian American Youth* (Teachers College Press, 1996) and *Up Against Whiteness: Race, School, and Immigrant Youth* (Teachers College Press, 2005). Her articles have appeared in such journals as the *Harvard Educational Review*, the *Journal of Negro Education, Anthropology and Education Quarterly*, and *Amerasia Journal*. Her research focuses on the ways race, class, and gender inform the educational experiences of Asian American immigrant students.

Arthur Lipkin is an associate editor of the *Journal of LGBT Youth* and a member of the Massachusetts Commission on Gay, Lesbian, Bisexual, and Transgender Youth. He also directed the Safe Colleges Program of the Governor's Commission on Gay and Lesbian Youth, the Massachusetts Department of Education's Project for the Integration of Gay and Lesbian Youth Issues in School Personnel Certification Programs, and Project 10 East at Cambridge (Mass.) Rindge and Latin School. He is the author of *Beyond Diversity Day: A Q&A on Gay and Lesbian Issues in Schools* (Rowman & Littlefield, 2003) and *Understanding Homosexuality, Changing Schools* (Westview Press, 1999). He was an instructor at the Harvard Graduate School of Education from 1993 to 1999 and taught in the Cambridge (Mass.) Public Schools for twenty years.

Deborah Meier is a senior scholar and adjunct professor at New York University's Steinhardt School of Culture, Education, and Human Development. A board member of the Coalition of Essential Schools and several other education organizations, Meier has spent more than four decades working in public education as a teacher, writer, and public advocate. She began her teaching career as a kindergarten and Head Start teacher in Chicago, Philadelphia, and New York City. She started a network of highly successful public elementary schools in East Harlem, and in 1985 she founded Central Park East Secondary School, a New York City public high school in which more than 90 percent of entering students went on to college, mostly to four-year schools. From 1997 to 2005, Meier was the founding principal of the Mission Hill School, a K–8 pilot public school in Boston. She serves on the editorial boards of *Dissent* magazine, *The Nation,* and the *Harvard Education Letter,* and has received honorary degrees from Bank Street College of Education, Bard College, Brown University, Clark University, Dartmouth College, Harvard University, Teachers College of Columbia University, Yale University, and numerous other institutions. She was a recipient of a MacArthur Fellowship in 1987, and her many articles and books include *The Power of Their Ideas: Lessons for America from a Small School in Harlem* (1995), *In Schools We Trust: Creating Communities of Learning in an Era of Testing and Standardization* (2002), *Will Standards Save Public Education?* (with J. Cohen and J. Rogers, 2000), and *Keeping School: Letters to Families from Principals of Two Small Schools* (with T. Sizer and N. F. Sizer, 2004), all published by Beacon Press.

Michael Nakkula is a practice professor of education within the Division of Applied Psychology and Human Development at the University Of Pennsylvania's Graduate School of Education, where he teaches courses on adolescent development and the intersection of counseling and education within urban public schools. Prior to assuming his current faculty position, he was the longtime codirector of Harvard's Risk and Prevention master's program, where he designed and studied a number of initiatives that support developmental opportunities for low-income youth. For this work he was named Harvard's initial recipient of the Kargman Junior Chair for Human Development and Urban Education Advancement (1998–2004). Among his many publications, Nakkula is the lead author (with Eric Toshalis) of *Understanding Youth: Adolescent Development for Educators* (Harvard Education Press, 2006).

Sonia Nieto is professor emerita of language, literacy, and culture at the University of Massachusetts, Amherst. She has taught students at all levels, from elementary through graduate school, and she continues to speak and write on multicultural education and the education of Latinos and other culturally and linguistically diverse student populations. Her book *Affirming Diversity: The Sociopolitical Context of Multicultural Education* (5th ed., Pearson/Allyn & Bacon, 2008, with coauthor Patty Bode) is widely used in teacher preparation and inservice courses. Other books include *The Light in Their Eyes: Creating Multicultural Learning Communities* (Teachers College Press, 1999), *What*

Keeps Teachers Going? (Teachers College Press, 2003) and three edited volumes: *Puerto Rican Students in U.S. Schools* (Teachers College Press, 2000); *Why We Teach* (Teachers College Press, 2005); and *Dear Paulo: Letters from Those Who Dare Teach* (Paradigm, 2008). She has received many awards for her advocacy and activism, including three honorary doctorates.

Pedro A. Noguera is a professor in the Steinhardt School of Culture, Education, and Human Development at New York University. He is also the executive director of the Metropolitan Center for Urban Education and the codirector of the Institute for the Study of Globalization and Education in Metropolitan Settings. An urban sociologist, his scholarship and research focus on the ways in which schools are influenced by social and economic conditions in the urban environment. He has served as an advisor to and engaged in collaborative research with several large urban school districts throughout the United States. He has also done research on issues related to education and economic and social development in the Caribbean, in Latin America, and in other parts of the world. Between 2000 and 2003, he served as the Judith K. Dimon Professor of Communities and Schools at the Harvard Graduate School of Education. From 1990 to 2000, he was a professor in social and cultural studies and director of the Institute for the Study of Social Change at the University of California–Berkeley.

Desirée Baolian Qin is an assistant professor of human development at Michigan State University. She received her doctoral degree from the Harvard Graduate School of Education and has done postdoctoral work at New York University and Teachers College, Columbia University. Her research focuses on adolescents from immigrant families, with a specific focus on the ways immigration, culture, gender, and ecological contexts (e.g., family and school environments) influence adolescent development. She is coeditor (with Marcelo Suárez-Orozco and Carola Suárez-Orozco) of the six-volume series *Interdisciplinary Perspectives on the New Immigration* (Routledge, 2001), and coeditor (with Marcelo Suárez-Orozco) of *Globalization: Education and Culture in the New Millennium* (University of California Press, 2004). Her research has appeared in *Anthropology and Education Quarterly* and *International Migration Review*. Her most recent work on Chinese and Sudanese American adolescents will be published in the *Journal of Youth and Adolescence, Family Relations, Youth and Society*, and *New Directions in Child and Adolescent Development*.

John Raible is an assistant professor for diversity and curriculum studies at the University of Nebraska–Lincoln. He works at the intersection of teacher education and family education. His research focuses on multicultural identities within interracial contexts, such as in interracial families formed through adoption. He worked for fifteen years as a multicultural educator in public schools in a number of settings, including New Mexico, California, and New York. He has taught "Introduction to Multicultural Education" at the University of Massachusetts and at Westfield State College in Massachusetts. He also has worked as a consultant on cultural identity and adoption and is one of the adult adoptees featured in the film "Struggle for Identity: Issues in Transracial Adoption."

Michael Sadowski is an assistant professor in the Master of Arts in Teaching (MAT) Program at Bard College, based in New York City and Annandale-on-Hudson, New York, where his course, "Identity, Culture, and the Classroom," explores many of the issues addressed in *Adolescents at School*. Prior to teaching at Bard, he was an instructor at the Harvard Graduate School of Education; editor of the *Harvard Education Letter*, for which he received several writing awards from the Association of Educational Publishers and the National Press Club; and vice-chair of the Massachusetts Governor's Commission on Gay and Lesbian Youth. In addition to *Adolescents at School*, he is the editor of *Teaching Immigrant and Second-Language Students: Strategies for Success* (Harvard Education Press, 2004), a contributor to the *Encyclopedia of the Life Course and Human Development* (Macmillan, 2008), and the author of numerous journal articles and book chapters. A former full-time English and drama teacher, he continues to coteach at the high school level with faculty at New Day Academy, one of the Bard MAT Program's partner public schools in the South Bronx.

Carola Suárez-Orozco is a professor of applied psychology at New York University's Steinhardt School of Culture, Education, and Human Development and codirector of immigration studies at NYU. She publishes widely in the areas of cultural psychology, immigrant families and youth, the role of the "social mirror" in identity formation, immigrant family separations, the role of mentors in facilitating youth development, and gendered experiences of immigrant youth. Her books include *Children of Immigration* (Harvard University Press, 2001, with Marcelo M. Suárez-Orozco), *Transformations: Migration, Family Life, and Achievement Motivation among Latino Adolescents* (Stanford University Press, 1995, with Marcelo M. Suárez-Orozco), *The New Immigration: An Interdisciplinary Reader* (Routledge, 2005, edited with Marcelo M. Suárez-Orozco and Desirée Baolian Qin), and *Learning a New Land: Immigrant Students in American Society* (Belknap/Harvard University Press, 2008, with Marcelo M. Suárez-Orozco and Irina Todorova).

Beverly Daniel Tatum, a clinical psychologist, is the president of Spelman College in Atlanta. She is the author of *"Can We Talk about Race?" and Other Conversations in an Era of School Resegregation* (Beacon Press, 2007), *"Why Are All the Black Kids Sitting Together in the Cafeteria?" and Other Conversations* *about Race* (Basic Books, 1997), and *Assimilation Blues: Black Families in a White Community* (Greenwood Press, 1987). Her work also appears in edited books and journals, including "Talking about Race, Learning about Racism: An Application of Racial Identity Development Theory in the Classroom" in the *Harvard Educational Review*. Her areas of expertise include black families in white America, racial identity in teens, and race in the classroom. Prior to her leadership at Spelman, she was the acting president of Mount Holyoke College in South Hadley, Massachusetts, where she also served as dean.

Eric Toshalis is an assistant professor of secondary education at California State University, Channel Islands. He received his doctorate from the Harvard Graduate School of Education in 2007. His prior academic work includes a teaching credential and MEd from the University of California, Santa Barbara, and a Master of Theological Studies degree from Harvard Divinity School. A former middle and high school educator, Toshalis has worked with youth and adults in schools as a coach, mentor teacher, community activist, teachers' union president, afterschool group leader, and curriculum writer. As a researcher, he is largely concerned with the way teachers and students variously resist schools' tendency to reproduce social inequality and how such resistance might be promoted in classroom teaching and teacher education. He is the coauthor, with Michael J. Nakkula, of *Understanding Youth: Adolescent Development for Educators* (Harvard Education Press, 2006).

Angela Valenzuela is a professor in both the Cultural Studies in Education Program within the Department of Curriculum and Instruction and the Educational Policy and Planning Program within the Department of Educational Administration at the University of Texas at Austin. She also serves as the director of the University of Texas Center for Education Policy and associate vice-president for university-school partnerships in the Division of Diversity and Community Engagement. Her research and teaching interests are in the sociology of education, minority youth in schools, educational policy, urban education reform, and immigrant education. As this book goes to press, she is currently in Guanajuato, Guanajuato, Mexico as a Fulbright Scholar, conducting a study on binational relations between Mexico and the United States.

Michael L. Wehmeyer is a professor of special education, director of the Kansas University Center on Developmental Disabilities, and senior scientist at the Beach Center on Disability, all at the University of Kansas. His research interests include self-determination for students with disabilities, gender equity in special education, technology use and intellectual disability, and instructional strategies for students with severe, multiple disabilities. His recent publications include *Promoting Self-Determination in Students with Intellectual and Devel-*

opmental Disabilities (Guilford Press, 2007), *Self-Determination: Instructional and Assessment Strategies* (Corwin Press, 2007, with Sharon Field), *Exceptional Lives* (Merrill/Prentice Hall, 2007, with Ann and Rud Turnbull), *Mental Retardation and Intellectual Disabilities: Teaching Students Using Innovative and Research-Based Strategies* (Merrill/Prentice Hall, 2005, with Martin Agran), *Personality and Motivational Systems in Mental Retardation* (Academic Press, 2004, with Harvey Switzky, Linda Hickson, and Robert Schalock), and *Theory in Self-Determination: Foundations for Educational Practice* (Charles C. Thomas, 2003, with Brian Abery, Dennis Mithaug, and Roger Stancliffe).

Index

Information contained in figures
and tables are indicated by an italic
f and *t*, respectively.